THE IMPORTANCE OF LUNCH

THE
IMPORTANCE
OF LUNCH

and other real-life

adventures

in good eating

JOHN ALLEMANG

RANDOM HOUSE CANADA

Parts of this book have appeared, in somewhat different form, in *The Globe and Mail*.

.

Canadian Cataloguing in Publication Data

Allemang, John
      The importance of lunch

ISBN 0-679-30986-1

1. Food. 2. Gastronomy. 3. Cookery. I. Title.

TX631.A44 1999   641'.01'3   C98-932553-9

Cover and text design: Sharon Foster Design
Cover and interior illustrations: Susanna Denti

Printed and bound in the United States

10 9 8 7 6 5 4 3 2 1

TO

P. H.

WITH LOVE

CONTENTS

HEAD CHEESE AND
THE HUMAN CONDITION ... 346

Acknowledgments

This is a book about the pleasures of eating. And because there is no pleasure without pain, it's also a book about the ways our pleasures have been compromised in the name of health and fashion and progress. I write for people who enjoy food and not for those who like to treat mealtime as an excuse for an anxiety attack—though if you want to understand the stresses and insecurities of modern life, this isn't a bad place to start.

I'd like to think I've been preparing for this book since I used to discuss the juiciness of my hamburgers with the waitresses at Fran's restaurant back in grade seven. But it actually started with a cranky article I wrote for *The Globe and Mail* about the high anxiety levels of modern cookbooks.

Doug Pepper, then editorial director of Random House Canada, read my diatribe, took it to be aimed at some of his best-selling books on healthy cooking and dashed off a critical letter to my newspaper. The fact that this book is published by Random House shows you how big-hearted a person he is.

It takes more than magnanimity to make a book. My agent Bruce Westwood used enthusiasm, charm and Veuve Clicquot in equal measures to push the project along. Whenever I think I'm passionate about food, I talk to Bruce and realize I've still got a long way to go in my struggle to be a hedonist.

While Doug and Bruce got the book started, Anne Collins of Random House gave it shape and turned my collection of dog-eared printouts into something more substantial. There's a hard-boiled, no-nonsense editor lurking in that woman somewhere, I'm sure. But it was her much-tried patience and unfailing sense of humour that allowed me to keep what remains of my sanity and complete *The Importance of Lunch* while I still had teeth to eat with—I owe her the title as well. Tanya Trafford's pain-free editing and genial tolerance for my lies about meeting deadlines made her dislike of retsina a little easier to accept. Her love of meat loaf is another matter.

Parts of this book first appeared in the pages of *The Globe and Mail*, where I've been fortunate enough to have worked and played for much of my adult life. Nancy Lugsdin gave me my first opportunity to write on food for the *Globe*—about Alsatian wine and cuisine, as it happens, an ancestral taste I've managed to hold on to wherever else the trends have led. Katherine Ashenburg when she was Arts editor rightly decided that food was one of the arts and encouraged me to go wherever my enthusiasms led—to Calvin Klein underwear models, blood oranges and bad imitations of Dante, as it turned out. Her successor Cathrin Bradbury saw the value of the column, even when its anti-trendiness went against the results of *The Globe*'s focus-group surveys. Though she managed to turn me into *The Globe*'s television critic in the end (which explains all the *South Park* and *Frasier* references), her support has been essential to this book.

I've felt strongly about food for as long as I can remember, but a number of people have given me knowledge to go with the feelings, and opportunities to put my thoughts into words: Christopher Driver and Aileen Hall at *The Good Food Guide*, who took me in when I was a student and then a young journalist; Professor Elaine Fantham, who first taught me the importance of both long lunches and Norman Douglas; the late Joseph Hoare, whose sense of delight is with me still; the iconoclastic Laas Turnbull, who made me a wine writer for a brief and boozy time; Roberto Martella, whose love of simple traditional food has always been contagious; my great friend Michael Lloyd, who proved to me that Greek drama, Irish bogs and pints of Guinness are subjects of equal and endless fascination; and Aliana Ho of the Hong Kong Tourist Association, who has shared so many ideas about food with me over so many steamer baskets of dim sum that I almost retitled this book *The Importance of Har Gow*.

My old Wadham pal Brian Langille, who knows the importance of many things, has been an inspiration for this book in more ways than one. It pains me to think that we once had a life-and-death battle about the tightest band on late-night television, but we've made up for it since over many plates of good food.

Finally I have to thank my children, Sam and Liz, for teaching me humility and proving to me that I could put together a book while listening to punk-rock guitar solos and girl-power anthems. They are passionate about food and disagree with me on almost everything I say, which I've found tremendously stimulating. Obnoxious, but stimulating.

My acknowledgments to my wife, Patricia Holtz, go far beyond thanks. Everything in this book is as much hers as mine. She was my first editor and remains my best companion.

THE IMPORTANCE
OF LUNCH

YOU THINK YOU KNOW SOMEONE WELL, and then a chance remark exposes an unbridgeable gulf. I was talking to a friend, someone I met in university over twenty years ago, and mentioned a new restaurant that had opened up near his office. The room was bright and airy, I told him, with high ceilings and Gothic windows that seemed to lift the spirits on a cold December day. The cooking was modern but sensible, or did I mean sensible but modern: barley soup accompanied by crusty focaccia that you could dip in garlic-scented olive oil, sandwiches layered with smoky portobello mushrooms or meaty swordfish, warm cornmeal pound cake in a sugary espresso sauce to prolong the meal well into the afternoon. Just reciting the menu was enough to make me check the calendar and decide how soon I could afford to book a table again.

Then came those fateful words.

"I don't eat lunch," he said.

Now perhaps I'm easily shocked—I couldn't bring myself to read, let alone steal, techniques from that *Cosmo* article on "The

Ten Things He Can Do to Drive You Wild." But when someone I considered a friend of long standing, someone whose champagne I've guzzled and whose neighbours I've insulted, says he doesn't make time for the midday meal, I'm stopped short.

What to say? Maybe his cholesterol's up and his doctor told him to cut back? Maybe he's on a year-long lunchtime fast with the proceeds going to the eradication of world hunger? Maybe he's just one of those superior beings who doesn't get hungry between breakfast and dinner, who puts in value-added time at the desk or on the StairMaster while you spend an hour or two marvelling at the way the sun streams through the Gothic windows and lights up the focaccia, to say nothing of your waistline.

Being a firm believer in the institution of lunch, and in anything else that makes eating a pleasure worth prolonging, I like to think his non-observance will catch up with him. He'll begin grabbing a chocolate-chip muffin at eleven a.m. just to tide himself over, or nibble on a Mars bar around three p.m. for a quick energy fix. Maybe he'll take up smoking to suppress the pangs of hunger or start moaning to his colleagues about the drawbacks in the company dental plan just to get away from his work. His eyes will suffer from staring at the computer terminal. His shoulders will seize up from repetitive strain. Don't eat lunch? No, and you've stopped living too.

Humans were not meant to go from morning to night without food. No matter how sedentary we've become, we still need to eat. And because we've become so deskbound, we need the distraction—no, the exercise—of a lunch break.

Easier said than done, of course. While I'm trying to preach the virtue of midday gluttony, the medical profession—a group collectively responsible for much of the anxiety we now feel about putting food in our mouths—has discovered that rats live longer on low-calorie diets. This is very disturbing news.

It's disturbing not just because a few more rodents were used up in the name of scientific progress. No, what really weighs heavily on the embattled psyche is the message this breakthrough proclaims: Less is more in the world of food. Long life at any price is the goal of the human race. That's how those who ignore the supreme importance of lunch will judge the news passed on by the rats that lived, and died, at the subsistence level. Their interpretation is completely wrong.

Food has been taken over by the paramedics and the valetudinarians, those anxious, unhappy people who think we eat in order to survive. They tell us to swear off animal fat, renounce red meat, switch our allegiance to the bran of the week and turn our feasts into a self-congratulatory penance. The pang of guilt we feel when we reach for the butter is their doing. The health warnings that have found their way onto bottles of wine give them smug satisfaction. The idea that lunch could be the road to ruin has its scientific backup in their pronouncements. When we look upon a carrot and think beta carotene or milk and think calcium or full-fat cheese and think yecccchh, we have become slaves to their mind control.

Food is a pleasure. That needs to be said again and again in these mean, self-lacerating times. A strongly flavoured old cheddar is one of the supreme accomplishments of the human race, right up there with Darwinian theory and early Motown. But you will be hard pressed to taste the cheese that used to console our ancestors at the beginning, middle and end of the working day — who's going to make the good cheddar self-righteous diners avoid, when there's easy money in turning out low-fat mozzarella or no-fat skim milk? Pigs have been reworked to be acceptably lean (which is why your pork is so tough and bland), trendy ice cream is now virtually cream-free, the quest for the low-fat french fry drives modern science and beer is trading alcohol for water. All too often these phony lifesaving qualities — milk as tonic, meat as protein supplement, cereal as medicine, vegetables as roughage, bluefish as a source of omega-3 — become an end unto themselves, and when that happens the sensation of taste is made to seem frivolous, pretentious or even irrelevant.

It all sounds like the worst of wartime cooking, except now we want our meat shortages, rationed eggs and near beer. Progressive children are sent to school with dusty rice cakes for their recess snack. The young and unformed are at least self-interested enough to beg chocolate-chip cookies from an unenlightened friend. But when adults are teaching their offspring that cakes are meant to be dry and dusty things, low in both fat and fun, how long will it be before no one remembers what a cake should really taste like, or what it is for?

What is any food for? You don't need a lot of it to stay alive. The rats have proved that. But for those of us not confined to lab cages there are still choices to be made. The big decision is not so much about choosing one food over another — sprouts versus french fries, say, or rice cakes versus cheesecake — as it is about deciding why we eat. Health doesn't need to be neglected for food to taste good — a crisp Northern Spy apple, garlicky hummus in pita, warming barley soup — and yet for some reason food is allowed to taste bad once it is declared to be good for you. A french fry needs some fat to be a good fry, if flavour has anything to do with it, and a cheesecake made with gelatin instead of butterfat will taste like — well, whatever unflavoured gelatin tastes like.

If you wash your raspberries in a Clorox bath for fifteen minutes to remove impurities, as health fanatics enthusiastically recommend, will the quality of your life be enhanced? Hardly. Will you live longer? Does it matter? Life is not a disease. Bad food is not the cure.

But good food is. It delights and distracts, connects and consoles, re-establishing the priorities of pleasure we may have lost sight of during the more officially approved parts of the day. It doesn't do this, of course, if you skip lunch, hurry dinner and turn breakfast into a hurdle on the way to somewhere else. Food, to become good food, needs attention and concentration, respect and even devotion.

I realize that in the greater scheme of things, the gullet and the gut don't seem to count for much. And yet who can stand to spend much time in a world, however solemn and rarefied, where the cooking is mediocre? Consider the remarkable wisdom of the European Union, a prime example of a body that passes itself off as singlemindedly devoted to high-minded tedium. Did the EU establish headquarters in Brussels and Strasbourg because the standard of debate was likely to be higher there than in Hamburg or Birmingham? No, the European commissioners thought first of their stomachs, as all reasonable people should do, and now relieve their boredom with lashings of frites and foie gras. Self-serving to the end, they recognize the importance of lunch.

The Eurocrats' priorities can be a model for us all. When smart young high-school students, for example, at least the ones not taken in by the propaganda of rice cakes, come to choose their universities, they should think first about the kind of food they're going to eat three times a day for four years. It's a lot easier, after all, to plod through *Das Kapital* if you're fortified with a plate of Singapore noodles (though why you would read Marx when you could be eating more noodles or moving on to the steamed fish with ginger is a more difficult question).

They leave school and find a job—near a good Italian panini place so they're not stuck with the cafeteria's meat pie—and then meet the person with whom they plan to share their life—making sure that the inamorata's appetite extends beyond well-done roast beef and tuna salad on white, crusts off. They buy a house—

with a bakery just around the corner—and all too conventionally produce children (who are raised on dim sum and sushi but quickly develop a preference for Kraft Dinner and tofu dogs).

And then, as winter turns to spring, it comes time to plan the summer vacation. Now if ever a part of life needed a good-food component, this is it. In the pursuit of the edible, it's not enough to take a vow that you will toss back a roasted pepper and goat's cheese sandwich for lunch once a week. I'm afraid the idea of eating well has to take over your sense organs at least three times a day, every day. Including holidays. I know there are people who can make do with Civil War battlefields and fast-food pit stops, that some folks get their thrills knocking back dehydrated carrots at backwater campsites. But for the more self-affirming members of the human race, it's important to increase and improve our pleasures wherever we can.

Now I don't mean to suggest tossing out the plans to visit the squares of Savannah in favour of an ascent of the Michelin high spots. Food fanatics who fixate on the best of the best court disappointment almost from the start, wrongly assuming that three-hour lunches are inherently superior to a quick plate of local crudités and a tin pot of new wine. Whenever I find myself listening to someone's reminiscences of treks to the great kitchens of the Rhône Valley, I think back to the delights of Corsicana, Texas, a place uncharted in the annals of gastronomy that should reset all fixed ideas about the accessibility of good food.

Corsicana is not a place to go to with a mind that is closed to the possibilities of discovery. If you can only feel content in a restaurant that has been written up in *The Sophisticated Traveller* and keeps a corner table free just in case Princess Caroline pops in, then you must steer your prejudices off the Interstate somewhere before the Corsicana turnoff. But the rest of us know that just as the Virgin Mary reveals herself in odd places like Fatima and Lourdes rather than Paris and the Côte d'Azur, so the true believer must always expect to find good food just around the next corner.

I went to Corsicana, an hour south of Dallas, to see a historic onion-domed synagogue. The synagogue happened to be just a block away from a bakery famed worldwide for its Christmas fruitcake. The bakery, it turned out, also produced some of the best cookies I have ever tasted, made from innumerable combinations of chocolate, pecans, eggs and gooey coconut. As if that weren't enough to put Corsicana on the gastronomic map, it also was home to Bill's Fried Chicken restaurant, which attracted Town Car retirees and garbage collectors alike to its spread of fried chicken, breaded catfish, baked beans, collard greens, coconut squash and cornmeal biscuits.

So who is happier (not to say better fed): the person who found high-end French food to be much as expected or the one who will forever be astonished by the hidden joys of Texan cuisine? And once you accept that food does not exist in some sort of official hierarchy, that there is room for negotiation and reassessment in the thorny matters of taste, then there's a powerful sense of liberation.

Take something as simple as a recipe, the text on which we base a cook's reputation. At the top end of the ladder — or should that be larder — are the upscale recipes, the sort you find in magazines such as *Gourmet* or *Food & Wine* that set the tone for the kind of food smart people will eat for at least the next month. These precious documents always manage to tie in with some important trend emanating from California or New York, and they are always the work of restless artificers, clad in the most fashionable baseball caps, who are incapable of banal or pedestrian fare. Goat's cheese–stuffed chilies with roasted tomato-fennel sauce, risotto cakes with wild mushroom and salsify, tuna tempura with eggplant caviar and mango compote — the titles alone are enough to make the cultured palate tremble.

The recipe at this level is an essential element in the sophisticated life, even if sophisticated people prefer to let other people cook their tuna tempura for them. But very rapidly, as one retreats from the avant-garde toward the rank and file and the need to keep pace with surging trends diminishes, the recipe turns into something very humble and ordinary.

But nonetheless delicious. And this is the strange thing about recipes: those with the most unimpressive pedigrees — by the standards of people who presume to hold forth on food at least — are often the ones that give the most pleasure for the longest time. I doubt that you or I will be knocking back goat's cheese–stuffed chilies in a fit of nostalgia twenty years hence, or that we will pass on its treasured recipe to future generations. One meal, surely, is enough, or perhaps even too much.

But that broiled-coconut-and-brown-sugar topping on the cake you bought in a small-town bakery, however modest its beginnings, somehow lasts. Why is this? Because it reminds us of an uncomplicated childhood, because it's free of the instantly passé fashionability that stamps its own best-before date on recipes of the moment, because it aims to please in a way that more ingenious, carefully constructed cantilevered desserts don't allow. Such simple, likeable recipes exist in an entirely different world from the cutting-edge creations assembled each month in the glossy magazines. They do not proclaim their links with young Soho chefs who only cook with Third World produce, nor do they make a point of using ingredients that must be ordered from a former anthropology professor experimenting with pre-Columbian seed varieties. They are safe, unthreatening, relatively neutral in their cultural heritage and calculated to please as many people as possible.

In politics that is a good thing. In food, at least according to the arbiters of taste, it is bad. Veteran restaurant-goers, people who feel that a dish previously tasted is a meal wasted, insist on being wowed by their food, as if it were a stand-up comedy act at the Just for Laughs festival bidding for a network deal. Theirs is the passive pleasure of the supercilious observer, and they are never more content than when a waiter looks at them soulfully and tries to move some old shellfish with the words, "Our plat du jour is fresh abalone, imported from our own beds in the South China Sea, grilled over seasoned rosewood and served on a purée of wild persimmon scented with lemon grass and Old Order Mennonite maple syrup."

There's a place for such esoteric one-upmanship, just not the central position it now occupies in the loftiest food circles. Hand your kitchen over to the passing trends and you lose the grounding that makes for confident and competent cooking. A few years ago, it became fashionable to serve grilled fish practically raw on one side, and diners ate it as if there were no other way. Now it is hard to persuade some chefs to cook anything rare, meat or fish. Excessive salt was proscribed by doctors for ages, and we congratulated ourselves for only eating unsalted butter. Then the Mediterranean diet took over the kitchen (backed by the big bucks of the international olive oil lobby) and brought with it pancetta, tapénade, anchovies and other ingredients that could put a salt lick to shame. What is the point of harbouring strong feelings about food if they can turn 180 degrees over the weekend?

Food in our age has become a battleground, where everyone's an aspiring critic and an easygoing meal gets displaced by competitive eating. It may seem a splendid idea at the time to dazzle your guests with a decadent all-black menu: Guinness and black bean soup, blackened blackfish with black rice, licorice ice with blackberry coulis à la Conrad Black, café noir. But the better, more humane, more relaxing plan is to treat food as a simple pleasure, not as a test. Any deliberations over a menu should start with a few basic questions, some culinary, some sociological. What's in season? If it's in season, will they be sick of it already (asparagus being the best example of a food that quickly wears out its welcome)? How much time do I have? And if I'm feeling lazy or oppressed, how much money do I want to spend on shortcuts (Quebec duck pâté, frozen cheese fondue, the Portuguese bakery's crème caramel that could almost pass for homemade)? Is the cooking to be the centrepiece of the evening, or is it a means to an end, the background music for talk or wine tasting or—help!—fundraising or—yikes!—romance? Are the other people around the table likely to be interested in discussing the nuances of Thai spicing or are you better off saving that coconut chicken recipe for more dedicated companions who will applaud your mastery of obscure Southeast Asian flora as long as they get to hold forth on their last visit to the best French restaurant in Hong Kong?

Your traditional dinner party has three courses. People who cook for show see this as a dearth of opportunities. They try extra hard with every course, believing that with only three chances to impress, they have to hit the bull's eye every time. But dinner is not some all-or-nothing game of chance. Honest, homely cooking —vegetable soup, roast meat and mashed potatoes, a cake or a custard—cooked with confidence and served without pretension can win over even the most critical (especially the most critical, come to think of it; they tire of the new and make a fetish of good old-fashioned cooking). And even simple meals give openings for compulsive show-offs: a sprinkling of Stilton or Roquefort on the soup, a rum sauce with the roast beef, custard made with maple syrup or vanilla bean instead of vanilla essence, interesting drinks throughout, expensive chocolates as a bonus at the end (preferably supplied by a thoughtful guest).

It's easy to hand out this advice. It's harder to follow it. Children, when they come due for a special dinner, order a meal that is decidedly unspecial: chili, burgers, tortillas, pasta or something equally humble and fun. Adults are much more ambitious.

When the question of my birthday dinner came up—one of my contemporaries had just been inducted into the Hockey Hall of Fame, which gives you pause—my first response was to behave like a savvy adult. I thought of the things I like that common sense and a poor credit rating normally prohibit: caviar, foie gras, maybe some truffles that had mysteriously turned up at the Italian grocery down the street. (I don't know why I wanted truffles. Any contact I've had with them has been a disappointment.) Or maybe salmon in a beurre blanc or roast duck with a spiced pear compote or perhaps an expensive piece of beef marinated in balsamic vinegar and served with a Roquefort sauce that dribbles over into the homemade frites and turns them into what poutine might have been if it hadn't been corrupted by the less tasteful elements of Quebec nationalism.

Then I thought more reasonably about the special meals I really do enjoy eating, the nibbling kind that let you sit undisturbed to ruminate happily about the strangeness of life: an endlessly various antipasto platter or a tray of French and Italian cheeses with a crusty baguette and a nice bottle of inky red wine.

And then I thought a bit longer, and decided that what I really wanted for my birthday dinner wasn't so much special food as the sight of other people around me eating contentedly. If this sounds a little too selflessly Christian—"Do I detect the smell of burning martyr?" Basil Fawlty used to say—I plead innocent. What I was aiming for was just a semblance of harmony at the dinner table, without which a special meal turns bitter on the tongue. As much as I like stinky cheese and prosciutto wrapped around pear and juicy duck, there are those in my milieu who resist these foods audibly and visibly, and sometimes tangibly. And so I ordered my children's favourite party food: tortillas.

Imposing your values on others is obviously one of this world's supreme pleasures—look at how much fun Conrad Black seems to be having—but at a dinner that's meant to be fun I find that it just as often leads to indigestion. You may think that nothing could delight your friends more than a chance to honour your continued survival with a good meal, but the egocentricity that is first nature to a birthday unbalances even the best judgment. Save the mackerel pâté and the marinated octopus and veal kidneys in mustard sauce for the most like-minded of your intimates —parties are for spreading joy, not concentrating it at the head of the table. We had tortillas to the delight of all, if not of one.

The moral so far? Be flexible about food, I suppose, and remain open to the possibilities, if that doesn't sound too touchy-feely. Have strong feelings, fine—food is responsible for some of the strongest feelings we can have, thank goodness. Just don't get too caught up in trends, or medical warnings or stratified traditions about where the best food is to be found, or self-absorbed prejudices about whether tortillas and lunch should both be avoided.

Because in good cooking, as in good living, there is always room for adjustment. My birthday-dinner chef de cuisine created the usual fun fillings for my messmates' corn-flour tortillas— spiced beef, avocado, tomato salsa, sour cream, jalapeños, grated cheese and so forth. But then, making a beautiful creative leap, she added a bowl of sautéed shrimp flavoured with cilantro and another of oysters cooked with a little black bean sauce.

It was a wonderful solution, partly because it didn't incite my dinner companions to riot and partly because it was so unexpected. I had been trained to see tortillas as kid food, entertaining and appetizing and nutritious, but still kid food. And then someone fiddled with the rules just a little, and a simple dish was elevated into something memorable.

Marinated Salmon

My favourite lunches start, and often end, with an antipasto assortment featuring no end of little dishes such as this modest treatment of raw salmon. A little plain on its own, it's used to balance the more assertive flavours on the plate. Marinated salmon prepared this way is as much texture as it is flavour, especially when served wrapped around a spongy ball of mild bocconcini cheese.

Use the centre cut of a fresh fillet of salmon. With a sharp knife, slice the fish into thin strips no more than ¼-inch thick. Pour out enough extra-virgin olive oil to coat a serving plate and lay out the salmon slices so that they lie flat. Squeeze the juice of a lemon evenly over the fish and add some finely chopped dill, 2 tablespoons of capers, a few thinly sliced rings of onion and a few shakes of salt. Turn the slices after thirty minutes, spoon the oil and lemon juice over the fish and let sit for another thirty minutes. Although the salmon can be served right away, it develops a luscious softness with a day in the refrigerator. Before serving, garnish with a little chopped parsley.

Thai Beef Salad

Seeking order and elegance in her life, my teenaged daughter will stay up until two in the morning watching TV cooking shows. Since I'm partly responsible for the makeshift lifestyle that forces her to turn to the tube for her role models, I can't complain too much. Besides, I have a guilty secret of my own: I once hosted a cooking show.

I should have known better. The producer was a New Yorker who'd just arrived in town and bragged about once having worked

as a cameraman for the Yankees. Maybe that part was true—
nothing else was. When I met him at his hotel, his girlfriend, who
doubled as co-host, was ironing his pants in the middle of the
suite. Too young, or too vain, I didn't see anything wrong. As we
filmed in smart downtown restaurants, my complete lack of experience apparently no barrier to the work-in-progress, the producer seemed to take special pleasure in stopping the shoot to
call for endless plates of food, on the house of course.

Our last show was at a stylish Thai restaurant called the
Bangkok Garden, run by a woman named Sherry Brydson who
had worked as a journalist in the Thai capital before returning to
Canada to make outstanding use of money she'd inherited from
her grandfather Roy Thomson, a billionaire press lord. As jour-
nalists, Sherry and I should have been more skeptical of our roles
in the producer's charade. But we both enjoyed our food too
much to doubt the greedy enthusiasm of others. And when our
New York friend fled town with his companion a few weeks later,
we were left with lasting memories of our phantom interview
over a platter of delicious beef salad.

Grill one pound of beef tenderloin rare and slice very thinly
against the grain. Remove the leaves from 1 bunch of cilantro
and 10 stalks of mint. Thinly slice 3 shallots, 2 fresh hot peppers
(Thai bird or finger peppers, skinny and an inch or two long, are
best) and 2 green onions. Mix with the leaves. Take 1 tablespoon
of rice, stir-fry it briefly in a dry, heavy pan and then grind it fine
in a mortar or spice mill. Arrange Boston lettuce leaves and other
vegetable garnishes (sliced cucumber and strips of sweet red pepper, say) on a platter. Then combine the salad vegetables with
the beef, the ground rice, 4 tablespoons of fresh lime juice and 3
tablespoons of fish sauce (nam pla). Mix well, check the seasonings and serve on the platter.

Cauliflower in Green Sauce

The gentleness of the still-warm cauliflower and the sharpness of the dressing make for a lively antipasto dish. Cut 1 large cauliflower into florets, making sure to use some of the stem, cut into chunks, for a variation in texture. Steam just until tender, remove from the pan and allow to cool slightly. In a food processor, prepare a green sauce of ½ cup olive oil, the juice of 1 lemon (2 if small or dry), 4 to 6 drained anchovy fillets, ½ teaspoon of red pepper flakes, 1 handful of well-rinsed parsley and a generous sprinkling of fresh ground pepper. Blend until the sauce is smooth and thick, then toss with the cauliflower. Garnish with a scattering of capers or black olives, and lemon wedges.

Pork in Tuna Sauce

Another antipasto dish, which doubles nicely as a main course for lunch on a warm summer's day. This is a variation on the classic Italian vitello tonnato, inspired by my local bargain-priced Hungarian restaurants that manage to bring plate-sized schnitzel within reach of the working man by using pork instead of pricier veal. Since pork has more flavour than veal, it actually stands up better to the potent tuna sauce. In a heavy skillet, heat 1 to 2 tablespoons of olive oil. Over medium heat, brown 2 pork tenderloins on all sides. Add ¼ cup of red wine to the pan and a few twists of ground pepper, then increase the heat briefly so that the wine bubbles. Reduce the heat to low, cover the pan loosely and leave the tenderloin to cook 15 minutes more. Remove the meat to a platter and cover loosely with foil. Bring the pan juices to a boil and reduce to a couple of tablespoons. In a food processor, blend half a tin of drained anchovy fillets, 1 tin of drained tuna,

1 tablespoon of capers, 1 cup of mayonnaise (homemade is preferable), 1 small clove of garlic, the juice of 1 large lemon wedge, 2 tablespoons of fresh parsley and a sprinkling of pepper. The sauce should be smooth and uniform in colour. Taste and adjust seasonings. When the pork has cooled, cut the meat into the thinnest-possible slices. On a serving platter, coat the bottom with several spoonfuls of the sauce. Set a layer of meat on top in overlapping slices, coat these lightly with more sauce and repeat until meat is arranged. There's no harm in handing leftover sauce round separately for those who like their tuna sauce in excess. Leftovers make not a bad sandwich, though you have to make sure the sauce doesn't squeeze out the sides.

Blood Oranges

IN A WORLD full of overstimulated supermodels, you'd hardly think there was a need for something called the Elite Model Action Drink. If anything, what's really required is a beverage that would calm down the manic mannequins and return the runways and fashion-mad TV networks to something more serene and fulfilling. But since the entire planet seems to draw inspiration from shapely things in their Calvin Klein briefs, it's not surprising that someone tried to put all that energy in a bottle.

What is surprising is the ingredient list of the Elite Model Action Drink: ginseng, guarana and blood oranges. Ginseng you may know as the ginger-like root prized for its tonic qualities in the Asian world. Guarana, a berry found in the Amazon jungle, provides much the same kind of stimulation in South America. Both are regarded as aphrodisiacs by people who think aphrodisiacs grow on trees.

But blood oranges? If blood oranges are supposed to be aphrodisiacs, I want my money back, because they haven't worked. If anything, they've had the opposite effect.

I don't know if you remember the theory floating around a few years ago that suggested Canadians were sex-crazed because of their harsh and endless winters. With so few other distractions available in the Great White North, so the argument went, they habitually resorted to the time-honoured one. Someone even published an anthology of poems called *Love Where the Nights Are Long* that claimed to prove a national obsession with cold-weather indoor activities.

Then along came blood oranges at the darkest, coldest time of the year, and suddenly winter didn't look so bleak. The idea that anything grows between December and March is amazing enough to those of us shivering in the upper reaches of the Northern Hemisphere, but that the produce in question could be such a stunning fruit—this was enough to lure any red-blooded Canadian out of the sack. The superficial miseries of winter weather—what drove us into hibernation in the first place—seemed to melt away in the presence of the blood orange's sunny glow.

Peel open a ripe, heavy blood orange and the flashes of red among the orange—anthocyanin pigments, if you must—light up the room. People come over to stare and, while the rarity of the blood orange is a draw, the penetrating fragrance is the real stimulus. And then there's the taste: an intense blend of sharp, invigorating acidity and a balancing sweetness that is almost berry-like.

Certainly the taste of a blood orange could perk up even the most torpid supermodel. It's one of those sensations, all too rare in the edible world, that makes you sit up and take notice. The acid bite threatens to bring tears to your eyes, only to be overtaken at the last moment by the succulent sweetness and the arresting citrus-berry flavours.

You know, this is starting to sound like a promising ingredient for an action drink. But the energizing qualities of the blood orange for me are balanced by something more contemplative. Blood oranges are expensive enough that most of us will eat them with respectful appreciation, savouring them segment by bloody segment rather than knocking back a jug of the fresh-squeezed juice as the carefree supermodels are inclined to do down in the palaces of Sicily. And blood oranges also carry with them a certain romantic dignity that makes it hard for me to associate them with hopped-up models. When you spot them at the produce store—the Sicilian bloods, not the unimpressive California efforts—what you usually notice first are the brilliantly coloured waxy tissue-paper wrappers. The pictures on the labels, designed to lift spirits weighed down by winter, are classic Old World images, almost magical in the way they elevate fruit to an icon. This orange is more than just a food—it is also a messenger from a far-off land of mystery, a legendary place where the sun retreats in winter to grow mythic fruit and who knows what kind of strange beasts roam the land, waiting for their encounter with Hercules.

Do I exaggerate? Blame it on the awesome finery of the blood orange, so unlike a low-key McIntosh apple. One label in my growing collection, which I plan to sell to Japanese collectors when the market is right, shows a golden dragon with one orange in its mouth and two entwined in its tail. How can you not be open to the suggestive powers of winter fruit after your eyes are blinded by that image? Another displays an ancient gold coin set against a radiating red sun and a brilliant royal blue sky. Several, alluding to the Sunny South from a Sicilian vantage point, show drawings of African figures. On one, Tutsi tribesmen kneel reverently before a giant red-flecked orange. On another, the Cherie brand featuring a demure black woman, is a ritual incantation I like to quote when I can't remember any Dante: *Se arance dolci volete gustare / La marca Cherie dovete comprare*—which translates something like, "If oranges sweet you want to try / Then Cherie brand you ought to buy." Take that, supermodels.

Blood Orange Salad

What do you do with blood oranges if you don't want to make a potent drink that will allow you to pose in skimpy underwear for days on end? Well, the tart juice is good as a means of acidifying sauces for chicken, the peeled segments look nice chopped up on fish and there are few sorbets tastier or tarts prettier than those made with blood oranges. A simple salad with sliced onion and olive oil makes a nice pick-me-up. Carefully peel three blood oranges, cut into slices horizontally, and then into bite-sized pieces. Add paper-thin slices of sweet Bermuda onion, enough to provide a contrast, but not dominate. If you like, you can also add small pieces of a ripe but firm avocado. Dress with olive oil, lemon juice and a little salt to taste.

But my favourite use for blood oranges is to do what the wise Sicilians like to do, at least for the first few weeks of winter: I just eat them.

PANCAKES, PROSCIUTTO AND THE PIZZA POLICE

THE BEST BREAD IN THE WORLD IS FRENCH bread. At least the French think so, and there's no quarrelling with French self-assurance when it comes to food. On the gastronomic map of France that hangs on my kitchen wall — and how many other countries make gastronomic maps of themselves? — Paris is labelled the *centre gastronomique du monde*, the food capital of the world. No wonder so many pilgrims go there to find tastes that have no rival.

I wanted to taste the best bread in the world. I liked the idea that it was conveniently located in a beautiful city well-supplied with museums and romantic views rather than in an industrial subdivision hard by a twelve-lane highway. Walking out toward Père Lachaise cemetery (Chopin, Proust, Piaf — even the French graveyards have class), I found a world-renowned baker who specialized in bread made from old country recipes. This baker, the best among the best, turned out to be a little different from his compatriots, a self-confident artisan even by the very high national standards. He scoffed at the long pale cylinder that passes for great French bread everywhere else. He made huge round loaves dusted with flour, dark sour rye bread that left a taste in your mouth for hours afterward and dense, barely leavened slabs fashioned from corn flour that kept their crust and flavour for days. I can't remember if he was wearing his Legion of Honour rosette, but I know that in the French hierarchy of national heritage, this baker and his bread ranked near the top. This is a country, after all, where government ministers have denounced bakeries that have the gall to buy prepared dough instead of whipping up their own.

I sat in my garret in the *centre gastronomique du monde* and savoured the best bread in the world. It was very tasty, and only one thought troubled me. I had tasted bread just about as good halfway around the world, in the Italian and Portuguese bakeries a few blocks from my house.

Now I'm not about to put forward the argument that my house is the *centre gastronomique du monde*, though it sometimes seems that way when I have three cats screaming at me to open up the can of beef chunks and a daughter pursuing her quest for the no-fat brownie. If anything I want to do the opposite. I would like to propose that those of us who enjoy our food treat such chauvinistic claims with a lot more skepticism. The best pasta comes from Italy. The best wine comes from France. The best chocolate comes from Belgium. The best peaches come from Georgia or Provence or Niagara-on-the-Lake. The best potatoes come from Idaho if you're American, Prince Edward Island if you're Canadian, Lincolnshire if you're British. What's best, all too often, looks like the product of savvy marketing, blinkered prejudice and smug insularity.

For years the French managed to convince us their wines were the best, and container-loads of screw-top plonk lived off the reputation earned by the priciest châteaux. Then foreign wines started beating out French wines in international competitions, and suddenly the bald statement of superiority wasn't enough. The French winemakers had to find a winning argument, and searching round they hit on the idea of *terroir*: the soil. French soil was one of a kind (most soil is, like fingerprints; yet most hands look much the same). Because California had not made a cult of *terroir*, because the freewheeling Americans couldn't see why good winemaking should be confined by property lines, French wines were deemed innately superior. At least by the French.

This is the reasoning of the chauvinist. Make up your mind first and search for proof second, if at all. While those who love food have long looked admiringly to France as a source of inspiration, the French have not always — by which I mean almost never — returned the favour. We think their passion for enlarged goose liver to be a sign of exquisite refinement, their taste for gnarly fungi rooted up by the snouts of trained pigs to be a mark of aristocratic breeding. But they, being historically a proud, disdainful and chauvinistic race, regard our heritage as barbaric.

The fast-food hamburger, they say, is the staple of people who have no interest in what they eat. Appalled by the North American preoccupation with hygiene, they ask how anyone could prefer cold skim milk to raw-milk cheese (grant them that one). They sniff haughtily at the idea that anyone even remotely exposed to the ideals of liberty, equality and fraternity would deign to eat the lowly peanut, let alone purée it and spread it on toast with grape jelly. But what they can't abide, above all, is the idea that people over here on the badly bred side of the Atlantic actually enjoy corn, the food that feeds the pigs that sniff out the truffles that flavour the tournedos that grace the meals that Jacques eats.

The French, apart from a few daring go-getters who have explored North America with an open mind, are convinced that corn is animal food. If they opened up a copy of *Gourmet* and found a picture of scallops seared with corn and cherry tomatoes, they would think it gaucherie of the highest order. What a preposterous idea, you can hear them whispering as they knock back their tripe à la mode de Caen (Such taste! Such refinement!), that the word gourmet could be associated with the feed flung at greedy pigs and scrawny chickens.

On those rare occasions when corn makes an appearance in European cookbooks, it's almost always as cornmeal, the coarse flour ground from the same dried kernels served without much flair to the beasts of the farmyard. Even then, when a highly decorated chef offers up a simple corn cake in tomato sauce, there's a sense of play-acting, like Marie Antoinette dressing up as a milkmaid at Versailles.

But if cornmeal offers the illusion of rough, honest peasant cooking—a heritage moment—fresh corn is seen simply as just another North American aberration, like churchgoing or monogamy. Believing very much in tradition, chiefly their own, the French can't place this sweet transatlantic newcomer. And because of their ignorance and indifference, we in the New World —I almost said the Free World—are able to do with it as we please, unrestrained by Old World dogma.

It's liberating for a cook in a way, to have a native ingredient that isn't tied down to specific roles and recipes. And what have we come up with in our liberated state? Not much. For all the corn that ripens along the highways and byways through the summer—it's practically become the North American hedgerow— there's still only one way to cook it. The accepted method is so universal, in fact, that I don't have to describe it, though I should make two quick points: the water should never be salted, and if you're going to boil, you might as well steam instead. It's faster and tastier.

Are we going to impress the French with our steamed corn? Hardly. Their thinking on the subject of cooking is much like their thinking on every other aspect of civilization: that it is the duty of man to improve upon nature. The grape turns into wine, the wilderness is remade into a formal garden, the savage becomes the philosopher and the cob of corn is transformed into pâté made from the pig that was fattened on it. You can't call yourself a cook, much less a chef, if all you do is boil water.

We see things differently, believing that not every meal needs to be an audition for the Legion of Honour. And yet the French, who know 121 different ways to cook a potato, have a point about corn's inbuilt limitations: anyone who proposes to cook with the golden kernels has to admit that human ingenuity is unlikely to improve on nature. Corn is not very giving of itself, unlike the tomato which spreads itself around, or very receiving, unlike the potato which takes on the taste of whatever it's cooked with. A kernel of corn is a self-contained bit of flavour, and as such works best in hodgepodge dishes — minestrone, fried rice or mixed-vegetable risotto — where it's just one of many ingredients. Some think its innate sweetness goes well with sweet shellfish such as scallop or crab, but I'm always bothered by the awkward independence of kernels, which makes it hard to integrate them with other ingredients. A crabcake or some other kind of fritter that pulls together all the bits and pieces might be the best solution for those who want to keep up with the French.

But whether you're breaking new ground with your corn or going the ritualistic route, your meal is still only as good as your raw ingredient. For some reason I don't understand, having been prodded away from botany and toward Latin at an early age, a cob of corn that happily bides its time while connected to the stalk suddenly starts converting all its sugar to starch the moment it's picked. A low temperature will slow the process, which is why you take your cooler with you when you go corn-shopping, but it won't stop it.

The French contempt for corn may spring from this diabolical transformation. The starchy ears that took their own bittersweet time reaching Paris didn't seem all that special. North American corn-breeders, thinking like Frenchmen, have tried to counteract the forces of nature by developing supersweet varieties with burlesque-house names like Kandy Korn. If you buy one of these types direct from the grower, you may be getting corn that is as much as forty-four per cent sugar. The advantage of these varieties is that they can hang around a while, maybe take a trip to Paris, and still taste sweet. Don't be surprised, though, if the French see this as just another sign of the decadent North American sweet tooth and go back unconvinced to their foie gras.

The French at least have reason to be chauvinistic. Their pride is reserved for their own products. But what would they make of the North Americans who ostentatiously turn their backs on their own local foods so that they can loudly worship something from far away?

I'd made my lunchtime sandwich with the ingredients collected on one of my world-class shopping trips to the neighbourhood stores: the almost-burnt Calabrese loaf from the bakery, the bitter radicchio from the shop that sells fig-syrup cookies in fig-syrup cookie season, the sweet-sour cultured butter from the supermarket that puts the better in big-is-better and the tender prosciutto that came direct to my deli after a twelve-month run on the aging hooks at a warehouse near the airport. I was enjoying my meal immensely, maybe too immensely for my workmates. It was something I'd learned in Europe, to show the joy you felt in eating delicious everyday food instead of hiding it away.

I took it as a good sign, and evidence of my balanced approach to the pleasures of life, that when one of my carrel colleagues who'd overheard my ecstasies asked if I'd ever been to Parma, I thought he wanted to talk about Italian art.

"No…," I began slowly, my thoughts racing around to recover whatever picture-book memories remained of elegant frescoes and soaring cathedrals. "No, I haven't got there yet," I said on further reflection, as I desperately tried to remember the name of the sixteenth-century painter whose name sounds a lot like parmigiano. "But I hear," I added, for I knew I was talking to a worldly man who expected everyone to have a nodding acquaintance with the glories of the Italian Renaissance, "that the baptistry's something else."

It's usually a safe thing to praise the baptistry, sight unseen, in any Northern Italian city. A baptistry is a connoisseur's kind of building that package tours, in their hurry to see the obvious, tend to miss. You get bonus points just for mentioning it.

"No," said my urbane friend, looking a little pained, "I meant, have you ever been to Parma and tasted real prosciutto di Parma?"

Uh-oh, I thought. I could see where this one was heading. In praising my prosciutto sandwich so enthusiastically, I'd made it pretty clear that my local industrial-subdivision version would do quite nicely. Guys who've sampled the pleasures of Parma don't see it that way.

I should mention that real prosciutto di Parma has traditionally been hard to find here because of the kind of concerns that government health inspectors always bring to traditional foods that predate technology. This gives European chauvinists, who like to think that all North American foods are pasteurized and processed and tasteless, another reason to feel superior.

So if you wanted to taste the original prosciutto, true prosciutto if you like, you pretty well had to travel to Europe. But my problem is that on those rare occasions when I find myself in Europe, I tend not to be thinking of prosciutto, and when I am thinking about prosciutto, I tend to be making my lunch or forming my dinner plans back here. Which makes it so much easier to go to the local deli and buy local prosciutto rather than sit at home mournfully and pine for Parma.

But my better-travelled friend didn't care. He heaped praise on Parma's ham while damning ours. He preferred it by far on flavour, but he also insisted that the texture was far superior. Real prosciutto melts in your mouth, he said; the stuff made in countries that lack Renaissance baptistries is necessarily dry and stringy.

I put up a bit of a fight—suggested that maybe he'd hit on a bad piece from the wrong airport warehouse or someone had cut it wrong or that he'd had his taste buds thrown out of whack by a childhood addiction to Roman nougat—but deep down I knew I was licked. There's no way you can argue with someone who's been to the source, tasted a food the way it's supposed to taste, when you haven't.

You've probably encountered this sort of thing yourself. You ask someone how he liked the dim sum restaurant you recommended a few weeks before and he says, "It was all right, but the only good Chinese restaurants are in Vancouver / San Francisco / Hong Kong." Or you find yourself praising the foie gras coming out of Quebec and New York and someone else pipes up, "Of course that's duck foie gras. The real thing comes from goose, though you have to go to Strasbourg to get it."

Or is it Budapest? I can never quite remember, overcome as I am by the thought that wherever we are, the great food is somewhere else. North America being a bit of a come-lately in the refinements-of-civilization process, I can understand why they might do some things better in the long-established habitats of the Old World. But it's still chafing to be told that whatever you're enthusing about, whenever you're actually enjoying what you're eating, someone does it better somewhere else.

So the peaches for sale here will never taste as good as the ones plucked warm from the tree in sunnier places. Or the mackerel we buy at the market is too long from the sea to be good. Or the suburban mozzarella's not a patch on the buffalo-milk version from Italy, the McIntosh apple is not half as good as the English Cox's Orange Pippin, the coffee down the street is no match for Tazza d'Oro's in Rome, the wine store's bottled retsina can't compare with carafes of draft retsina drunk amid the olive groves of Delphi. And if you want to sample the original bock beer, skip the local imitation and fly straight to Munich.

Travel broadens the mind. But it also closes it. Yes, the only way we can set our standards—on whether governments should monopolize liquor sales, say, or strawberries have to taste unripe and hard—is to find out how they do things elsewhere. But having discovered that they actually have us beat at a few things— they do have a few thousand years' headstart—we can't mope eternally and long for that next flight to Parma.

All right, we can long. But at the same time we can make do and then some with the pleasures accumulating around us: the good affordable prosciutto, the rich, malty microbrews, the spongy bocconcini that may not be made from Italian buffalo milk but still tastes pretty fine with tomatoes and olive oil and chopped basil. And don't forget corn and peanut butter. Dinner shouldn't always be about perfection, and if it is, it will always be found wanting. However distant our local equivalents are from the Eurocentric ideal, they still taste better than sour grapes.

For all that the connoisseurs crow about their matchless travels, it's surprising what you can find in our quiet little gastronomic backwaters if you just keep your eyes open and shop often enough. While I haven't yet come across the hop shoots that figured in a memorable Alsatian meal—must ask Labatt's to spare me a couple—the quail eggs of my once-in-a-lifetime *oeufs de caille Maintenon* at London's Connaught Hotel are a common-enough sight around Toronto's grubby Kensington Market (where you'll never, unfortunately, come across Madame de Maintenon; some pretensions you have to supply yourself). In my watchful ramblings over the years, I've discovered live frogs and turtles in my local Chinatown, fresh salmon eggs at a tiny Japanese variety store and no end of rarities at farmers' markets across the continent—meaty white puffballs, aromatic quince, elderberries, wild persimmons, cactus paddles, huge stalks of sugar cane and tiny ground cherries (which under the high-toned name Cape gooseberry can pass themselves off as a rare imported delicacy). If you're looking for a way to make your kitchen Michelin-worthy, and you can't afford a view of the Seine, all it takes is some wide-eyed market-going and those obscure three-star ingredients will suddenly appear.

Visionary shopping may not be a concept the world is quite ready for. But it should not be undervalued as a way to expand our resources and keep the culinary Eurocrats at bay. Just as Wayne Gretzky was said to see the entire ice surface in a single glance, so an astute shopper can give a store the instant once-over and spot the last carton of wild mushrooms lurking beyond the curly endive. I don't need to tell you which one lives in a fabulous mansion and is the subject of adoring articles praising his prodigious talents and which one wanders the streets in anonymity. Life is indeed unfair. But I know whose cooking would be more interesting.

And who sees more of the real world. Urban streets (this is market-going in its broadest sense) are full of mulberry trees. When the purple fruit ripens in early summer (look for the stains on the sidewalk and the drunken birds milling about), collect enough to put in a pastry shell with a little custard and pass the result off as the kind of dessert you only read about in exclusive travel magazines. Our forests harbour tiny wild strawberries that, under the name of *fraises des bois*, command some of the highest prices going at Paris gourmet shops. True, you have to crouch on the ground for hours and pick the fragile little berries while mosquito gourmands sample your delicate flesh, but winning that third Michelin star takes just this kind of effort.

Though come to think of it, one of my best finds took very little effort beyond skilled use of the practised eye. I went into an Italian grocery store in search of balsamic vinegar and, scanning the produce shelves, noticed a basket full of yellow flowers. Devoted readers of Italian cookbooks will know right away that these were zucchini blossoms, and that they were put on this earth to become fiori fritti. I bought a six-quart basket's worth and persuaded my wife to deep-fry them in her best tempura batter. The novelty value certainly enhanced their taste—and why not?—but even after the novelty wore off at about the fifteen-flower mark, they were still delicious, with maybe the slightest cabbage-like sweetness to go along with the crunchiness of the battered blooms.

The strange and interesting thing about evanescent foods such as the zucchini blossom is that they exist only at the top and bottom of the food-distribution scale, on the tables of plutocratic restaurants (where they would probably be renamed courgettes) and on the shelves of the local ma-and-pa operation. Someone had a garden rife with zucchini. The male blossoms, the ones not connected to a growing vegetable, would die off if left to themselves. What a shame, the gardener said—or, alternatively, I can get thousands for these from Paul Bocuse—and gave them a more rewarding end on the table. The shoppers busy buying the usual tomatoes and broccoli never noticed, leaving all the more for those of us who believe that the treasures are waiting to be found.

Not all of our culinary heritage takes hold quite so firmly. I must have been on the receiving end of too many pancakes as a thick-haired lad, because to this day even the prospect of a flapjack—a mere glance at the disturbing Aunt Jemima's smiling face, come to think of it—is enough to make me lose my appetite.

It's not enough that a food be handed down by our ancestors. If that were the case, I'd be eating hardtack instead of biscotti. And it's also not enough for a taste to take hold just because a food is present when our earliest memories begin. Otherwise I'd still feel some kinship with the pancake. But those thick, doughy roundels with their inescapable baking-powder edges, lathered with butter and soaked in maple syrup, weren't designed to establish a lifelong appetite. As far as I can tell, the indigestible pancakes we ate on Sunday morning before staggering off to church served a higher purpose: they allowed my father to exploit the unpredictable art of culinary improvisation before his awestruck children.

Things could go wrong and often did; that was part of the fun, and fun is as much a part of culinary heritage as flavour. Experimental shapes, oddball ingredients, burnt offerings—whatever version came out of the pan, you ate in your turn. When the last one was devoured, the next one was ready, and so on until Sunday School called. If you started eating early enough, you could feel truly sick as the three crosses of St. Luke's came into view.

So strong was my association of pancakes with Sunday mornings that for years when I heard the story of the Israelites in the wilderness, I visualized the manna they found on the ground as thousands of silver-dollar pancakes that had fallen from heaven. But as with all childhood obsessions, when I reacted against pancakes, I reacted against them strongly. For years I avoided them and consigned even the thought of their existence to that ethereal plane where Sloppy Joes, banana Popsicles and Tahiti Treat sodas all languish.

Then suddenly one Sunday, while exploring the spiritual possibilities of an Indian vegetarian restaurant, I realized that what I
was eating under the name of masala dosa was a pancake. Thin as
lace, crunchy around the edges with a lively, slightly sour taste,
filled with cilantro-flavoured potato and served with a coconut
chutney, it was a marked improvement on the non-compact discs
of my childhood. But the family resemblance remained.

I thought of how much I liked this latter-day version of the
pancake and then realized how many other exceptions to my no-
pancake rule had also passed the test over the years: Hungarian
pancakes filled with apricot jam and chopped walnuts, Chinese
steamed pancakes stuffed with pork and vegetables in a jammy
hoisin sauce, corn tortillas layered with whatever was handy, curried goat rotis from Trinidadian takeouts folded up into a sandwich
and buckwheat crêpes freshly cooked on the portable griddles
that supply such spiritual uplift to the market squares of Brittany.

I went home determined to make a pancake that would rise
to these worldly standards (while not dishonouring my father's
legacy of sometimes-wayward culinary improvisation). Starting
out as a crêpe novice, I copied a recipe from Anne Willan's thorough *French Regional Cooking* and emerged with something very
close to the ideal, if you accept that a pancake can be a highly
irregular polygon. And if you also accept that I'm not contradict-
ing nearly everything I said before by suddenly seeking inspiration
from the French—at least this isn't the kind of French food that
overawed North Americans plan gourmet holidays around.

The crêpes, made from fine upstanding Canadian buckwheat,
tasted surprisingly good on their own. The variations were innumerable—that much at least was like my childhood version—
starting with just a pat of butter and/or sprinkle of sugar and
moving on to jam, chestnut purée, chocolate sauce or liqueurs
such as Grand Marnier if you like it sweet, or to grated Gruyère,
egg, ham or even sardines if you wanted savoury.

Of course the stronger the flavour of the additions, the less you appreciate the wild, racy taste of the buckwheat. Which tends to be the kind of thing we do with our heritage foods in a mixed-up era that combines democratic freedom of choice with a sense of overstatement that can quickly turn tyrannical. Purists who like to keep things the way they were don't stand a chance. Solemn prosciutto becomes a hip pasta topping, corn is thrown into sushi rolls, summer sausage is reissued in a reduced-smoke, low-fat version, and when it comes to pizza, anything goes.

Actually, when it comes to pizza, many North Americans don't realize that there is such a thing as an original heritage version. As far as the takeout crowd is concerned, the pizza is something that arose inevitably after the invention of the telephone, the car, the canned pineapple and that uniquely North American product called double cheese. Which is why some people must have been surprised when a delegation of Neapolitan know-it-alls took it upon themselves to show New Yorkers where they'd gone wrong.

It was a mission akin to English cricketers trying to show the Boston Red Sox the error of their ways—"That green wall out there is monstrous, for a start"—but the emissaries from Naples had a point that needed to be made. Even Americans, great innovators though they are, may have decided that this time they had exercised their constitutional rights a little too enthusiastically. Could it have been the California chefs' toppings of snow peas and duck sausage that made the New World audience realize they'd finally crossed the line? Or were they remembering the congealing cheese, sloppy sauce, cardboard crust and four a.m. heartburn of too many bad takeout 'zas?

Like St. Paul attempting to make sober Christians out of the fornicating Corinthians, the Neapolitan pizza preachers spread a gospel that condemned so that it could uplift. You can't make pizza at home, they said. You need a wood-burning oven that reaches a temperature of 750°F. The dough must be fat-free — no olive oil. You can't use canned tomato sauce or plum tomatoes from the tin: only raw ingredients will do. The diameter of a pizza must never exceed twelve inches. Ergo, no Bigfoots. The edge of the crust must be raised, like a handle. And never mind the non-dairy "cheese" that turns up in the more depraved American pizzerias; not even regular North American mozzarella is good enough. Only full-fat Italian buffalo-milk mozzarella will do.

It may be that, like St. Paul, the visitors set standards that are impossibly high for the average sinner. Certainly there are few of us who would be able to eat pizza with any frequency if the Naples rules prevailed, and I have to believe there was the promise of a free lunch that kept the New Yorkers from striking back with a traditional Bronx cheer (tongue-powered only; no mechanical aids allowed).

But rigid as the guardians of Old World tradition may be, they have their purpose, and it is not just to exasperate. If their purist policing doesn't actually restore wandering cooks to the straight and narrow, it at least stops us in our tracks and makes us consider our failings.

So have we gone too far? Of course we have. This is North America, world of the new. There is nothing we do that doesn't offend some hidebound Old Worlder. But even here, where arguments for quality subside in proportion to the volume of money earned, a little introspection is useful, if only to stay one step ahead of the market.

Reflecting on what we have done to the pizza, it's easy to see why the Neapolitans are piqued. A crust that is interesting in and of itself has become a rarity. Toppings are forced to carry the weight, and this is where we go desperately wrong. First mistake: to cut corners by using canned pizza sauce (and too much of it), making for a soupy, slippery mess. Second mistake: to go overboard on the cheese, which prevents the underlying sauce from cooking and leaves a heavy feeling in the diner's gut. Third mistake: to impose an inordinate number of toppings, destroying any sense of subtlety or individuality while making the poor crust even soggier. And all too often the combinations are too salty ("It felt like an earthquake in my mouth," said one Naples pizzaphile of a cheese, olive, peppers and sausage takeout) or too weird (snow peas, of course, but also the cherry pie-filling pizza I sampled at an upwardly mobile pizzeria in Bowling Green, Kentucky; my daughter loved it).

Without being quite as absolutist as the Neapolitans (whose ultimate aim seems to be to export their expertise while deflecting homeward a few of Little Caesar's millions), I can see better ways to make pizza. Your kitchen may not extend to a wood-burning oven (try the barbecue, if you must), but a pizza cooked on a baking stone in an oven preheated for at least half an hour is a good equivalent. When it comes to toppings, work with some of the Italian traditionals — marinara, margherita, francescana — before taking creative flight. Tomato sauce must be used sparingly, only painted on in a drab terra cotta, and cheese should be seen as an occasional ingredient, not a compulsory layering. In fact, one of the best pizzas I've tasted — the onion and rosemary variety from Rome, not Naples — does without both tomato and mozzarella. And when the cultural guardians aren't watching, I like to sprinkle on some blue cheese. I'm sure it's someone's heritage I'm carrying on, I just don't yet know whose.

The pizza police from Naples have it lucky. They know what they're talking about when it comes to their regional cuisine. We ignore them, in our refusal to be confined by someone else's traditions, but we may also envy them for the confidence they can bring into the kitchen. They have rules and history to go by, recipes handed down in the family, and farms that have produced the same ingredients for the same dishes since time immemorial.

When it comes time for dinner, they don't have to invent. Their heritage and traditions supply all the answers while the restless and rootless innovators in the New World are still stuck on the questions.

What does it mean to cook regional cuisine in North America? Every fashionable chef does it, or claims to do it. But can it be anything more than a marketing ploy—kind of like the French notion of *terroir*—when no one here is any longer tied to the land or the conditions it enforces? What, for example, do regional chefs do in winter, especially in those parts of North America where winter effectively lasts until summer? Even in an era where science has prolonged growing seasons by creating hardy new varieties and taught farmers techniques to triumph over the moody indigenous weather, the strictest of regional chefs depend on the wider world's produce well into spring.

As an exercise in culinary heritage, an attempt to concentrate flavours by excluding what doesn't belong, this is absurd. And yet who do we go and blame for our limitations? Those impulsive, desperate Old World ancestors who long ago decided the unknown had to be better than the known and booked passage to North America. The idea of putting together an interesting regional menu was hardly uppermost in their minds when they came to these parts. They did, in fact, manage to create regional cuisine out of necessity, living off their gardens, traplines, flour mills, smokehouses, cold-storage cellars and wits. No, if the blame is to be fixed anywhere, it is on us, for no longer being content with an ancestral diet that allowed strawberries for only two weeks if you were lucky and rutabagas for the other fifty.

All right, so it wasn't as desperate as all that. But anyone who insists on cooking truly regional cuisine hereabouts still has to make the kind of compromises that no one in these parts is prepared to make. And the big question, for those who want to find and sustain a culinary identity: What do you do in winter?

Well, you learn to cook rutabagas and potatoes and cabbage and apples fifty different ways, while waiting for the first asparagus or strawberry. True genius always begins with such mind-numbing limitations. The great cook is the one who can make something interesting out of a limited set of ingredients for the twentieth day running. It's certainly not the charlatan who plunders the planet for ingredients and the food magazines for ideas, and then dubs the result regional cooking.

The modern concept of regional cooking, so popular in food magazines that want to say something good about what they'd otherwise consider the middle of nowhere, is too artificial to be tolerated. Where, after all, do you draw the line? At fruits and vegetables grown in the province or state? But what does a political boundary have to do with regional cooking? At ingredients grown within a day's drive or bicycle trip or carriage ride? But if you can grow bok choy near Toronto in July, does this mean you're allowed to cook with its Floridian counterpart in May? And what do Asian vegetables have to do with North American regional cooking that has any sense of history? You can grow maple trees in China, but that doesn't make maple syrup part of Chinese regional cooking, does it?

It's possible to argue the point with such powers of logic that you end up banning everything but the indigenous plants and animals found here the day before the first European arrived. And yet that kind of food, whatever it was, is more alien to our current mix of habits, customs and grateful borrowings than sushi or soul food. Clearly the idea of regional cooking in a climatically challenged New World territory settled by all kinds of people over a relatively short period of time is bound to be an artificial concept. And yet artifice is what good cooking is all about, transforming the raw into the cooked, the wheat into bread, the pig into prosciutto, even the ear of corn into something that would delight a New York magazine and unnerve a Frenchman.

People who love good food believe in a wide-open world where everything's at our beck and call, or at least at the end of a cheap deregulated plane flight. But the cooks who have to choose what to make tonight crave the confinement that a sense of heritage provides. Provided of course that the local prosciutto is as much a part of the current definition of heritage as the rutabagas taking up space in the basement. We have to be flexible here.

Eggplant Pâté

One of the great pleasures of being a student in a cosmopolitan city like Toronto has always been the opportunity to eat good, cheap and adventurous food in the city's innumerable ethnic restaurants. Once a week back in the '70s, usually after my last lecture on Friday morning if I'd arranged my timetable right, I'd search out a new spot, and a new cuisine, to add to my knowledge. When I discovered a diner named the Bucharest back in those pre-glasnost days, I was overjoyed and spent the whole week of classes trying to imagine how Romanian food would compare with the scrambled eggs and cauliflower I ate at Toronto's first Czech café or the chicken paprikás served up at the Hungarian cellar where I went for a few pints after a hard game of squash.

The Bucharest was run by a serious man named Aisic Ilie, who proudly put the name of the Romanian capital on his sign but couldn't persuade many of his customers to stray beyond liver and onions. The long diner menu, with its obligatory hamburgers and Western sandwiches, made me think I should just order a Coke and clear out. But when Mr. Ilie, who moved more like a priest than a counterman, finally approached to take my order, I found the nerve to ask about the shortage of Romanian items. Without saying a word, he drew away, returning shortly with a bowl of a garlicky dip. Though it was nothing like what I expected from the Soviet bloc, I should have recognized it right away from an earlier foray across Toronto for Egyptian food. But it took me a few bites, and a quick refresher course in the geography of eastern Europe, to realize that this could be the Romanian take on baba ghannoush, the eggplant and olive oil purée found wherever Muslim armies and cooks held sway. I've since had dips like this in Palestinian, Turkish, Bulgarian, Lebanese, Israeli, Greek and Cypriot restaurants, but Mr. Ilie's came as the most welcome surprise.

Broil 1 large eggplant and 2 or 3 sweet red peppers until soft, on a charcoal barbecue if possible. Peel the skin from the eggplant and let the pulp dry out in a sieve. Peel the skin and remove the seeds from the peppers and mash together, by hand or in a food processor, with the eggplant and 2 cloves of crushed, finely chopped garlic. Slowly mix in 4 tablespoons good olive oil, 1 teaspoon ground allspice, the juice of 1 lemon and salt and pepper to taste. Chill, then serve with raw chopped onion and fresh tomato. Letting it sit for a day will soften the sting of the garlic a little.

Peanut Butter Noodles

Peanut butter is a far more useful and versatile ingredient than it's given credit for. Add it to a pork or chicken stew, Filipino-style, and it gives a depth of flavour that puts commercial meat stocks to shame. Cooked with noodles, as in this recipe my wife has been cooking since her days as an underpaid editor at *Cosmo*, it supplies a filling and appetizing meal for a song. If you're not counting pennies or worrying about advanced life forms, you can add some quick-cooked chopped chicken (or pork) and shrimps (in the shell) to this dish. But it can stand up perfectly well on its own as a casual dinner.

The best kind of peanut butter for cooking is the unsweetened and unhomogenized variety. But for it to work well, you have to make sure the oil that separates from the butter is stirred in evenly. Too dry or too oily, and the peanut butter won't be as effective in a cooked dish. Cook the contents of a 14-ounce box of spaghetti in advance, and drain. When ready to make the dish, briefly soak the noodles in a large pot of hot water to separate the strands, and drain again. Heat 2 tablespoons of peanut oil in a heavy skillet, add 1 tablespoon of finely chopped garlic and 2 tablespoons of chopped fresh ginger and cook until they soften and have lost their fiery edge. Stir ¾ cup of chunky, unsweetened peanut butter into the pan and then add 3 tablespoons of soy sauce, 2 tablespoons of sesame oil, ½ tablespoon of fish sauce (nam pla), ½ tablespoon of Worcestershire sauce, 1 teaspoon of red pepper flakes, ¼ cup finely chopped green onions and enough hot water, chicken stock or vegetable stock to moisten (up to ¼ cup). Stir the mixture gently until the peanut butter is the consistency of a thick sauce and coats the noodles (more liquid may be needed). Cook over a warming heat for a couple minutes more, then blend the sauce with the spaghetti. Stir in ¼ cup of thinly sliced red pepper and ½ cup of bean sprouts. Garnish with chopped green pepper, a handful of bean sprouts, some cilantro, a dash of red pepper flakes and some coarsely chopped peanuts (or cashews if you're classy; but then you'd want to use cashew butter in the sauce's recipe). A sprinkling of lightly toasted sesame seeds also looks nice, and enhances the sesame oil aromas.

Thin Buckwheat Pancakes

One of the great pleasures in walking through Paris in the cold-weather months is coming across a sidewalk crêpe stall. Except for the fact that it takes only a minute or two for a chestnut crêpe to be cooked and consumed, this is food that is in no way inferior to the pompous feasts of the most admired Michelin restaurants. Most of these thin pancakes cooked in Paris for your instant enjoyment are offered with sweet fillings, but as good as they are, I prefer the savoury crêpes (cheese, ham and / or egg) served in the markets of Brittany. This recipe is based on one found in Anne Willan's *French Regional Cooking*.

Cut up 4 ounces of butter and clarify by melting it over a low heat, skimming the froth from the surface and letting what remains cool until tepid. Pour the butter into a bowl and dispose of the milky sediment at the bottom of the pan.

Mix together 1 cup of buckwheat flour and 1 cup of white flour in a large bowl, then add 1 teaspoon of salt. Make a well in the centre, pour in 1¼ cups milk and stir it into the flour with a wooden spoon until it makes a thick and very smooth paste. Beat well for 1 to 2 minutes, then add 1¼ cups more milk in two batches, continuing to beat well. Let the batter rest for 30 to 40 minutes. Then add 1¼ cups water and beat well. Add more water if necessary to obtain a batter with the consistency of thick cream; beat well, then add half the clarified butter and stir until no trace is visible.

Spoon a little clarified butter onto a broad round pan and heat until a drop of batter sizzles at once. Add 2 to 3 tablespoons of batter to the hot pan, turning the pan quickly to coat the base evenly. If the pancake doesn't spread, stir a little more water into the batter. Cook over a fairly high heat until light brown, then turn and brown the other side. At this point you can add cooked or quick-cooking ingredients, or you can remove the slightly undercooked pancake to a plate and reheat later. As each pancake is removed, add a little more clarified butter to the pan.

These pancakes are tasty on their own with just a little melted butter, but they also go well with jam or marmalade, sweet chestnut purée, grated Gruyère or sliced ham. Fold in half or in quarters and leave on the heat until filling is warmed.

⊂━━━≣ Smoked Salmon Pizzette

The dairy coolers at Italian bakeries and delis often hide plastic bags of white blobs that on closer examination turn out to be lumps of pizza dough. You can make your own, of course, but this is one time you're better off taking the shortcut. Don't cut corners on the ingredients though—because the sour cream, salmon and caviar are uncooked, you need the best-tasting products you can find.

This recipe is based on one created by California celebrity chef Wolfgang Puck. It's just the sort of thing Neapolitan traditionalists despise about the effete New World, but for once I'm with the beautiful people.

Preheat your oven to 425°F. Shape the pizza dough into 4 circles, each about 6 inches in diameter. Lightly brush the top of each one with good olive oil and a little sea salt. Place on a cookie sheet sprinkled with cornmeal and bake for 10 minutes or until the crusts are golden and the dough feels baked through—there's nothing worse than uncooked pizza dough. Lift the crusts onto individual plates or one large platter and, while still hot, spread the surface of each one with 1 tablespoon of good, rich, full-fat sour cream—do not give in to that inner voice that tells you yogurt would be healthier. Cut 4 ounces of smoked salmon into thin strips and arrange as artistically as you want across the sour-cream backdrop, then sprinkle with finely chopped chives and a little black pepper. A few dabs of caviar on each mini-pizza makes this superior bar snack even better—the real thing from Iran or Russia is best, but salmon eggs would be a thematically appropriate alternative. Serve sliced as a pre-dinner nibble, or whole as an informal first course. Tastes best eaten with your hands.

POTATOES

EXAMINING THE POTATO on its own—knobby, mottled, dirty-looking even when it's clean—I can't get too excited. An unpromising vegetable in its natural state, it all too readily makes the transition when cooked to an unevocative dullness. Its easy versatility, its apparent willingness to submit to every form of debasement, has given us a world beset by lumpy mashed potatoes, boring boiled potatoes, mealy baked potatoes and fresh-from-the-freezer fries that should never be dignified by the word French.

Confronted at every turn by potatoes that settle for second-best, my thoughts drift back to a dish that showed the way things should be. It was 6:15 a.m. in a place called Forrest City, a town on the Arkansas side of the Mississippi that hasn't yet got around to capitalizing on local-boy-made-bad Sonny Liston, and the wake-up call had just shocked us into consciousness.

Living the Interstate life, where any moment spent off the highway is a moment wasted, we were keen to grab a quick bite and push off. One faction voted for eating the Pizza Hut leftovers from the night before. This is the same faction that swears by mcrowaved curly fries and Pringles' reconstituted potato rounds. Saner views prevailed.

A crowded parking lot surrounding a hut named Clint's Deli

pointed the way. We asked for the usual permutations of eggs and bacon, and as an afterthought—it would probably mean heartburn somewhere near Little Rock, but the South has its ways—we ordered the hash browns.

It was a revelation, if you're allowed revelations ten feet away from an Arkansas sheriff not long after dawn. The hash browns I remembered from my greasy-spoon days were grey, crusty hunks of bitter spud. These were more like creamy potato pancakes, smoky from the bacon fat they'd been cooked in, as light and sweet as a potato dish could ever hope to be.

My sense of contentment—the best potatoes work well at inspiring contentment—carried me far past Little Rock and buoyed my spirits even as the rest of the family bought Socks the Cat souvenirs in Bill Clinton's birthplace of Hope and talked about hanging around for the annual watermelon festival. It has remained with me ever since.

Thinking back to the joys of Clint's, I picked up the phone one morning, around the time I figured the first wave of hash browns would have been served, and called the pride of Forrest City to ask for the recipe. Unfortunately, Clint's was no more, sold to a chef who planned to open a French restaurant as even off-ramp Arkansas moved upscale. The French, I fear, do not know a lot about hash browns.

They know their potatoes, mind you. They showed the world the two-stage process for making fries (no, not thaw 'n' bake. First, deep-fry at low heat, to cook the chips through, and then at high, to crisp them). They do a nice variation on scalloped potatoes, by layering the thin slices with minced garlic and topping the lot with cream. They even make a dish that finds its way into cookbooks as the grandly named pommes de terre sautées à la lyonnaise and still looks suspiciously like the truck stop eye-opener of fried potatoes with onions. But when it comes to hash browns, I've learned to look south.

Southern Hash Browns

With Clint's Deli out of the picture, I pulled out Mrs. S. R. Dull's book *Southern Cooking*, first published in 1928. Between the recipes for boiled collard sprouts and congealed fruit—which sounds like the sort of thing you might get on gourmet night at the prison farm—she gives these instructions for making hash brown potatoes: Dice cold leftover potatoes (about a cup, she says, which doesn't sound like much). Put into a pan and with a biscuit cutter chop again, sprinkle with a little flour to hold together and chop some more; then add salt and pepper. In a heavy frying pan, put about 2 tablespoons of bacon drippings or butter, pour in the potatoes and spread them out to about the size of a saucer, half an inch thick. Cook over medium heat until the bottom is well browned, and the flour used as a binder is well cooked. Lift up with a battercake turner—found in the battercake section of your local Southern-style cookware shop—place on a plate and serve.

Sausage and New Potato Salad

Perfect summer food.

Cook on the barbecue or in the pan 1 pound of fresh German or Italian-style pork sausage. This can be done in advance, although the dish tastes best when all the ingredients are freshly cooked and still a little warm. Steam 2 pounds of smallish new potatoes and then cut them in half and set in a large serving bowl. Add the sausages, cut into bite-sized pieces, and 1 onion and ½ red pepper, both finely chopped. Pour a Dijon mustard vinaigrette (5 ounces olive oil, 1 ounce good vinegar, 3 good tablespoons mustard, whipped together over it all), stir well and garnish with plenty of chopped chives.

FADS AND
FASHION

EVERYONE WANTS TO BE AN ARTIST IN the kitchen but some cooks, hoping to rise above the rest, are determined to become architects as well. Not content with displaying their talents on the relatively flat surface of a plate, they have redirected food heavenward and put a little more hauteur into haute cuisine. Rib-eye steaks are stood on end, squid swim erect on a mound of roasted red peppers and chicken breasts perched on building blocks of green asparagus are themselves crowned with an overhang of allumette potatoes.

Though not quite in the realm of the World Trade Center, these vertical meals regularly ascend to a height of six or seven inches. Some, slipping the surly bonds of earth, propped up by groaning mounds of bok choy, stewed rapini or weighty nuggets of barley risotto, can go even higher. Stand a ruler on end, helicopter in a sprig of organic basil to top it off, and you begin to get an idea of the modern meal's upward thrust. The first requirement for doing justice to these skyscraping suppers is a high ceiling. The second is the mouth span of an anaconda.

The trend toward tall food, which is far from being the looniest thing we've inflicted on our food in this insecure era, got its start in a city where verticality is accepted as a virtue. New Yorkers, long used to the idea that the maximum amount of height must be extracted from the measliest bit of real estate, had no trouble accepting the idea that a pyramid of food was somehow superior to a low-rise.

One must pause here for a moment's reflection, since these are the same New Yorkers who not so many years ago oohed and ahed at the low-density minimalism of nouvelle cuisine, where tiny quenelles of shrimp were isolated across a kiwi-and-tomato coulis like cottages on the shores of the Hamptons. But only for a moment. Memories are short in the food business, and very selective. What seemed brilliant yesterday will be revealed as trite tomorrow. The important thing for industry leaders is to stay one step ahead of the changes, and not have the foresight to see that the day will soon come when you will laugh at the folie de grandeur of the tall food you now claim to adore.

Somewhere, someone is already laughing, of course—food fads have a built-in obsolescence. Before you enrol in the tall-food seminar at your local cooking school, it may be wise to ask whether the trend has already spent itself, like some giant spaceship that rises off the ground in great bursts of flame and smoke, only to collapse limply in pieces within moments. The signs of creeping suburbanization have been there for some time: a photo spread in *Gourmet* of steak slices climbing a mountain of thinly sliced raw cabbage, a feature article in *The Wall Street Journal* (not usually the handbook of cutting-edge chefs) detailing monstrous chicken-salad sandwiches and towers of tuna, a legion of chefs out in the culinary hinterland beyond New York busy consolidating their position as the local tall-food upstarts.

Sitting on the terrace of a lively restaurant in, by Manhattan standards, the middle of nowhere, I suddenly found myself the target of this rising trend. A conversation with long-lost friends braked to a halt as dinner appeared on the distant horizon. Larger and larger it loomed, and as we gaped in silence—more stunned than awestruck—the menu monoliths, Stonehenge-like in their bulk, assumed their place on the table. It became hard to talk of anything else. We first tried to figure out what strange new shapes had entered our lives—an upright rack of lamb ceases to look like an edible—before breaking out the slide rules to calculate how they managed to prop it up so high. I hope we remembered to eat it. I think we did, though the taste escapes me.

Tall food is meant to overwhelm and that is not necessarily a good thing for a cook who wants to keep the conversation going. The old chefs who used to waste their time sculpting swans out of lard were equally intent on making an impression, and perhaps succeeded in stopping short the high society of their time. But they were not creating food. Their modern counterparts work with ingredients that are meant to be eaten, but it's difficult to believe their carefully cooked fantasies taste better for being painstakingly arranged like a class photograph, in order of height. Saucing becomes meaningless when a salmon steak rises high off the plate, and with the airborne meat as the centrepiece, the accompanying vegetables are reduced to the role of props. Do you really want to eat a dish composed on the basis of erect bearing and supporting strength?

Food should be a comfort. Instead, in the kitchens and workshops of the superstar chefs, it has become supportive only in an architectural sense. These guardians of the gas-fired flame feel the need to amaze and overwhelm. Their status is directly connected with a sense of superiority that must be reinforced with every aspect of a meal—if everything they dished out looked and tasted just like something you could do at home on a good day, why would you take out a second mortgage to sample it at their restaurants?

But bringing food back into the home doesn't by itself keep you safe from the intimidating power of fads and fashion. Because wherever you turn, in your desire to make food a part of everyday life, there's a certain someone standing in the way.

She seems folksy and almost accessible, that ever-smiling ex-model with the youthful blond bangs concealing the rows of wrinkles. But the real Martha Stewart is far more imposing than any restaurant chef, if only because she infiltrates the home in so many different ways. Let's see where we stand now. There's the syndicated TV show, a triumph of superwoman domesticity that makes you look upon yourself and despair. The TV show spins off into a video empire, so that if you failed to understand how to make the edible stained-glass window on your gingerbread house the first time round, you can take a refresher course.

Or, if you prefer to be browbeaten by Martha in smaller doses, you can catch her appearances on the CBS show *This Morning*, where she has evolved into the correspondent with special responsibility for Life—basically whatever's left after the far less influential politicians and celebrities have said their bit. CBS, seeming to acknowledge Martha's aspirations for global conquest, sent her off to Cuba to cover the lifestyle side of Pope John Paul II's landmark visit. Castro was still in power when she left, but at least he was hand-rolling his own cigars and ordering political detainees to faux-finish their cells.

Then there are Martha's books, on such diverse but necessary subjects as pies, tarts and weddings—no word yet on whether the Pope approved her revised version of the Bible, the one where Jesus now praises the woman named Martha instead of rebuking her for fussing over household tasks. In the meantime, seek her divine inspiration in *Martha Stewart Living* magazine, or in her weekly column offered up to a waiting world that can't wait for the monthly Martha. If you don't feel like reading, you can always catch her motivational speeches on the lecture circuit.

And I'm told there's some connection with Kmart, though I've never ventured inside a Kmart to see. I wonder if Martha and I have that in common.

If so, it's the only trait we share, my modelling career having been cut short by my height being cut short, and my hair having fallen out at about the time my wrinkles needed hiding. No, I lie. We do have a common interest in food, and yet why do I think that Martha would consider me only a tangent to her well-rounded circle? Martha believes that every meal, every part of every meal, is an event that deserves the most deliberate attention to detail. I think life is too brief to worry about not owning special chive scissors, and if we become enslaved by our batterie de cuisine we lose sight of the idea that cooking is a pleasure. And who, we should always be asking, prepares and cleans up for Martha? Or, to put it another way, how long do the credits roll in the story of your life?

Martha insists that the setting is as important as the food, that the Limoges and Wedgwood and the view out the French windows of the cherry orchard in bloom are necessary parts of the pleasure. I persist in feeling that the way of life she embodies makes the rest of us feel inadequate, since we pine for the eternally elusive orchard (or paddock or chicken run or in-house dairy) instead of calculating the number of good meals we could make because we're not busy pruning (and grooming and feeding and milking).

Martha says the meaning of life lies in doing everything yourself. I say the main advantage of modern society is that other people work for you, as you for them, and that you don't have to stuff your own boudin noir or breed your own sheep to make a pale imitation of Roquefort—somebody else has already done it. (Of course you wouldn't ever breed sheep, even if you envied Martha for doing so. But the advantage of living in the twentieth century is that you shouldn't have to feel bad for not doing it.)

Martha, above all, thinks food is about entertaining. I think food is a pleasure in its own right — if people want entertainment with their meal, they must supply their own, or hire Drew Carey as the after-dinner speaker. That said, it's surprising how entertaining guests can be when the smoked-salmon-and-sour-cream pizzette hit the table. The best test of good food — anti-Martha cuisine — is if the invitees make more noise when they eat it than when they first see it. ("Ooh! Ahh! Where did you learn to do carrot origami?")

Come to think of it, has anyone ever eaten Martha's food, or is it just shown to the camera and then paraded away, like couture on a runway?

Too much of the food we consume has been cooked for show. No one would wear a Versace catsuit for dinner with friends — people with Versace catsuits don't have friends in the conventional use of the term — and yet what we put on the table has the same aspirations to impress, astonish and in some desperate way validate our membership in the avant-garde. The excitable trend-spotters who show us the lead believe that our taste buds, like our world, must turn upside down every year. Combining the clairvoyance of Nostradamus with the mutability of Madonna, they dream up the fashions that wiser people will spend the rest of the year trying to avoid.

There are trends and fashions that have a justification for entering our kitchen, that follow on some historical process or economic change. The Vietnam War spurred on the hippie movement, which included the back-to-the-land types who found a higher purpose in the kind of market gardening and cooking that inspired the influential Alice Waters and her produce-friendly style of Californian cuisine. The war also caused the dislocation of peoples from Southeast Asia, who brought their cuisines to North America and Europe and eventually made us familiar with the lemon grass and coconut milk that are a part of any outward-looking chef's inventory.

But then there are the other trends, the more noxious kind formulated entirely at random that exist only to separate the know-it-alls from the out-of-its. I remember when some arbiter of taste in his New Year's message decided that the hot dish for the coming months was none other than Welsh rabbit. I have to admit that designating melted leftover cheese as the latest thing was an inspired choice. It was harder for reasonable people to dismiss it as the creation of some fashionable flake because it was both traditional and simple, two qualities the more predictable trendoids avoid at all costs. It didn't seem, at first bite, like a food that would wow the jaded jet-setters of your acquaintance. It sounded more like what you get when the big trend for the year before was accumulating hard cheese at the back of the refrigerator.

But the problem for me was that I've been eating Welsh rabbit for years with no awareness I was leading the avant-garde. I'd even mastered the Druid incantation that keeps the heated cheese from going all watery. And yet like all those deranged people who wore underwear outside their clothes long before Madonna got around to it, I couldn't see why my simple tastes had to become a trend, why I had to feel self-conscious about the meal I was sitting down to. There had to be a reason, though it was much more likely a conceit in some fashionable mind than any great hunger after the collapse of communism for melted Caerphilly.

I think the logic must have gone something like this: people in this frantic, over-leveraged world are looking for food that is simple, traditional and cheap. What better than a warm, filling meal that the worn-out cook could make out of leftovers the minute she walked through the door? Then again, it may have more to do with the Celtic revival, New Age earth worship and the search for Camelot. I just don't know. Spotting trends is such a tricky business.

Using the same logic that well-paid experts in the field use to counsel restaurateurs, supermarkets, canned-soup makers and the like, you can come up with all kinds of absurdities that are disturbingly close to reality. Take the demographer's standard insight that aging baby boomers will want to seek more vicarious excitement as the boundaries of their life begin to close in. The consequence at the table? Food from the world's conflicts will become newly popular, and regional recipes brought back from the factions fighting it out on the streets of [insert front-page trouble spot here] will take pride of place among adventurous diners bored by foods that lack the frisson of danger. Call it discomfort food.

Of course you could just as easily turn the demographer's observation around. As baby boomers grow older, their tastes will become more conservative even as their better judgment says they must follow trends or die. That's where Welsh rabbit comes in, certifiably fashionable and yet totally unchallenging. And that's why we see all kinds of plain food submitting to the influences of upward mobility. In the wake of four-cheese macaroni and baked potatoes with truffle oil, you can predict with certainty that shepherd's pie will undergo a Pygmalion-like transformation. At the finest hotels and the most luxurious tables, the working man's Monday-night leftover dish of ground grey roast beef and lumpy mash will be soon be made with hand-creamed Yukon Gold potatoes and hand-ripped single-estate Shropshire lamb. It will cost $30 a plate, the ultimate confirmation that this is food to be taken seriously.

Will the fondness for baby vegetables finally be revealed as a trend-spotter's fabrication—because why would anyone prefer a food in miniature? Then it will follow, according to the inevitable oscillations of fashion, that giant veggies will finally come into their own. Huge overgrown pumpkins and squashes will make the groaning board groan even louder and connoisseurs will become conversant with the results of elite English marrow-judging competitions just as they now memorize the placings at the Great Australian Shiraz Challenge.

After the cocktail craze and the single-malt cult, beer will come back with a bang. Aging baby boomers, desperate to relive their past glories, will get together at each others' homes on Friday nights and chugalug cases of suds bought with fake ID. Take-out double-cheese-and-pepperoni pizzas will be the de rigueur accompaniment. Children and careers will not be mentioned. Fashionable dining out, meanwhile, will become even more in-your-face. A couple years back, every trendy restaurant worth its unrefined sea salt was full of fur-clad models chowing down on twenty-four-ounce steaks between puffs of hand-rolled Cuban cigars. This could be the year they finally bring their drug habits out into the open, shooting up from designer hypodermics while knocking back bowls and bowls of figure-flattering shark-fin soup from hand-slaughtered sharks. Or maybe not. Maybe this will be the year they go all nostalgic and sentimental, reverting to the model's traditional fare of no-fat yogurt, cigarettes and fingernails.

Food trends have their use and their purpose, as they persuade our diets to acknowledge an ever-changing world. Somebody in Italy had to pick up on the possibilities of the tomato, and the results on balance aren't all that bad. We should congratulate the people who caught our attention with Thai food, olive oil, balsamic vinegar, sushi, warm salads, low-salt potato chips, Middle Eastern dips, bitter salad greens and pommes frites.

But the honour roll is awfully short compared to the duds that have held us in thrall. Do you remember those rubbery mousses that once stuffed every veal chop and chicken breast? Or the blackened fish of Cajun cooking that everyone said was the next trend, until they had a bite? Like vengeful Jeremiahs, the prophets have cursed us with nasturtium salads, fish cooked on only one side, anorectic spa cooking, the return of meatloaf, the triumph of rice bran, black bell peppers, white eggplant and baby vegetables that look like they should have a speaking part in a Disney cartoon.

We like to pretend there is something absolute about food, that good can easily be distinguished from bad. How else, after all, can we invite people round for dinner with any confidence if everything is relative on the plate? How else can we despise other people's trends while adoring our own?

Yet we know not just that taste is a personal thing—why else prefer lamb to beef, or cilantro to parsley?—but that personal tastes are fleeting. This seems obvious enough when we contrast our childish enthusiasms for vinegar-and-gravy fries with our grown-up passion for garlic mashed potatoes. But even in adulthood, long after we've settled on a career to carry us through to retirement and a mate who's built to last, we're still adjusting our culinary likes and dislikes.

Look at the way our feelings about food have been mutated by our changing notions of health. Fat, so long the symbol of a rich and satisfying diet, has been successfully demonized by cookbook authors writing for an aging readership grown nervous about mortality. For a low-fat diet to be embraced with any kind of zeal, however, the taste buds must be transformed. It's this seemingly radical change that Dean Ornish describes when he urges the shift from whole milk to skim in his *Everyday Cooking with Dr. Dean Ornish*: "At first most people find that the skim milk tastes like water, not very good. After a week or two, it tastes fine. If you then go out to dinner and are served whole milk, it doesn't even taste very good—too greasy, too rich, like cream."

As a fan of whole milk, of anything that's greasy and rich and creamy, I don't like this idea that my enthusiasm is so unfixed and evanescent. I'm pretty certain skim milk never tastes fine, even after years of trying—it's just that your sense of superiority has conquered your sense of taste. Anorexia is the ultimate expression of this perverse desire to let the mind fool the body. Yet even if I want to believe in good and bad, right and wrong, I can't deny the conviction that people I'm certain are misguided bring to their eating habits. Hard-working Scots for generations have eaten their porridge with cream. Try that on your health-conscious friends, who would gag at the first taste of something so lush. Similarly with tea: people who like it with milk are appalled if you offer them cream, but those who drink it straight up can't understand why anyone would adulterate a good brew with milk. And pity the poor children of the whole-milk household who claim they will never recover from their first taste of skim at a friend's; the friend's distaste for whole milk is just as strong and certain.

Dogmatism I can at least respect. Food, even bad food, should inspire strong feelings. It's too important a part of our lives to be turned into fashion's toy, a lifestyle adjunct used to carry messages about our sophistication and style. For proof, consider what happened to the artichoke.

How in the world could anyone develop a fondness for this difficult vegetable and feel a need to inflict it on others—unless they were enslaved by fashion? Yes, we have to salute the genius who first cleared away the leaves and choke to uncover the succulent little heart (though I'm pretty sure this was a last resort in time of famine after the household pets and the ceiling tiles had already been consumed). But why would anyone take this marginal pleasure and turn it into the sadistic host's instrument of torture, forcing guests to feign glee as they suck the bitterness from one unyielding leaf after another? When sensible people can buy their artichoke hearts in bottled form—one of those instances where a processed vegetable is clearly superior to the painstakingly homemade version—who persuaded *Saveur* magazine to run a ten-page spread on the artichokes of Syria? Apart from the Syrian Artichoke Marketing Board and the Hafez-al-Assad Goodwill Foundation, I mean.

While bottled artichoke hearts take on the oily, tart and herbal qualities of their marinade, a fresh artichoke doesn't have much flavour at all—"delicate" is the kindest description its supporters can come up with, which assumes that the harsh taste from the leaves isn't still lingering in your mouth. And another thing against fresh artichokes: they make your wine taste nasty and metallic—as good a reason as any not to bother with them.

The rage for artichokes can be explained up to a point: novelty value, the popularity of the Mediterranean diet, the bonding experience that hands-on leaf stripping brings to any social gathering. But how do we account for the revival of such deservedly dead vegetables as turnips and Brussels sprouts during the comfort-food craze of the last few years? As usual, the answers have less to do with the foods themselves and more to do with the changes that have come about since Mom used to boil the spinach to death and declare it good for you:

- Health mania: the post-war children whose mothers were so concerned about what was good for them are now old enough to be sensing their own mortality. It's unlikely that a few cubes of long-cooked beet in a deep-fried won ton will enable them to join the ranks of the immortals, but it's easier to fight cancer by eating marinated cauliflower than by changing your genetic code.

- Economic recessions: since the 1980s one led to the grosser excesses of the Reagan years, it may at first seem odd that the 1990s one gave us cooked greens and deep-fried root vegetables. But if you think of the more recent recession in religious terms, as retribution for over-the-top charity balls and cocaine-fuelled corporate raiding, then the rustic peasant diet that has taken hold in recent years—and branched off into Third World and vegetarian cuisines as a further rejection of capitalist indulgence—comes to be seen as a form of repentance.

- The corporate recovery: the economy may have improved on paper, but only because businesses determined to maximize profits (and position themselves for the next recession) turned leaner and meaner. Somewhere, the bosses are living for today with their cigars and U.S. Prime steaks. But for harried employees, expense accounts get a thorough examination, and stockholders' interests extend right down to the garnish on the appetizer plate. It's a lot easier to sell the virtues of grilled chicken on a bed of beet greens than lobster in cream sauce. If the CEO stops by the table for a chat, all he'll see are the foods his mother said were good for him.

- Nostalgia: speaking of Mother, we may not have cared for the way she boiled spinach or stewed cabbage, but we fondly wish to relive the happy days when her cooking filled the house with its own peculiar aromas. Grilled mahi mahi and mango sorbet in a macadamia-nut tuile hardly have the same effect. So when we see a mess of greens on our plate—good thing the old lady never cooked chitlins—the oppression is temporarily lifted from our souls and we are transported back to those innocent times. Of course, the bitter greens of the Golden Age weren't even all that good for you. When Mom boiled spinach for a prolonged time, the nutritional value decreased rapidly, the colour turned an unappealing grey-green and the metallic taste of oxalic acid was concentrated enough to make you gag.

The fashionable old-fashioned vegetables cooked by modern chefs, superior though they may be in taste, are not necessarily the stuff of health food either. A recipe gleaned from Patricia Wells' *Trattoria* requires the patient cook to boil spinach in six litres of salted water for three minutes. The spinach is drained, then rinsed with cold water, then drained again. Then it's chopped and the remaining liquid is vigorously pressed out one more time. With its vital juices discarded, the spinach is then sautéed with garlicky olive oil, flavoured with salt, pepper and lemon juice, and served. It may not be very good for you, but it's still very good.

Cooking, even fashionable cooking, must not lose track of taste. If vitamin A intake is paramount in your mind, take a pill — that way at least you won't ruin the spinach for the rest of us by steaming it with a puritanical disregard for flavour. If it's nostalgia that's governing your appetite this season, at least blend your style sense with common sense. When you put some care and effort and imagination into cooking mashed potatoes, a tired old dish is transformed; do the same with Brussels sprouts and they taste no better than they did when you boiled them with mutton for your Beatlemania party back in 1964.

Still, those of us who've left behind the Big Gulps and corn dogs of a best-forgotten youth have no reason to be complacent. Why do I even look at the tofu section of a Chinese menu or think of ordering an Italian dish that comes with stodgy baked polenta or feel tempted by the prospect of starchy fried plantain at the latest Latin hot spot? When the lasagna recipe calls for a layer of ricotta, what madness is it that makes a cook obey? Ricotta, as far as I can tell, has no flavour. Any texture it has can be likened to meat that's already been chewed or the paper you had to eat after your teacher discovered you passing notes around the class. But compared to an artichoke or a ceiling tile, it's relatively inoffensive.

Food preferences are so bizarre. Does anyone really crave whitefish or smelt or orange roughy? Is there a reason why some people start to tremble ecstatically when you bring up the subject of the omelette? Can the taste of veal really be so beguiling that you will endure a crisis of conscience to choose it over beef or chicken? Sure, there's osso buco, but that's at least made with a cut of meat that has some flavour, and most people like it for the sauce and saffron rice, anyway. And what about asparagus? Its taste is bitter, its texture is stringy, its price is inexplicably high and its dimensions make it uncookable. How this stalky fern came to be regarded as an exciting vegetable, I'll never know — the phallic shape may be a factor, but if that were enough of an explanation, we'd all be hungering for geoducks.

Desperate to flee fads and status-consciousness, to elude the trend-setters and the healthmongers alike, we seek refuge with ice cream. Here the rules of fashion and the principles of Darwin do not apply, at least not in any way a reasonable person would understand. If only the fittest survived, healthy freezers would be devoted exclusively to mango sorbet, lemon granita and other fruit essences. And if à la mode were more modish, high-fat ice cream would have died out along with its most ardent devotees, cookie dough never would have found its way into a Häagen-Dazs tub and Ben and Jerry would have gone the way of Cheech and Chong.

But as Howard Stern serves to remind us, evolution is not entirely rational. Faced with a choice between what has officially been declared hip or healthy and what actually tastes good, a surprising number of people go against all reason and consume the saturated fats that will ultimately consume them. How bad is it? For two scoops of premium — i.e., high-fat — ice cream, the saturated-fat content is more than half the recommended daily intake. Have a second helping and you risk eating into tomorrow's allowance, if there is a tomorrow.

Nobody wants to hear bad news about what we eat — apart from diet flagellants and a few doomsday nutritionists — and there's a natural tendency to shrug off the food warnings that come our way by heading in the opposite direction. Fettuccine

Alfredo is a heart attack waiting to happen? Yeah, well I'm carbo-loading for next year's marathon. Takeout Chinese food clogs the arteries? I hear won ton batter's high in fibre.

But who are we trying to fool? Ice cream is not health food. It doesn't figure prominently in the diets of those half-starved lab rats who live twice as long as their well-fed cousins. When the research scientists at Häagen-Dazs first pondered a new line of ice creams for our valetudinarian times, they didn't come up with High-Fibre Brown Bread Sherbet or Tofu-Flavoured Nice Cream. Aiming directly at creaky baby boomers who wanted a break from the worries of the world—one of those after-hours trends that pretends not to be a trend—they created the most escapist and decadent flavours possible: Triple Brownie Overload, Caramel Cone Explosion, Cookie Dough Dynamo, Cappuccino Commotion.

Now I suppose there's a therapeutic argument at work here that says the ice cream makers were simply trying to appeal to our inner child, the one who used to gorge contentedly on the birth-day brownies, sneak the Halloween caramels and lick the egg beaters as the cookies baked. If I had to come up with a defence of these flavours before a jury of serious people, I'd certainly cross my fingers and say something like that. But the fact is, they were a knock-off of even weirder flavours from the highly idiosyncratic Ben & Jerry's.

Where Häagen-Dazs seems to feel that they have done their bit by slipping a few pieces of cone into the silky ice cream of their Caramel Cone Explosion, Ben & Jerry's took excess to the limit: mouth-filling chunks of mint cookies were worked into Mint Chocolate Cookie, Peanut Butter Cup was filled with whole peanut-butter-cup chocolates and Chocolate Chip Cookie Dough incorporated gobs of gooey dough into high-fat ice cream—or is it the other way around? My personal favourite, over several years of nibbling, was Rainforest Crunch. In true Ben & Jerry's style, it overflowed with large pieces of actual rainforest—or at least its ice cream version: nut brittle made from cashews and Brazil nuts grown in Latin America as part of a Ben & Jerry's project to increase farm incomes and spare the rainforest. If it were just plain old supermarket-freezer peanut-brittle ice cream destroying my digestion and clogging my arteries, would I have brought myself to devour it with quite the same degree of wild abandon? I doubt it.

Ben & Jerry's ice cream is sold at a premium, but the sermons on social justice come free. The label of Heath Toffee Crunch that I discovered one tooth-destroying day carried the fighting words: "We support family farmers because we believe they are central to the heritage and quality of life in Vermont and across America." To trumpet their Wavy Gravy flavour (made not from gravy but caramel-cashew Brazil-nut ice cream with roasted almonds and a chocolate-hazelnut fudge swirl), they sermonized as follows: "The ideals of social justice and a healthy planet are the legacies of the Woodstock Nation. It's up to all of us to bring them home." The moralizing is unrelenting. When I toured the Ben & Jerry's plant in Waterbury, Vermont, a few summers back, the guide offered a frozen prize to the first person who could answer this skill-testing question: "What percentage of pre-tax profits does Ben & Jerry's donate to social justice?" Two scoops of Chocolate Fudge Brownie to the man who said 7.5 per cent.

This is called having your cookie dough and eating it too. But for all the glee with which Ben & Jerry's promoted political causes and high-fat food, the style-conscious '90s necessitated second thoughts. A slip in profits forced them to redefine the legacies of Woodstock Nation so that it now includes a greater emphasis on low-fat products. Don't tell David Crosby.

Of course, dope was a low-fat product (unless you added it to your brownies), so maybe there's nothing odd about the company that made cookie dough a flavour now putting its faith in the recuperative powers of skim-milk frozen yogurt. But I sense a loss of principle—the self-denial side of skim milk (and is there any other side?) just isn't in the self-gratifying Woodstock tradition. Häagen-Dazs, meanwhile, has also shifted priorities, moving from the silly self-indulgence of Cookie Dough Dynamo to the sophistication of Dulce de Leche—caramel ripple the worldly South American way.

To escape the trends that pursue us wherever we go, we have to look for something more timeless, foods less likely to sell their soul for a little transitory fame on a fashionable menu. Actually, I thought the original dulce de leche—a luscious Hispanic fudge made from condensed milk and sugar—did the job quite nicely. In that slightly pathetic way of people who are determined to defy food trends, I used to carry home a bar of the stuff whenever I went to the parts of the world where it was a staple. Every night I would make myself eat a slice, determined to enjoy a food because I liked the odd, haunting, ancient taste of it and not because I'd read about it in a restaurant review. But all the time, forcing it on family and friends who couldn't get away fast enough, I was serving as a storm trooper for the culinary avant-garde. And now the big corporations have moved in (Häagen-Dazs is a part of Pillsbury, which is owned by the ominous-sounding Diageo PLC, than which you can't get much bigger), and it's time for the more independent-minded of us to move on.

So I tried to think of a way to defy the fashionable eaters, to hit them where it hurts, and here is my response: processed vegetables. What better way to offend the fresh-is-best crowd?

It was a time when the markets were overflowing with seasonal produce and the street-corner greengrocers turned their sidewalks into a gallery of still lifes. The stalks of broccoli spilling out of the old bushel baskets had the vigorous sheen of the newly harvested, and green-topped beets promised a tender, lively taste for salads and soups. It was that moment in the year when you couldn't steal a peek at a basket of red peppers without being jostled by packs of chefs specializing in what they like to call fresh-market cuisine.

The fresh-market part I have no quarrel with. No one could argue that the undercooked beet greens and virginal florets of broccoli in their cooking were not long from the ground. But the bit about cuisine—now that was more questionable. Cuisine, contrary to the current wisdom that predicts a long and stylish life for any cook who consorts with raw or nearly raw vegetables, is not about getting to the market early in the day. Freshness isn't everything. Ripeness isn't all.

Yes, I'm as grateful as anyone for the timely arrival of cheap and healthy-looking produce. Who couldn't use a little colour in the neighbourhood after months of staring at chewing gum squashed onto the sidewalk? But I also know that a vegetable in and of itself is not much of a meal, certainly not after the first six or eight plates of raw vegetables and heaping bowls of steamed vegetables and mugs of yet another puréed vegetable soup. As impressive as the sidewalk cornucopia must be in places with a confined growing season, some of the best vegetable flavours are to be found year-in, year-out in tiny bottles and jars lining drab supermarket shelves.

This is heresy, of course. Proponents of the dullness that is the modern diet despise foods that have been adulterated and processed by human hands. But in this, as in so many other things, their experience is as limited as their imagination. Sure, packaged broccoli-soup powder and the pimento blob that decorates the pickled olive aren't vegetables at their most ambitious. But look further, taste with your mouth and not your brain, and you will become convinced that what vegetables need is more of a helping hand.

And one of the best places to look for help is Italy. Drawing on the ingenuity that comes from dealing with several millennia worth of abundance, tradition-minded Italian processors know how to capture the flavours of seasonal foods and even enhance them. Some of their specialties — marinated artichokes, pesto, sun-dried tomatoes — have enjoyed fleeting fame when briefly taken up by those who eat fashionably. But then they're dropped, leaving me to wonder why, if they were so good in the first place, they're so tiresome now.

At the risk of seeming several thousand years out of date, while the avant-garde has already had its way with jicamas and moved on to tomatillos, the Italians turn out products that make a point of defying fashion. You want freshness? Then go manhandle a gourd at a pick-your-own farm and come home happy with the thrill of the chase. But for intense and penetrating flavours, for haunting ingredients that pique the appetite and improve a dish in ways unimagined by more straightforward cooks, open up the neat and tidy jars from Puglia, Sardinia and other unfashionable addresses. There you'll find whole roasted artichokes and onions that carry a savage bittersweet taste from the grill, mild straw mushrooms soaked in rich olive oil, lush strips of tender eggplant that manage to have a taste and a texture you would never come across in the raw.

These marinated vegetables work well on an antipasto plate, where their intense taste becomes a reference point for all the other dishes in the mix. But with the spreads made from olives, artichokes, anchovies and dried tomatoes, it's almost enough to sample a little bit of each on a spoon as if they were varieties of caviar. It would be wrong to treat all food with this kind of reverence — most fresh produce couldn't stand such prolonged scrutiny — but if you find yourself with someone patient and kind, this is a very pleasant way to pass the time. (Of course, if they're that patient and kind, skip the spoon and savour the spreads directly from the more inviting surfaces of their naked flesh.)

The best of these marinades and spreads aren't cheap by the standards of bulk produce, though there are cheaper versions that make up in price what they lack in subtlety. If you invest a lot of money in your foods, you may want to get more use out of them: a steak sandwich with olive paste is a wonder, and you might think about substituting a spoonful or two wherever you would use mustard or horseradish—chicken with artichoke spread can be very good, though chicken with marinated grilled artichokes might be even better. Pious people of simple tastes will be happy just to use a little tomato paste to liven up bland foods like halved hard-boiled eggs—take out the yolk and blend it with the paste along with a little olive oil before replacing it in the white. A few dollops of olive or anchovy paste on pizza or pasta dishes gives them a life they never knew they had—but you have to watch out for the inherent saltiness of these products, an Old World value not nearly so well aligned with modern tastes.

Though as always in trying to describe contemporary fashions in food, we have to distinguish between what people profess to eat and what they actually do knock back when they're living it up. I once talked to an urban archaeologist whose specialty was studying people's garbage. Before investigating their trash on the sly, he'd ask them about their diets and get the well-meaning answers you'd expect: little red meat, hardly any fat, lots of vegetables, less and less junk food. Then he'd open up their garbage and discover that they'd out-and-out lied to him, as they probably had to every surveyor who asked official questions about their eating habits.

We mean well. We even buy those fresh vegetables and talk about cutting down on our sodium intake. But the fashionable chefs know us better than we know ourselves. They realize that whatever our statements to the contrary, we want our meals to jump out, to be special, to engage our senses rather than our sensibilities. A mild temperament may have been lauded by Jane Austen, but in a more competitive era, even one that pretends to enthusiasm for slightly neurotic eighteenth-century novels of manners, mildness just won't do. Big personalities rule the roost and a life that escapes notice is a life consigned to failure. Like mild weather and mild-natured people, mild food has been left behind in the pursuit of extremes.

It is an attention-grabbing world out there, and one of the many unhappy results in the modern kitchen is the use of fresh herbs to heighten the belligerence level on the plate. Herbs have a predisposition to dominate a dish. Yet people who wouldn't think of splashing Obsession on a newborn child or diluting a Chardonnay with Cointreau happily toss branches of rosemary or lime leaf over everything that passes from the stove to the table.

It's not that herbs are bad. They've been a part of the kitchen for thousands of years, after all, adding beguiling fragrances to foods that would have been remarkably bland otherwise. A single bay leaf tossed into a beef stew and left to diffuse its aromas for hours provides a depth of flavour that can't be achieved any other way. But for today's chef, herbs are an overamplified statement of freshness first, a flavouring second. Rosemary encountered now and then — on a roast lamb, say — suggestively evokes sheep-scavenged hillsides rising up from the wine-dark sea. But partnered with every pasta and every grill, used to prop up tall food and give a kind of evergreen landscape to plates already thick with flora and fauna, it screams excess.

Nothing in excess, advised the Greeks, sounding uncannily like a with-it government liquor authority; and even if they invented retsina, the rosemary of the wine world, the Greeks still paid lip service to mildness. In the kitchen, this translates into a healthy respect for the virtue of moderation, which sounds pretty ordinary when you're used to throwing chipotle peppers all over your soy-and-ginger-glazed ostrich breast. But ordinary food —

which is to say, food that doesn't immediately grab you by the boutonnière and yell in your face—may not be such a bad thing six days out of seven.

It's obviously not in the nature of mild food to put forward a strong case for itself. A good leg of lamb, well-roasted, is nice meditative fare, perfect for partnering with deep thoughts and a brambly Pinot Noir. But as a typically mild-mannered dish, it doesn't leap out at you from the menu until it's been complicated to the point where it ceases to be simple roast lamb. On the other hand, that roast lamb in the right circumstances can taste better than showier, tarted-up food. Neither crowded, smoky restaurants nor dinner parties devoted to the institution of chatter are capable of showing cooking at its best. One of the reasons the public face of food is so brazen—always wanted to use that word—is that it has to be able to catch our wandering eye.

I won't carry the painted-strumpet analogy any further, as telling as it is, but instead will reflect back on the best example of middling food I've eaten since I entered middle age: simple cabbage rolls, with just the slightest crunch in the leaves encircling a savoury mixture of coarsely chopped pork and paprika-scented rice. Easy on the spices, easy on the herbs, easy to like.

Brandade de Morue

Salt cod used to be a poor person's dish, eaten for lunch on Friday fast days by the devoted Catholics and dedicated garlic-lovers of Provence and the Languedoc. But as the North Atlantic cod fishery declines, the dried fish has become something of an extravagance. This doesn't mean that you have to serve this salt-cod paste with caviar and truffles in the usual way of gastronomic luxuries—olive oil and garlic will do just fine—though you can top it with a couple of poached quail eggs if you're made of money.

You can buy your salt cod either dried or reconstituted, with skin and bones or stripped down to something more workable in the time-challenged kitchen. As much as I enjoy the hardship element of cooking, I suggest you use the pre-soaked, filleted version, at least the first time you make this dish.

Start with 1 pound of dried salt cod or 1½ pounds of the hydrated version. Soak the dried cod for a day in cold water, changing the liquid a couple of times to help reduce the saltiness. Rinse it before cooking, then put it into a pot, cover with cold water and bring slowly to a boil. If the fish is especially salty, or you prefer a milder brandade, let the fish poach at a soft simmer for 5 minutes. Drain the fish and separate it into flakes, picking out any bones. Unless you feel compelled to use your antique Provençal mortar and pestle, place the cod in a food processor with 3 or 4 very finely chopped cloves of garlic. Warm (separately) 1 cup of extra-virgin olive oil and 1 cup of cream (the heavy 35% version is best). Partially blend the cod and garlic, then slowly add the warmed oil. Give another pulse or two, then add the cream. The brandade is best if it's not overprocessed, paste rather than mush. If it turns out to be unbearably salty, thin with mashed potatoes.

Brandade de morue goes best with garlic toast. Moisten slices of a baguette with olive oil, grill or toast quickly (they would have fried them in the old days), rub with a cut garlic clove and serve.

Hungarian Cabbage Rolls

Yes, there are those cabbage rolls that are made from hamburger, Minute Rice and tomato sauce. Then there's the real thing, made by Hungarian cooks who don't mind grinding down the meat from a smoked pork hock. I usually grab a few takeout containers from my local Hungarian store, the St. Clair Delicatessen, on the way home from work, and then let the microwave do its magic. With a thinly sliced cucumber salad, a glass or two of dry Riesling and a slice of poppyseed strudel, it's the perfect dinner at the end of the day for those who crave a little Middle European escapism.

Many Hungarian cooks like to use sour-cabbage leaves for their cabbage rolls, but Edit Szalay, who shared this recipe with me, prefers the milder taste of parboiled fresh cabbage. Ordinarily I'd opt for the stronger flavour of the fermented leaves, being a little too partial to aggressive tastes. But having enjoyed her version many times over, I have admit that moderation has its value. And, besides, with the smoked pork in the filling, there's no shortage of flavour.

Parboil ½ cup of uncooked rice for about 5 minutes. Drain and let cool. Grind ⅓ pound of smoked pork. If you're using pork hock, give the hock 20–30 minutes in gently boiling water to soften up the meat first. Trim away the tougher outside pieces and excess fat before grinding the amount you need. With the rice, mix the smoked meat, ⅔ pound of freshly ground pork, salt and generous amounts of freshly ground pepper and 1 tablespoon of paprika. To make the mixture bind better, you may want to add in 2 beaten eggs as well. Core 1 fresh green cabbage and place it in a pot of boiling water. With sturdy tongs, remove the outer leaves as they soften—you'll want about 12 to 14. (Use the rest of the cabbage, cabbage water and smoked hock bone and trimmings as the basis of a hearty cold-weather soup.) Let the leaves cool so that you can handle them easily, then thin the stalk-end of the leaf so the leaf is more uniform in size and easier to roll. Lay each leaf out flat. Take a small fistful of the meat-rice mixture and place near the broad end of the leaf, then fold over a thin strip from one side, tucking the fold in at the point where it comes in contact with the filling. Roll up the filling loosely and tuck in the other end when you're done. Repeat with the remaining leaves. Layer the bottom of a deep, broad casserole dish with sauerkraut (a milder cooked version is best; German imports are dependable), then set a layer of cabbage rolls on top, placed close to each other so they'll hold together. Cover with another sauerkraut layer, the rest of the cabbage rolls and more sauerkraut.

Heat the oven to 350°F. Meanwhile, heat 1 ounce of vegetable oil in a large pot and stir in 1 tablespoon of flour, then add 1 tablespoon of paprika and 4 cups of cold water. Stir well, then pour the mixture into the casserole dish so that the water rises a little above the cabbage rolls and sauerkraut. Cook at 350°F until the water starts to boil, about 15 minutes, then reduce to 275°F and cook for another 60 to 90 minutes. The first time you make this dish, you may want to test one of the rolls at the hour mark — the great variable is the rice, but it's better to overcook it than undercook it.

Porridge

What's happened to porridge? The bland quick-cooking stuff is one of those modern improvements that has managed to make itself obsolete. If you're really in a hurry, why cook porridge when you can toast a pre-sliced bagel or munch a cream-cheese-and-strawberry cereal bar or skip breakfast altogether?

But classic porridge isn't that much better. The best I can say about boiled oats with salt and cream — the classic way — is that it's solid and warm and non-threatening. Add a few spoonfuls of brown sugar and it becomes sickly sweet and indigestible.

Without trying to win over traditionalists who need to start the day with a solid mass of horse-feed, I'd like to suggest a few variations that might keep porridge alive in the twenty-first century. First of all, experiment a little more with your grains. Try rye or wheat in place of oats or in combination with them. Or, instead of the flattened "rolled" grains, try the nuttier wheat, rye and oat berries available at bulk-food suppliers, health-food stores and from Irish and English sources. With these, as with the non-instant, long-cooking rolled grains, you can save some time by treating them like beans and soaking them overnight before cooking. I cover my rye flakes with milk, not water, and leave them overnight in the refrigerator. By morning they're ready to eat, just as they are, like a cheap, simple and earnest muesli, or heated up with a little more milk.

When it comes to improving on nature, you can treat porridge like granola and add raisins (Australian muscats are the best), chopped dates, dried mango, roasted almonds or hazelnuts, or shredded coconut. But a more appetizing approach is to look on porridge as a savoury rather than a sweet, something in the class of risotto. This can mean adding some quickly sautéed bacon and mushrooms to the cooked wheat berries or, taking a cue from barley soup, some chopped onions and maybe some shredded leftover lamb. Many Chinese like to start their day with rice soups called congee that are flavoured with egg and green onions or root vegetables and pork—order some in dim sum restaurants for inspiration. But the best inspirations may come from Indian cooking, where you can have cracked wheat berries with cinnamon and date sugar (which tastes much like maple sugar) or improve the old breakfast standby, cream of wheat, with eye-opening ginger, cilantro and cashews.

Lightly brown 2 cups cream of wheat in a pan, stirring quickly for 2 or 3 minutes. Remove. Heat some peanut oil in the pan, then add 1 thinly sliced hot pepper, 1 finely chopped medium-sized onion and 1 tablespoon of finely chopped fresh ginger. Cook at a medium heat until ingredients soften. Add 2 cups of water (or stock, if you have any handy), heat to a boil and then add the toasted cream of wheat. Cook until it reaches a porridgy consistency, stirring constantly as you would for risotto. Toward the end of the cooking, add a few sprigs of chopped cilantro, a handful of roasted cashews (chopped if they're jumbo size), 1 tablespoon of butter to enrich the heaving mass of wheat, and salt to taste. If you're using salted cashews, be sure to give the porridge a good stir and a taste before deciding if you need more salt. Other ingredients can be added in the cooking to vary the taste, such as chopped roasted chicken, garlic, raisins and mushrooms.

TOMATOES

IT'S SEPTEMBER and the tomato's time is coming to a close. The shorter days and colder nights are slowing down the progress of the last green fruits on the backyard vines. My Italian neighbours, their cellars full of freshly made spaghetti sauce, have moved on to bottling the first of the autumn wine. Baskets of the bright red warm-weather crop can still be found at the market for those who want a last reminder of summer's easiness. But as the season changes, and the days turn crisp and clear and serious, it becomes time to move on, to potatoes, carrots, cabbage.

Who am I kidding? The tomato is the Baron Munchausen of our vegetable culture—immortal, unstoppable and unavoidable. Walk into any Burger King in December and you'll find the Whopper layered with tomato slices as if it were the height of summer. Spend a few more bucks, raise the level of anticipation a few notches, and the result is still the same: the wind may be howling, the snow may be falling and the Christmas bonuses may be replaced by a gloomy letter of woe. But still the winter ratatouille is on simmer, the mussels are being cooked with chopped tomatoes and the insalata caprese at the top of every Italian menu makes room for the pale pomodori of winter.

Unlike the seasons, which realize the dangers of overstaying a welcome, the tomato seems to think it's always wanted. August and September are its peak months in my part of the world, but the self-aggrandizing tomato has become a year-round fixture. So the season's almost over? Then make way for those rock-solid imports, or the pale greenhouse varieties or bottled salsa, canned Romas, spaghetti sauce in a jar, Manhattan clam chowder, V-8 juice, decorative tubes of Sicilian tomato paste that should not be confused with Crest, and the four hundred other products that carry our memories forward from the last of the summer vine.

The tomato is the supreme example of dietary imbalance. Your standard hamburger comes with both a sliced tomato and a thick spread of sweet ketchup. A pizza isn't considered a pizza without a soupy layer of tomato paste beneath the mozzarella. The tomato is an inevitable standard garnish, a sandwich ingredient, a fundamental part of many soups, the basis of long-cooked casseroles, the standard by which all other pasta toppings are measured, the main constituent of the inescapable salsa, the *sine qua non* of bruschetta, even the basic flavouring of curries at Indian restaurants that care nothing about their tomato-free traditions. (A dining hint: scope out restaurants' trash bins on garbage day, just to know what corners they're cutting and how many cans of tomato sauce they consume; but don't do it with your own garbage pile — that would be too discouraging.)

How bad has it got? Talking to a friend back from an autumn trip in Burgundy and Provence, I asked him what impressed him most. He thought for a moment, and I waited to hear him make me envious with his praise for the Côte de Beaune or the Palace of the Popes or the plainsong at a hilltop monastery where they bake their own olive bread.

"No tomatoes," he answered finally. Ten days of determined eating, and not a whiff of the great red interloper.

Now I'm sure he was playing to his audience; if his inquisitor had been, say, Greg Norman, his answer might have been, "No water hazards." But, still, try to imagine a trip anywhere in North

America that could prompt the answer "No tomatoes." It just isn't possible. You can't avoid them. Only by crossing the great water hazards of the Atlantic and Pacific can we realize how they've taken over.

There are many explanations for the tomato's supremacy. It's a colourful ingredient that plays well against the greens and browns of other foods. Despite being throughly domesticated in drabber parts of the world, it still evokes sunny, happy places along the Mediterranean or the Gulf of Mexico (its ancestral home). Its versatility allows it to intrude into almost any part of a meal or snack short of dessert (tomato sorbet having never caught on). And though essential to the success of the fast-food industry, it manages to retain a fair amount of flash: tomato focaccia, tomato and saffron soup, spaghettini with sun-dried tomatoes, grilled tuna with tomato salsa, tabbouleh. With so many food trends starting life in Italy and California, champion tomato producers both, this dominance is hardly surprising.

And there's one more factor, though I almost hate to admit it. Tomatoes can taste good.

Oh that's hard to say. It's like cheering for the Yankees or hailing a new Disney show or humming a Lloyd Webber tune. So let me back away from what I said just far enough to feel comfortable. Some tomatoes taste good but many don't, because breeders and growers have other priorities such as firmness or uniform red colour or a low-acid taste or a high yield or good keeping qualities. The reason we see so much tomato in cooked food is that so few tomatoes can be pleasurably eaten on their own.

Not that tomatoes are simple to cook with. Their high water content is one of the things that makes them easy to eat, but when their cell walls are broken down by heat and their juice is released, they both dilute whatever they're added to and turn out mushy themselves. As a result, they need either very short, easy cooking, lengthy simmering or long baking that dries them out without breaking them down (very thin tomato slices on top of a plain pizza show the virtue of this).

If, like me, you're persuaded that the tomato is bent on world dominance, there are a few forms of resistance. Leaving tomatoes out of the mussels goes without saying, but what about no-tomato minestrone, ratatouille based on eggplant and peppers, pizza with just a faint coating of tomato sauce (or with none at all: just olive oil, rosemary, onion slices and Gorgonzola)? And stay clear of authentic salsa—it's good enough to win you over.

Tomato and Bocconcini Salad

Tomatoes will always be with us, and so we must make the best of them. Even those opposed to the tomato's imperialist tendencies, like me, have to admit that there are ways to make it taste good. This dish looks best when the tomato slices are not much larger than the slices of bocconcini. The round balls of soft, snow-white cheese are usually found floating in buckets at better Italian delis. You can substitute fresh buffalo-milk mozzarella very nicely, but firmer pizza mozzarella gives a heavier taste that's out of place in this light summer salad.

Cut 4 to 6 tomatoes in ¼-inch slices, trimming away any woody bits from the core and discarding the fleshier end slices. Cut enough thin slices of bocconcini or buffalo-milk mozzarella to alternate in a one-by-one formation. Layer two rows of the tomatoes and cheese on a slant in a broad, shallow bowl, then dress with lots of good olive oil, chopped chives (some people prefer chopped green onion), a little chopped basil, salt (coarse sea salt works well here) and freshly ground pepper. Serve as a first course.

Breaded Beefsteak Tomatoes

You can use other varieties if you like, but with the huge meaty beefsteaks (and some bacon on the side) this dish becomes a summer meal in itself. Have a good quantity of toasted bread crumbs on hand. Spread out the crumbs on a broad plate or a sheet of wax paper. Cut your tomatoes into ¾-inch slices, discarding the small slices at either end. Gently cook ½ pound of sliced bacon in a broad sauté pan, extracting the fat, which you will use to fry the tomatoes. Set the bacon aside, wrapped up in paper towels. Bread 4 tomato slices (or as many as you can fit in the pan) on both sides and fry in the fat at a medium high heat for about 2 minutes on each side.

In our house, you eat the tomatoes as they come out of the pan along with a couple of slices of bacon, leaving some poor person standing by the stove to produce the next batch. You could take turns doing the breading and cooking, or permit the hungry cook to jump up and down from the table every two minutes.

Baked Tomatoes

A favourite easy-to-make-dish of my garlic-loving daughter, this recipe manages to give flavour to the dullest greenhouse tomatoes.

Heat the oven to 375°F. Slice your 4 to 6 tomatoes in half, hollow out a little bit of the core of each and spoon in a mixture of finely chopped garlic, parsley and a little basil. Paint the surface of the tomatoes with olive oil, grate a little Parmesan over the top and bake in a shallow, broad casserole dish for 10 to 12 minutes, or until soft. Chopped pine nuts make an interesting addition to the filling, in which case use fresh mint instead of the basil.

Fish in Olive Oil

When I spent three years studying Latin and Greek in England, one of the most fascinating books I read had nothing to do with the Classics curriculum. Claudia Roden's intimately observed *A Book of Middle Eastern Food* cheered me up whenever the climate turned cold and the work turned arid. And when I bicycled home from the market with a backpack full of green peppers and fish, needing to take a break from the learned preoccupations of the ancient world, there was this equally ancient Turkish recipe to help me out. It uses the canned tomatoes of winter to good effect.

Start with 2 pounds of fish. I always used mackerel in England, since it was fresh, cheap and full of meaty flavour. The original Turkish recipe uses swordfish, which works well when you can find it. Otherwise try slices of tuna, shark, kingfish or a fresh whole fish with enough flavour to stand out in a stew. Clean your fish and fry it gently in olive oil in a large pan until lightly coloured. Remove the fish to a plate, and in the same pan sauté 2 large sliced onions until tender, then add 2 large, seeded sliced sweet peppers (green or red) and cook until they soften. Add 2 crushed, coarsely chopped garlic cloves and fry for another minute. Finally, add 1 pound of peeled, chopped tomatoes, 1 bunch of finely chopped parsley (not a few stalks, an entire bunch), 1 tablespoon of tomato concentrate diluted in 1 cup of water and a handful of black olives. Stir well, bring to a boil and simmer for 10 minutes.

Return the fish to the pan and spoon the sauce over it, covering it completely. Cook for another 15–20 minutes, or until done. If I'm using a whole fish, I like to take out the skin and bones and cut the meat into large chunks before putting it back in the sauce. Season to taste with salt and pepper, chill and serve cold.

THE THRILL OF
MORTALITY

ON A GREY LONDON DAY, IN THE YEAR
of Our Lord 18—, as unrelenting rain
lashed the streets of Whitechapel... No, that's not right at all. I
was just being melodramatic. It was actually a typical dinnertime
in smug old Toronto, middle of the working week. Two adults,
home late from the unrelenting office, need a quick dinner. The
previous few days have seen a parade of easy options, falafel sandwiches from the friendly Lebanese place, pork chow mein from
the Chinese takeout at the foot of the street, Taco Bell's child-
friendly burritos, barbecued chicken from the Portuguese churrasqueira. The time had come to reclaim the kitchen and create a
real meal.

It was the work of a moment, as all modern meals are supposed to be. Boneless, skinless, fresh-from-the-package chicken
breasts in the effortless urban style were set in a shallow glass
casserole, marinated with extra-virgin olive oil and sprinkled
with oregano and flakes of red pepper. While the chicken roasted
in the oven, a mix of salad greens was arranged in a painted bowl

and grated rösti potatoes browned in the skillet. A lively Riesling was poured and sipped with a sense of accomplishment. The chicken emerged, golden brown and fragrant. And dry as my old hiking boots.

Should we blame the cook? No, and not just because she's got a knife in her steady hands. The fault—the malaise if you will—runs deeper. To discover what went wrong, compare the plainly roasted boneless, skinless chicken breast with the Portuguese barbecued chicken that never fails to please. And what important differences do we see? The Portuguese version of chicken is preceded neither by the word boneless nor—here I warm to my theme (and your destruction)—skinless.

A chicken breast brought down to its bare essentials, sans skin and bones, will almost certainly dry out in the oven no matter how much extra-virgin olive oil you apply to the exterior. With a piece of meat that dense, by the time the innermost part is cooked through, the outer parts are overcooked. A whole chicken spreads out the meat more evenly and allows heat to get at the hard-to-reach parts via bones and the bird's inner cavity. But the most important thing missing from the skinless chicken breast is the skin. And when we talk about skin, we don't just mean the crisp outside layer that concentrates the flavour of hot pepper and salt and garlic and meat juices so nicely. We also have to appreciate the value of the fat underneath.

There, I've done it. I've said good things about fat and lured you into the grease trap of Hell. Let the heavens open up and rain down three-legged toads. Society has turned against fat in a big way, and now that tobacco has been successfully marginalized, the fat-eradication program can proceed in earnest. Chicken comes tough and skinless, cheese is shunned as death food, the Centre for the Study of Science in the Public Interest has proscribed almost every cuisine in the marketplace and if they ever notice the fat content of mother's milk, we're really in trouble.

Is it too late to say that we're going too far? Yes, if you patronize the Chinese restaurants that remove the skin and the bones (and much of the flavour) from their black bean chicken to placate nervous Westerners. Yes again, if you bite into a steak and wonder why you've paid good money for something that tastes like compressed cardboard. The fear of fat has long since ensured that cattle are brought to market leaner and duller. Real beef can still be had, but only for a price, in high-end steakhouses and exclusive meat boutiques, where a rib-eye is prized for its rich and juicy taste and not for its cholesterol-avoidance strategy.

Fat in excess is certainly a bad thing, but it's not something to be feared to the point where small children are forced to drink skim milk and teenaged girls subsist on fat-free frozen dairy desserts (contents: milk ingredients, sugar, glucose, modified milk ingredients, cocoa, mono- and diglycerides, guar gum, xanthan gum, cellulose gum, seaweed). Fat transports vitamins through the body, stimulates the flow of saliva, aids in cell development and keeps a body feeling satisfied between meals, staving off those urges to take a cellulose-gum break. In cooking, fat helps transfer heat from the pan and lubricates the food it's a part of. Meat low in fat toughens easily, and since dry meat requires a sauce you'll probably end up with your dose of fat anyway — unless the no-fat lobby has got to you so successfully that you think a sauce can only be made from puréed fruit, vegetable-water reductions and modified milk ingredients.

I admit I have a distorted outlook on fat, having somehow failed to be swayed by the scare stories that so successfully demonized this essential ingredient. Did it come from watching too many nature shows as a kid, the ones where the bears stored up all that fat to get through the long winter? It's hard to believe the bears would have made it through hibernation by switching to no-fat yogurt. Was it the happy memories of shoestring potatoes cooked in beef suet, before the vegetable-oil brigade took over and made deep-fried potatoes more of a hit-or-miss proposition? Or maybe it was the farmer's market I was taken to as a small fry, where a religious community known as the Brethren had a stall devoted entirely to the gifts of the goose: goose-down pillows, goose-wing dusters (very useful for taunting squeamish friends), a whole bird for the Christmas feast and a small but high-priced tub filled with the bird's rendered fat, better known as goose grease. Though I'm not sure what the goose grease was intended for—I tried it as a sandwich spread, without much success—the important thing was the reverence in which it was held. How could fat be such a bad thing when a hard-working religious group gave it pride of place in their market display? But then, of course, goose grease when transported halfway round the world to a less nervous culture is nothing less than the gras in the fabled foie gras.

What's most important about fat is that it's full of good taste. Take it away and you'll make a meal that might be better for you but is certainly worse to eat.

Look what happened to the pig. In places where food is valued for its own sake, and not as a vaccine against mortality, pigs have status. But in diet-conscious countries where fat is a dirty word not spoken in polite company, the corpulent porker is a thing of shame. Desperate to please nervous consumers, pork producers have streamlined their animals in the hopes of making the word pig less of an insult. Trimmed lean pork is now presented as a chicken equivalent, the ideal substitute in a healthy stir-fry or a quick grill. The only problem is that chicken is cheaper to produce, and when taste is no longer paramount—the standard supermarket chop has the flavour and texture of a grilled Victorian novel—what's the point of buying pork? And by transforming the image of the pig so completely, naive pork producers have also sacrificed the reputation of the traditional products that made the meat so loved in the first place: juicy smoked sausages, fragrantly cured hams, boldly flavoured salamis and, above all, the melt-in-the-mouth fattiness of pâtés and terrines.

Pork is bad enough. Pork fat is worse. Mix the pork and the pork fat with the liver of a pig and you have a mixture that offends most of the principles on which the modern diet is based. Almost no one thinks of making charcuterie any more. It's hard enough finding such obligatory items as pork belly and fresh pork liver (to say nothing of pig's head or bottles of fresh blood for homemade black puddings). But even supposing you turn up the rare butcher who keeps a stock of pig parts in his shop, will you have the courage to buy and cook all that fat? Those who aren't put off pork by ancient religious laws—have you ever stopped to wonder why God was so finicky about his food? Shouldn't He have been omnivorous as well as omnipotent?—are scared away by the equally harsh rulings of all-knowing dieticians.

So even those of us bold and irreligious enough to like a little charcuterie miss out on the pleasure of making it ourselves. We let other people do it for us and enjoy only the finished result, as far as our nervousness and upbringing allow. The fat blended into a slice of terrine goes unnoticed in restaurant meals. It has transformed itself in the cooking and coalesced with the chunks of pork shoulder or duck or veal, taking on a pretty pink tint from the baking that makes the terrine look like nothing more forbidding than well-marbled rare meat.

There may be flecks of green pistachios or knobbly walnuts suspended in the slice that elevate the dish from its humble, pig-sticking origins to something more chic and refined. Instead of the bacon slices or strips of back fat that used to envelop the traditional terrine, the restaurant chef surrounds the square on the plate with the lively green of cooked leeks. Fruit compotes will fill out the rest of the canvas, perhaps lightly pickled crab apples or figs stewed in Cabernet Sauvignon or berries partnered with a simple and absurdly showy icewine jelly. The dish in the end becomes a balanced-diet blend of meat, vegetable and fruit that strives to convince you that it suits this time and place (and get a ruling from the holy men while you're at it: maybe the old laws can now be updated).

The sleight-of-hand approach is one way to sell pâtés and terrines to the modern diner. But the other, far superior approach is to appeal to the sense of risk that surfaces in over-cautious times. I have to admit that this is where my preference lies, partly because I need to feel the frisson of mortality when I eat—my version of scaling Everest—but mostly because I like my pâtés the deadly old way, without elaboration. Serve up a pot of pork rillettes bare of vegetables and fruits and other pretty distractions: the shredded pig sits there in its container immobilized by something solid, something shiny, something congealed, whose name polite society dares not speak. There is nothing to conceal the fact that what you are eating is meat in fat, or to be more accurate, fat on meat.

The juicy, meaty taste characteristic of the best pâtés comes about only with the help of lubricious pig fat that takes on all kinds of interesting complexities as it undergoes the chemical transformations of slow baking. You may swear by your vegetable pâtés, your shellfish terrines, your so-called rillettes of salmon. But they are nothing compared to the real charcuterie made from pork. I'll grant you that smoked mackerel blended with butter makes an arresting little spread, that scallops and lobster and crab layered airily in a terrine constitute one of life's gentler luxuries (provided the gelatin's held at bay), that there is something racy about eating a dish called pâté au chocolat (even if the result isn't so far from what you get when you filch the icing from a chocolate cake). They are all edible and sometimes interesting, but they are in no way a substitute.

For proof, take a charcuterie vacation in France, just to see what one country can do with the spare parts of a pig. There are other places where pork is revered—Italy's prosciutto, Germany's bratwurst, China's barbecue, the vinegared vindaloo of Goa—but no one can match the French talent for transforming the raw materials in so many ingenious ways. The distance is huge between a terrine of melting foie gras and a pot of rillettes—basically a coarse meat spread, looking disturbingly like dog food. And yet rillettes can in no way be said to be inferior in flavour, certainly not by me, who once spent a memorable hour spreading potfuls onto crusty French bread between pitchers of Vouvray after a hard walk along, around and occasionally into the Loire river.

You need a high-energy occupation like river-walking if you're going to spend much time around the rillette pot. Even as a fat advocate, I have to admit this isn't a food that suits an inert lifestyle. It came as a wonderful surprise when I discovered that my summer vacation in Quebec's Eastern Townships would include rillettes from the Saturday market as well as dubbed Adam Sandler videos and sightings of Donald Sutherland in the local supermarché. But the much-anticipated plans to read long-winded novels and go for leisurely drives had to be modified tout de suite —after a baguette's worth of all that pork paste, the guilt-filled modern body needs hard hours of kayaking and mountain biking, fat-fuelled parasailing and Donald Sutherland–stalking.

The good thing about rillettes, on the other hand, is that because they're so fatty, they're very spreadable. That reduces an eater's stress levels considerably, which has to be good for your health. Another dietary plus: the bread you put the spread on doesn't need butter. But who am I kidding? If you're troubled by fat, you haven't read this far.

Overcoming a reluctance to cook pâtés and terrines may be harder than just eating the stuff. Older handbooks, such as Jane Grigson's *Charcuterie and French Pork Cookery*, make it sound like exceptionally complicated work, and undoubtedly it is when you undertake your first galantine. A pork terrine isn't nearly so demanding, except of your spare time. The traditional process of turning raw meat into upscale sandwich paste is more methodical than it is difficult. My basic, time-honoured, time-consuming pâté de campagne uses up large chunks of several days of your life (not counting the portion it will deprive you of once you've eaten it). Given the choice of being there for the kids—where is that there, by the way, where this self-sacrifice takes place?—or marinating a dead pig's back fat and belly overnight, then watching the oven for hours the next day until the pâté finally seems to pull away from the sides of the terrine to swim in its own fat, most people will go with the kids.

Modern cookbooks, such as Patricia Wells' *Bistro Cooking*, are more conscious of life's conflicting pressures, though in their blithe, think-positive style they ignore what's lost in our range of flavours by accelerating cooking to fit the shrinking time hole. Wells even swears by a microwaved rabbit and hazelnut terrine that needs only thirty-five minutes of cooking (though this comes from a woman who can bone a rabbit in ten minutes).

The old books recommend hand-chopping for the meat; most people will use a food processor. The trick is not to let the meat turn into hamburger or mush: a pâté must have texture. It must also be highly seasoned (sauté a little in advance as a test) and not overcooked. Otherwise, it's boring old meat loaf, which even the sternest high priests of religion and nutrition can't bring themselves to admire.

Children devour Froot Loops. Adults, the more adult of them anyway, can find good things to say about liver. This difference in tastes tells me that certain appetites are learned, and others unlearned, with the passage of time.

But not all. There are some aromas and flavours that take hold of the smallest child and don't let go until the faculties fail. The one I'm thinking of in particular—and even now I feel one of those Proustian reveries coming on — is the smell and taste of smoked meat.

Proust, being a rather delicate soul, would be distraught to be mentioned in such company. To associate hams, hocks and pork bellies with the author of *A la recherche du temps perdu*, the man who raised the teacake to high art, is like casting Ernest Borgnine in *The Importance of Being Earnest*. But just because smoked meat hasn't yet prompted a great roman-fleuve is no reason to deny its evocative powers.

The smoking of meat over fire — take this, you Proustian tea-sippers — is one of those basic and defining activities that reaches back to the origins of humanity. When you arrange slices of salami on an antipasto plate or carve off a few hunks of ham from the bone, you're prompting an instinctive reaction in your messmates that goes back well beyond Proust's temps perdu. Much as the smell of burning leaves penetrates through to the pleasure centres of the brain and persuades people to write songs and buy Ralph Lauren, the fragrance of smoked meat stimulates a powerful and instinctive response that makes you want to grab a club and hunt a beast.

Proust-like in this respect at least, I'll take an example from my own experience. A few years back, my mother and stepfather were in the habit of visiting the small town of St. Jacobs in Southern Ontario to buy a salami known as summer sausage that has been popularized by the old-fashioned Mennonite sect. You can find thinly sliced non-sectarian versions of this Germanic delicacy in the supermarket, but somehow it never tastes so intense and smoky as when you buy it in a hunk at the source, preferably from a bearded elder named Noah or Ezra. Visit an apartment where a piece of summer sausage resides, and you'll be convinced you're in a back-country smokehouse. Considering that it's being stored in a plastic bag within a refrigerator to mute its power, this salami is clearly not to be trifled with.

Generous beyond belief, or desperate to clear the air, my stepfather liked to offer my family a share of the summer sausage whenever we dropped by. I would always hesitate, hating to deprive anyone of their smoked meat, but my children made sure that I finally accepted.

It was their determination to possess this food, still wrapped in the mottled cloth bag that had hung for a week over smouldering maple, that makes me think the appeal of smoke is innate. My son, not one to show interest in regional cuisine, would have eaten the whole piece for dinner, given the chance (he has since sworn off meat, which at the rate he was going was probably necessary for his self-preservation). My daughter, even then a dedicated vegetarian, was strong-willed enough to keep from eating any. But she still asked to hold the summer sausage on the drive home, just to be close to the smell. When I cut off slices for my son's suicidal meal, I'd give my daughter a piece of the smoked cloth bag, just so she could sniff it. Though her mind tried to convince her otherwise, the primeval longings were still there.

As they got older and even wiser, of course, they learned to ignore their instincts and shy away from such foods. Almost all the modern trends in eating are heading in the opposite direction from the ideals represented by smoked meat. Smoked meat is salty and fatty (the dehydration and concentration of the smoking process see to that). Whether Germanic, Polish or Ukrainian by origin, the browned hams and hocks and sausage rings hanging in old-fashioned butchers' come from culinary traditions that may never catch fashion's eye. And most noticeably and offensively of all, these indelicate delicacies are smoky. Smoke is carcinogenic any way you look at it, and to proclaim an interest in smoked meat is to make yourself a risk-taker in a risk-free world. When the best-selling cookbooks are those promising miracle cures from regimented diets, taking a risk is a wacky thing to do. But, damn, it tastes good. And I bet I could still turn my children's heads, maybe even reawaken some suppressed childhood desire, just by walking a slab of summer sausage through the house.

We should own up to these urges, rather than slotting them into the category of forbidden vices. Maybe it's possible to nibble around the edges of the smoky world, sampling a little smoked salmon here, a little — is there such a thing? — Montreal-smoked brisket there, with a sip of peaty single-malt whisky on the side to chase it down in good company. But, frankly, I think it's better to confront the urge head-on. Make your lentil soups with a smoked ham hock. Reclaim the antipasto plates given over to grilled veggies by filling them with handcut shavings of summer sausage. Face the demons, go whole hog, buy the fatty bacon, the smoked pork chop, the knackwurst, plus a little weisswurst for contrast, and put together a comforting and filling Alsatian choucroute garnie. This is life as it was meant to be lived, and not yet outlawed.

Of course the law is already having its cold-hearted way with smoke. I mean the evil kind emitted by cigarettes (and cigars and pipes), not the stuff that gets applied to the flesh of animals and fish for our dining pleasure. But the two forms of combustion, one officially proscribed, the other still socially acceptable, aren't quite as distinct as we like to pretend.

It would be nice to think that there was a single, logical way to deal with the question of smoking at and around the dinner table. But unless you are a public-health officer who can focus exclusively on the medical consequences and ignore the absurdities that result, logic by itself won't work. Whatever the courts ultimately decree, no one who thinks about food can pretend that tobacco can be neatly isolated from the other things we ingest, imbibe and inflame around the table.

I belong to that category of people who hate cigarette smoke: prim, upright folks who instinctively ask for a no-smoking table when they make restaurant reservations and go so far as to post no-smoking signs around their not entirely hospitable home (though ours is in polite and formal Parisian French, to undercut the hostility and turn it into something semi-witty). My head jerks around accusingly when I smell cigarette smoke where it shouldn't be—office washrooms, subway platforms, bus shelters—and even where it's still allowed, out in the open air. I consider my meal ruined if the no-smoking table I'm assigned to is right beside a gaggle of smokers, and I make myself tell the truth when someone asks me whether I mind if they smoke. Yes, I do mind.

Though I find myself coughing when I'm forced to inhale someone else's smoke at close quarters, I refuse to use the socially acceptable cop-out and say I'm allergic. No, it's more that I hate it: the smell that lingers on the clothes and in the hair, the irritation to the eyes and nose, the rudeness that comes from thinking you have the right to impose your habit so completely on me. A libertarian with food, I'm the typical puritanical neo-fascist when it comes to smoking. But here's where I start having problems. When I'm in a Chinese restaurant, where a lot of the young people smoke Marlboros, or when I'm around poseurs who light up Gitanes, or for that matter when a whiff of marijuana drifts across the urban sidewalk, I find the smell enticing. There's a penetrating herbal fragrance to all this smoke that anyone seriously committed to food has to acknowledge and even admire.

The passion for cigars that transfixes the media and occasionally even surfaces in real life makes the connection more potent. Tobacco is still an agricultural product, albeit one much corrupted by the big cigarette companies. It should not be surprising if good growers and manufacturers, like their counterparts in the vineyards and wineries, can bring out powerful and beguiling scents from their noxious weed that would make life seem a little less of a struggle and a little more of a pleasure. Not one for me, perhaps, but then I can admire the artistry of a good single malt without drinking it.

And at the same time, please note all the odd things we do around the kitchen that might be at risk if we took as hard a line there as we already do with cigarettes. I don't just mean alcohol and animal fats, which already come in for their share of attacks from prim do-gooders. But given the aggressive uptightness we can summon up for the evils of smoking, why should we be so accepting of other culinary offences?

If you can't stand the reek of cigarettes on your clothes at the end of the evening, how can you put up with a chef who salts his food so heavily that you wake up parched at three in the morning? If the smoke from a neighbour's pipe seems so intrusive, what about the sizzling chicken in fermented black beans that sends up clouds of smoke as it's carried to your table or the decorative fireplace that taints the room with the smell of burning logs? Who condemns flambé desserts, or the sprigs of raw rosemary scattered around the pasta that assault your taste buds and make it impossible to taste anything else, or the wasabi horseradish dips with sushi that bring tears to the eye, or the fragrance of a wild-raspberry eau-de-vie at the end of a good meal that fills the air like an exotic perfume?

We'll say nothing about the reek of barbecuing meat and scented candles, the family pets who are welcomed a little too lovingly at the table, the loud music that overpowers conversation, the conversations we'd rather not have to hear, the table-mates who aren't stylish or witty or beautiful. Some things we must learn to put up with, some to ignore and some, quite possibly, to appreciate.

But simple appreciation is a challenge when so many people see the act of eating as a physical assault and are determined to save us from ourselves. I'd always thought fruit juice was safe. After all, it comes to us almost directly as nature intended and was the sort of thing our parents tried to foist on us in the name of all that was good instead of Coke or candy. And then someone confided to me as I was finding pleasure in my lunchtime pineapple juice that I was wasting my time.

Fruit juice, they said scornfully, is empty food. It lacks the upright and exemplary fibre of real fruit but carries with it all the sugar and calories of a soft drink. Without the fibre, I was instructed, the sugar is absorbed faster into the bloodstream. And as the blood sugar level rises (here comes the apocalyptic part), the pancreas secretes insulin to lower sugar levels back to normal. But insulin also makes you turn those calories into fat (particularly if you're sitting around the cafeteria being hectored by some health tyrant instead of clearing your head by strolling the boulevards).

The long and the short of it, and the wide and the wider, if I have the argument right, is that fruit juice makes you gain unwanted pounds. That is, unless you are a baby, in which case fruit juice works its dastardly deeds in a different way. Infants fed too much apple juice (which could be as little as 500 millilitres, or a couple of Tetra Paks) may fail to grow or develop normally. In the smaller stomach, adult-sized portions of well-meant juice take the place of more nutritious foods. Add in the fact that a naturally occurring sugar in apple juice is indigestible, often resulting in diarrhea, and you have a drink to be castigated.

I've said nothing about allergic reactions or pesticide residues, or even the increased presence of pulp in modern fruit drinks, which is the chief source of breakfast-time misery to my own in-house dieticians. They prefer no-fat, no-stress filtered water when they can get away with it, which is more and more often as the news on fruit juice turns more and more one-sided.

I take all these points and I feel appropriately chastened. In this era of watchful eating and competitive nutrition, no one can afford to be unenlightened. The social stigma is too great. I don't actually know how much of this is true, though it has the ring of truth. Which is to say, it's just persuasive enough to stir up some guilt and make me wonder whether I destroyed my children as I'm destroying myself. On the other hand, I still have to drink, and when I'm alone at breakfast or lunch, there's no doubt I'll still drink fruit juice. I happen to like the easy energy that an eye-opening mug of tart, sweet orange juice gives me in the morning. At lunch, I enjoy the extra flavours and fragrances juice brings as opposed to something neutral, like water, or something ersatz, like Coke or hazelnut coffee or those bastardized drinks that blend a little aromatic concentrate with water and sugar to make what is basically a flavoured IV drip.

And at dinner, I like my fruit juice in its traditional fermented state, empty calories carried to their emptiest extreme. Which shows the emptiness of this kind of thinking. Wine is not much of a nutrient, and certainly lacks fibre unless you buy those unfiltered Cabernets that Robert Parker so admires and make sure to shake before serving. On the other hand, it is that rare thing, a pleasure, both as a taste in itself and as a way of pushing aside the daily distresses to the margins of consciousness.

But the distresses will return quickly enough. The simple appreciation of wine becomes complicated when you set down your glass to slice a piece of the cheese it accompanies so well. Instead of enjoying a taste that has delighted and sustained human beings for centuries, you may, in the eyes of your government overseers, be undertaking a deadly risk. The United States routinely bans many of the world's best cheeses and Canada has tried to, backing off only when brie-loving Quebec separatists got into the act and turned a health issue into a battle about nationhood. And what violations do these offensive lumps of curd have in common, to be targeted by the feds? They're unpasteurized raw-milk cheeses, and therefore defy all that science deems safe and sound.

Most cheeses manufactured in North America satisfy all the government regulations that purport to protect our health. The milk they are made from has been pasteurized or heat-treated to a point where noxious bacteria shouldn't be able to survive. All is well, except that the government-approved cheese has very little taste. If you ate it, you almost certainly wouldn't die, at least not in the short term. But why would you want to eat it?

"They made it a wasteland," observed the Roman historian Tacitus of his countrymen's heavy-handed military tactics, "and they called it peace." The health bureaucrats' approach to cheese is much the same. They attack living cheeses filled with the microflora that produce weird and wonderful flavours in order to make their countries safe and orderly. But peace has its costs: you lose the powerful, penetrating taste of a runny Epoisses from the depths of Burgundy, and have to be satisfied with the shelf-ready blocks of shrink-wrapped cheddar that make our long lives seem like an endurance test.

Not being much of a scientist, I have difficulty determining how big a threat raw-milk cheeses pose. My instinctive reaction is to say it's not very great, because I have survived this long after eating cheeses that can chase away unwanted teenagers on smell alone. Instinctive reactions, of course, are viewed with contempt by the people who actually study the microbes under the microscope and know the damage they can cause, particularly to pregnant women and those with weakened immune systems. And yet for all the apocalyptic warnings rising up out of the labs and research institutes, it's necessary to remain skeptical about a wholesale ban.

If the micro-organisms that can find their way into raw-milk cheese are all that deadly, shouldn't there be more evidence of the harm being inflicted? While many cases of food poisoning (to say nothing of miscarriages and stillbirths) are never traced back to their source, the horror stories cited by supporters of cheese blacklists are meagre in number. A greater number of examples can easily be found for products that aren't prohibited but merely monitored for safety (hamburger meat and prepared salads in particular). Almost any processed food has the potential to kill, but the only way to solve that threat would be to ban human beings. The European Union, faced with the same issue, chose to allow the sale of raw-milk cheeses, accepting that the risk to most people was negligible.

At the same time, the raw-milk cheese debate is not just about scientific evidence pro and con. Political factors enter into it and so does dairy-industry lobbying. Yes, the big cheeses want to protect their turf against both foreign invaders and a domestic cottage industry that could pose a threat similar to what the microbreweries mounted against the industrial beer plants. But more important than a fractional loss of market share is the pristine image of milk products in North America. The dairy industry has spent a good part of the last two decades facing down scares about the dangers of animal fats, and has spent massive sums promoting its pasteurized, calcium-rich, vitamin-supplemented products as an essential part of a healthy lifestyle. All that media massaging will be wasted if cheeses come to be linked in consumers' minds with sickness and even death.

Bland conformity is the price we are asked to pay for a risk-free existence. Which, when you think about it, is just a modern twist on Charles de Gaulle's exasperated question about his unruly compatriots: "How can anyone be expected to govern a country with 325 cheeses?" Easy. Just reduce the number of cheeses to a manageable few through health scares and commercial concentration — the two conveniently go together, as it happens — and the compliant citizens will fall into line. Good cheese, with its rude, boisterous smells and its unsightly mould and its unpredictable bacterial action and its scary decomposing appearance, is not a product that submits easily to centralized control. Which makes me wonder: could the mediocre cheese that North America produces so effortlessly be part of a plot to take away our liberty through sensory deprivation?

A victim of my culture, I still can't help but think about the rights and the wrongs of what I'm eating. It isn't enough that the garlic dip on my chicken kebab has a great flavour—I also find against my will that I'm congratulating myself for eating food that's good for my heart. And even as I'm ordering fish and chips, the first thought that goes through my mind is not how good my fry-up's going to taste but how rebellious I am.

Either way, the calorie-counters are in power, and their prescriptions govern the act of eating. But food shouldn't be bound by nutrition any more than sex is confined to procreation. And when I want to put the passion back into my mealtimes, I eat Chinese food.

Most of the Chinese people I've encountered love their food without hesitation. The amount of thought and conversation that goes into shopping for scallops or mustard greens is astonishing in people so famously devoted to the more worldly concerns of business or education. I like to think I share that passion, to the point that I can join their debates about whether blue crab is better than hairy crab or if Hunan's cuisine is superior to Shanghai's. But in every such discussion, there comes a point when I have to give up.

My Hong Kong dinner companions are endlessly excited about their food and, unlike many self-important Westerners, they feel no compunction in talking about memorable recipes, amazing fish markets, novel uses for obscure pig parts, the hierarchy of dim sum dumplings, anything remotely connected with the pleasures of eating. I always like to imagine, at mealtimes like this, the shock among Hong Kong's Asian population when the

British upper classes held sway—a group famous for following the dispiriting motto that food must never be discussed at the table. (To their credit, it should be admitted that the colonial powers usually served food that wasn't worth noticing.)

So we talk and talk about the crab dumplings and seaweed fritters in front of us without inhibition. The nutritional voices that usually creep into my head fall silent, chased away by all this common sense and uncommon enthusiasm. But then invariably one of my Hong Kong friends says something that still manages to stop me short. "This dish," she announces, pointing to the almond soup I'm just about to inhale, "is very good for your complexion."

With these well-meant words the spoon slips out of my fingers and the milky white broth trickles onto the Szechuan shrimp with snow peas that's probably good at hair restoration. Open-mouthed (but with an improving complexion), I stare uncomprehendingly at the person across from me: a moment ago she seemed to share my passion for robust eating. Now suddenly she wants to talk about health food.

For me it's an either/or proposition, the split between food that tastes good and food that is Good For You. I'm willing to acknowledge that ultimately breakfast, lunch and dinner exist to keep us safe and sound, like stoplights or human-resources departments. I'm not above patting myself on the back when I suddenly realize there's a brassica vegetable on my plate. And yet I've always believed that those who concentrate on the life-giving part miss out on the life-enhancing side.

I know that health food has come a long way in the last decade or two, to the point that it's never referred to as health food except by cranks like me. Fresh-market cuisine it's now called, with its emphasis on colourful vegetables that are barely cooked and herbs that attempt to make every dish smell like the

Provençal hillside as the sea breezes waft by. Or heart-smart cooking, with most of the dairy products politely shown the door and the fragrant garlic bulb given pride of place on the lean and mean menu. Or perhaps just Mediterranean food, with a repertoire that conveniently ignores all the salty, fried and syrupy food Mediterranean peoples have traditionally adored and substitutes something concocted in a Californian kitchen — but, hey, it's on the same latitude!

The surest sign of health food's entry into the mainstream is that the label of crank now belongs more fittingly to someone like me — the guy who will risk a future coronary if it means Gorgonzola instead of skim-milk mozzarella, the carefree nosher who lives to eat while others eat to live.

And then to be betrayed by my so-called allies from Hong Kong. I had always preferred to see Chinese cuisine as a refuge from the trend-setting preoccupations of the insecure West. Yes, I know that the early proponents of healthy diets used to point to the crunchy stir-fried vegetables on the Cantonese menus as the way we ought to go. But anyone who really understood Chinese cooking knew there was no end of pork fat and deep-fried dumplings and ten-course banquets with Courvoisier toasts waiting to confound the health brigade.

To their credit — which is really their unshakable confidence in themselves coupled with pride in traditions that won't change with the latest issue of *Food & Wine* — my exuberant Hong Kong friends don't shy away from barbecued pork belly or deep-fried crab rolls or stewed duck with salted vegetables. When they celebrate their autumn moon festival, it's not with a plate of lightly grilled vegetables but with the formidable moon cake that may combine salted duck-egg yolk with ham fat and rock sugar.

They are not timid, miserable valetudinarians. And yet to my everlasting surprise, every food they eat, no matter how delicious, has a medical use. This dish is good for the complexion, this one speeds digestion, that one is good for fighting off a winter cough, another can be recommended—nudge, nudge—to men who need a pick-me-up. I try hard not to remember which does which. And yet, as I grasp greedily for the coiled snake-meat dumpling and simultaneously see the knowing look in their eyes, I have that sinking feeling: by my appetite I'm betraying not a passion for food but some embarrassing physical need.

I refuse to ask which one. Some things should never be discussed at the table.

Rillettes

If you're travelling rough in the Loire valley—by which I mean if you're behaving like an ordinary human being, shopping for lunches in charcuteries or eating in no-nonsense cafés rather than dining in sumptuous Michelin-approved splendour—you will have frequent encounters with rillettes. Anyone who likes meat to be spreadable will recognize this shredded-pork-and-fat paste as one of the great triumphs in cooking, particularly if you've just made room for a few thousand extra calories by walking through the orchards and vineyards above the Loire. People who are nervous around fat, on the other hand, will suffer spasms of disgust at the sight of the glistening grey meat stuck in all that congealed whiteness. Knowing the pleasures of the pro-rillettes state of mind, I can only feel pity for them.

Prepared rillettes are harder to find in Canada, since even hedonists here shy away from so much obvious fat. You'll occasionally find expensive little pots of the stuff in gourmet shops—so far from the blue-collar cafés of the Loire—but if you can do your eating in the hungrier parts of Quebec, the odds improve significantly. Just as pockets of Shakespearean English are alleged to have survived in remote outposts of the unchanging Appalachians, so there are corners of Quebec where the old-style rillettes still find refuge. I remember a Saturday-morning market in a field near Magog, Quebec, where one stall was selling nothing else but meat in fat, made not just from pork but rabbit and duck as well. It reminded me how sad I'd feel if my country ever lost its most independent-minded province.

Cooking your own rillettes is time-consuming and real physical labour, but the technique is relatively simple. It may help to taste the real thing first so that you know what you're aiming for. You'll want about 4 pounds of pork, of which a good proportion will be fat. Some people like equal amounts fat and meat, some prefer to reduce the fat to a 1:2 ratio. A good piece of belly pork will supply the fatty meat and you may want to add a leaner cut to increase the meat presence. Cut the meat and fat into 2-inch cubes and put in a large ovenproof pot with plenty of salt and pepper, a bay leaf and 1½ cups water. Bring to a boil on the top of the stove, then cover and cook slowly in a 300°F oven for about 4 hours, or until the meat is soft enough to shred with a fork. Replenish the water if necessary so that the meat doesn't dry out, but make sure that it doesn't boil hard. In the last hour of cooking, add some grated nutmeg, chopped herbs and a crushed clove of garlic.

Drain the meat and fat, saving the cooking liquid (you can boil it down and add it to the shredded rillettes for extra flavour). Reserve the fat and let cool. Shred the meat with a fork, or break up with a blender—a food processor would be easier, but you don't want a homogeneous paste. Add the fat and the reduced cooking liquid back to the meat, make sure there's enough salt and pepper, then turn into glass pots or terrines, cover the surface with wax paper and leave in the refrigerator for a couple of days before serving. Tart gherkins or cornichons are always served as an accompaniment to undercut the fat.

A rillettes shortcut, not officially recommended by the French charcuterie guild: buy 2 pounds of pork loin and a whole duck from a Chinese barbecue shop. Separate the meat from the bones and the fat from the meat. Put the fat in a blender and blend with a little warm water until fairly smooth. Then add the coarsely chopped meat, and blend to a rough paste. Season to taste, and serve to guests who are open to new ideas.

Braised Pork in Milk

I always worry as I enjoy this rich and succulent but still very strange dish that it was created by medieval Christians to harass observant Jews, unless it was invented by the Jews as a parody of Christian excess. But more likely it was just an attempt to replicate the taste of milk-fed suckling pig in meat from an older animal.

English celebrity chef Alastair Little says you must first marinate your pork for two hours in a mixture of cider vinegar (3 tablespoons) and dry white wine (2 glasses). I never have, and don't feel any the worse for it. In a large, heavy pot, brown 1 pork shoulder in 3 tablespoons of olive oil; when coloured on all sides (which takes about 15 minutes), add 1 bay leaf, 3 cloves of garlic, 4 or 5 coriander seeds and a sprinkling of fennel seed. Cook several minutes more until the garlic takes on colour; then add 1 cup of whole-fat milk to the pan, and leave to simmer loosely covered on a medium-low heat. Turn the meat over every 20 minutes or so. As the milk cooks down (around the 40-minute mark), add another cup to pan. After the first hour, you may want to reduce the heat and leave at a low simmer for another hour. From time to time, scrape the solids down from the sides of the pan and into the juices on the bottom, to keep them from burning and to flavour the sauce. If the liquid begins to dry up in the second hour of cooking, add a third cup of milk. By the time the meat is tender (after 2 to 2½ hours), the sauce should have reduced to a cup or so of sweet golden-brown liquid. At that point, remove the meat from the pan, season it with salt and pepper as desired and let it sit covered for about 10 minutes before serving. Serve with a not-too-thick potato purée, braised fennel and a salad of greens with a little bitter radicchio.

Sauerkraut and Sausage

The legendary Alsatian choucroute garnie is one of those grand-standing dishes you rarely want to eat again after you've picked your way through it once. When cooked in the traditional manner, it features some half-dozen forms of pork products, most of them smoky and salty and fatty. There's only so much the tart pickled cabbage can do to counteract all that heavy meat. The best way to make this dish digestible and enjoyable is to reduce this overkill to something more bearable — three kinds of meat, tops. Then go plough a field.

In a large pot, melt 2 chopped onions in bacon fat, then add 2 pounds of sauerkraut and a 1-pound piece of smoked bacon, a bay leaf, a pinch of juniper berries and coriander seeds. Pour in 8 to 10 ounces of dry Riesling or similar tart dry white wine and the same amount of water. Simmer, covered, for 1½ to 2 hours (or longer if you like your sauerkraut to lose its crunch). About 15 minutes before the end, add a couple of weisswurst sausages and a brace of bratwurst.

Serve with mashed potatoes to absorb the sauerkraut juices, or whole potatoes that have been steamed on the top of the cooking sauerkraut. Dijon mustard is a compulsory accompaniment. If you are really a glutton for punishment, you can pad out the meat portion with smoked pork chops, butcher-shop frankfurters, a few pieces of salted pork (belly, knuckle) and some airy liver dumplings to lighten the load. Leftover sauerkraut and potatoes can be puréed with the pot juices and some stock to make a good day-after soup. Add some chopped bacon and smoked sausage before serving, and thin with a little warmed cream if it's too dense or tart.

CHICKEN

IT'S STRANGE THAT chicken has become our most versatile meat, considering how poorly qualified it is for the job. All chicken as currently sold in supermarkets and consumed in the home is basically the same. True, there is a difference between dark and light meat; but since most people eat one or the other, that difference isn't always noticeable. And yes, a few of us still eat chicken livers, which are fundamentally different in flavour and texture from a breast or a leg.

But compared with the huge number of options available with beef or pork, chicken on its own is the most predictable of meats: mild, unassertive, juicy and tender, at least if not overcooked. Its appeal has less to do with any innate virtues than with the needs we bring to it. Chicken is cheap, it's fast and easy to cook, it behaves predictably (unlike, say, stewing beef, which too easily ends up tough and tasteless after hours of cooking; and who's got the hours anyway?), it's marketed in a user-friendly way, it's perceived to be low in fat, it offends no one (among carnivores anyway), it doesn't come with nasty scales like fish or bothersome connective tissue like old beef and its recipes are amost universal.

My praise may sound faint, but I can't bring myself to damn chicken, much as I think its allure defines the failings of our age.

Going through my memory of favourite dishes, I'm ashamed to say that I can come up with many selections from the chicken portion of the menu: coq au vin, Thai curried chicken, my once-a-week treat of chicken, spinach and goat's cheese pizza, chicken kebabs with garlic sauce, chicken breast breaded with chopped pecans and cooked in a cream and mustard sauce, salty-skinned roast Portuguese chicken drenched with chili pepper and vinegar, chunks of Chinese chicken (with the bone in and the skin on) quickly cooked in a smoky wok with black bean and ginger.

Statisticians would argue that this proof is flawed by the fact that the chicken dishes in anyone's experience are likely to outnumber by far the mutton or wild boar selections. There are more of the best dishes because there is so much larger a pool to draw from. And they would be right, up to a point: people going to the trouble of cooking a good meal are more likely to lavish their talents and efforts on a meat like chicken that isn't by itself too obtrusive. With, say, a well-hung piece of beef, the best decision a smart cook can make is to leave it pretty much as it is. But that approach risks drawing too much attention to the raw material —which not everyone will appreciate in proportion to its cost —and drawing too much attention away from the skills of the cook.

Chicken, on the other hand, begs to be fiddled with. I know there are highly refined types who like to keep everything simple and spare, who think that just as the best treatment of a good strip loin is a few minutes on the grill and nothing more, so the best approach to great chicken is to ignore it while it roasts contentedly in the oven. But, first of all, there isn't a lot of great chicken around. And when you can find it, it just isn't all that different from the average stuff that populates the supermarkets. Feeling flush and adventurous in France one time, I bought poulet de Bresse, the highly regulated appellation-contrôlée bird that's the pride of Burgundy. It was all right, I suppose, though the reverence in which it is held meant that we had to chew each piece so thoughtfully that dessert was a head-clearing Tylenol.

Refusing to learn from my experience, always convinced that it's my fault I can't taste the subtle flavours that tickle the cookbook writers' fanciful fancies, I once bought a live chicken in Toronto's outdoor Kensington Market. The chattering creature I selected from the cages stacked on the sidewalk and watched meet its end might as well have breathed its last on some unpicturesque factory killing floor. I've travelled across Southern Ontario as the sun was setting trying to track down an Amish farm where the free-range chicken was said to be something special. City-dwellers with the same idea should remember that you really have to like chicken to lose yourself after dark on the free-ranging back roads of farm country.

The mistake I made with all these birds was to roast them simply. Roast chicken is fine, if you're looking for something that won't get in the way of the Meursault, or if you want a meal where the guests won't feel obliged to talk about the meal (except that someone will always say helpfully at the end, "This makes such a nice change after all those fancy and complicated dishes"). But even the best chicken—I'm not convinced there is such a thing, but let the Burgundians pretend—is too dull for our present palates to benefit from plain roasting.

No, what makes chicken the enjoyable everyday food it is, apart from the fact that they package it so presentably at the supermarket, is that it is such a good vehicle for other flavours. Having little taste itself, chicken needs sauces, and all those herbs, spices and other flavourings that make up a good sauce improve the dish many times over. If you set out to invent a pleasant way to refresh our mouths with the tastes of ginger, paprika, garlic, lemon, cumin, cilantro, fennel, turmeric—complete the list as you will—it would be hard to improve on chicken. For this, we must be grateful.

Chicken Liver Pâté

I've never been able to duplicate the light, airy, boozy chicken-liver mousses that are still served in old-school restaurants. I suspect I need to double the amount of butter, but I find it easier to let chefs overdo it behind the scenes than to get carried away myself. It took a while, but now I'm content with my denser, darker, earthier homemade version.

Trim the fatty tendrils off 1½ pounds of fresh chicken livers. Melt 2 ounces of butter in a large frying pan and sauté the livers until they are pink inside. Remove the livers and add 2 ounces of cognac or other good brandy to the pan and let bubble. Then add a small glass of port and let it seethe some more. Add 2 coarsely chopped cloves of garlic and cook for 2 minutes. Put the livers in a food processor for a few seconds, then spoon in the pan juices and garlic and grind for a few seconds more. Add salt and pepper to taste, chopped fresh tarragon if you have it, a little thyme (fresh or dried) and 4 ounces of chopped-up fresh butter. Grind until smooth and mixed, then spoon into a terrine.

Refrigerate until cool (it will keep several days), then serve dusted with a little chopped parsley.

Chicken with Nuts and Mustard

This recipe, based on one in Michèle Urvater and David Lieder-man's *Cooking the Nouvelle Cuisine in America*, makes perfect use of chicken's talent for carrying other flavours. The mild, juicy taste of the white meat is layered with the nuttiness of the pecans, the mustard's aromatic sharpness, the milky richness of the butter and cream. Since the chicken is largely a vehicle for the sauce, this is one dish where the skinless, boneless version works well.

While 6 tablespoons of unsalted butter melt over low heat in a small saucepan, lightly season 4 chicken breasts with salt and pepper and set aside on a plate. (The chicken can be cooked in single pieces but I prefer each breast cut widthwise into three or four smaller pieces—more surface area for the sauce.) As soon as the butter has melted, remove from the heat and whisk in 6 tablespoons of good-quality Dijon mustard. Dip each piece of chicken breast into butter/mustard mixture, coating the surface thoroughly. Then cover the exterior completely in a coating of finely chopped pecans (the best choice, I think), almonds or hazelnuts (which have a tendency to burn).

In a wide, heavy skillet, melt 4 tablespoons of unsalted butter with 2 tablespoons of peanut oil. As soon as the fat begins to sizzle, add the chicken pieces, leaving space around them so that the pan is not crowded. Sauté for about 3 minutes on each side, watching carefully to be sure the nuts don't scorch. As they turn a rich golden brown, put them in a baking dish and place in preheated 200°F oven. Continue sautéeing until all the pieces have been cooked. Keep the prepared chicken in the oven while you make the sauce. Pour off any loose fat from the frying pan, and if there are any scorched bits of nut in the pan carefully spoon them out as well. Deglaze the pan with 3–4 ounces of 18% table cream (stir in a few tablespoons more mustard here if you like a more mustardy taste, as I do). As the sauce reduces, scrape up any browned nut bits that have stuck to the pan and stir in; adjust seasoning with more salt and pepper if required. Chop in a few tablespoons of chives if you have some around.

This dish is excellent with basmati rice, which supplies its own nutty fragrance to add to the beautiful smell of the cooked nuts. Goes well with a fat Pinot Gris from Alsace or a buttery Chardonnay from Australia.

ACQUIRED TASTES

IN THE ANCIENT WORLD, THE KNOWLEDGE of faraway places was limited to the stories brought back by merchants or soldiers or slaves. For centuries before television, when other peoples' strange ways weren't nearly so accessible to a prime-time audience, these travellers' tales were the leading form of after-dinner entertainment.

Foreign parts, in the imaginations of those who lived normal, humdrum lives, became filled with horrible giants, deadly seductresses and infernal beasts on all-human diets. The average Egyptian or Indian or German who heard such distortions of his homeland would never recognize them — they were far too outlandish.

Myth-making didn't stop with the onrush of jet travel. We still feel compelled to misunderstand the outside world at almost every opportunity, not least when it's time for dinner. Think of the numberless crazes in Italian food we have suffered over the past few years. Do you remember Northern Italian cooking, which was the catchphrase invented to keep out the veal parmigiana crowd? So-called Northern Italian restaurants based their menus very squarely on pasta, preferred cream sauce to the usual tomato, filled the bowl with undercooked vegetables to take up space in the name of health and charged twice as much for food that was half as filling. Food magazines adored this craze: it played well with the need to divert busy people short on time and basic cooking skills. Anyone, after all, could put together a pasta dish with standard North American refrigerator ingredients in a few minutes. This was deemed a remarkable advance in our culinary progress.

Eventually, after six or eight years of linguine with broccoli in cream sauce, people began to get bored with the bland tastes of this invented place called Northern Italy. To the rescue came something presented as the new wave of Southern Italian cooking. After the languid seasoning of the North (sophistication, at that point, being equated with halfheartedness), the southern alternative offered bold, aggressive, macho flavours. It wasn't enough that your spaghettini came with tomatoes, garlic and black olives. To achieve that genuine rustic spirit, it also had to include green olives, capers, anchovies, sun-dried tomatoes and pancetta. The taste in your mouth by the end of the meal reminded you of the time long ago when you swigged garlic salt on a dare.

But it didn't remind you much of Southern Italy, any more than Northern Italian cooking reminded you of the North, or gourmet pizza with snow peas evoked real pizza or the Mediterranean diet conjured up the shores of the Med. The coarsening had begun, and the stereotypes that stood in for real Italian cooking bore as little resemblance to the original as a black-velvet *Last Supper* does to Leonardo's.

The difference between the real thing and the travesties passed off as Italian food to make a quick buck is immense. My lasting memory of the nation's cooking—sophisticated Italians will hate to hear this—is of healthy, simple, balanced meals, the sort that entrenched North Americans only serve to their special guests with reluctance and shame.

Grocery counters supplied a splendid lunch or the beginnings of an antipasto tray with their stunning selection of salami—the coarse fennel-flavoured finocchiona of Florence was the most intriguing, but every town had its specialties. Pasta was a likely part of any meal, but it was a small, uncomplicated serving—of thin spaghetti, say, lubricated with olive oil and flavoured with seared garlic and a little dried pepper—that tantalized the appetite without overwhelming it. Sautéed meat and grilled fish were standard main-course items, unless you preferred to slice a few slabs off a lukewarm roast of lamb or pork. Broths and salads were everywhere. A bowl of fruit was the standard dessert, because everyone knew there were few pleasures purer than a ripe pear or more bracing than a sweet-sour blood orange. Cheese was another good way to end the meal, the best choice when you could cut liberally from a wedge of nutty Parmesan. If you complain that each item sounds a little boring, I can only answer that the total effect of five simple courses was far more inviting than the take-no-prisoners style of show-off catering.

I admit that my exposure to Italian cooking was a little skewed. I wasn't staying at a grand hotel on Lake Maggiore or trotting off to a different deluxe ristorante every night on Capri. My meals were dished up at a student residence in Rome, which by North American standards makes them ineligible for consideration when the subject is cuisine. Cuisine in these parts is always something special, as you would guess from a word that takes such pains to distinguish itself from mere cooking. When we talk about Northern or Southern Italian cuisine, we don't mean to describe what ordinary folks in different parts of Italy actually eat week in, week out. The North American idea of cuisine is much more remote and superior than that, much like the foreign languages we were taught in school that didn't actually prepare you to say real things to real people.

But the great glory of Italian cooking is that it is inescapably real. What I ate was everyday food, not the sort of thing you could use to woo jaded palates into a New York restaurant. For that reason alone it deserves attention, since it managed to be delicious as well as cheap, nourishing and varied. When we look to foreign cultures for inspiration, there's no point in confining our vision to what some opportunistic restaurateur around the corner decided might pull in a crowd for the next few months. The tastes most worth acquiring are the ones that can fit into our lives, not the ones that force us to take a break from reality and play let's-pretend.

If you really want to know what Southern Italian cooking is about, don't line up at the trattoria of the moment and order the low-fat veggie pasta that looks suspiciously like every other pasta in town except that it has a few more black olives. The twenty-something chef who dashed off that dish was probably turning out much the same thing at the Provençal restaurant the month before and the Northern Italian restaurant the month before that (but with fewer olives). Far better to hang out with some real Sicilians who know what their cuisine is all about.

Unlike those modern chefs whose cultural achievements consist largely of recreating a recipe they read in a magazine, Sicilians can lay claim to several millennia of menu-building. Their cooking is a fundamental part of their culture, not some trendy fixation that is remade month after month to give bored people something new to do on a Friday night. Any group of people who rank food high among their cultural achievements—as opposed to making it a fashion statement or a business expense—earn my respect right away. And for the Sicilians, it's no idle boast made after a few cannoli too many. The story behind their traditional dishes extends back twenty-five hundred years and includes contributions from the Greeks, the Muslim Saracens and the Normans, who in one of those odd culinary-historic encounters that turns mere dinner into high culture gave the Sicilians a taste for salt cod.

When you're an island at the centre of the Mediterranean, your food becomes imbued with history whether you like it or not. The Sicilians I met during a Sicilian Cultural Society gathering—motto: Come for the lectures on dialect, stay for the cassata—seemed to like it very much. In talking to someone like me whose diet is very much a day-to-day kind of thing (do I still like rösti, am I tired of pesto?) they spoke with a tender delight about the dishes in front of them that had been brought back from the Crusades.

I thought I knew something about Italian cooking based on my student days in Rome. But nothing I had eaten prepared me for the hidden delights of traditional Sicilian cooking. Or for traditional Sicilian spelling. The first item I tasted—Sicilians can't be accused of pedantry—was called either *giggulena*, *gigiulena* or *giuggiulena*, depending on whom I asked. This fine product of the oral tradition turned out to be a diamond-shaped mass of sesame seeds, honey, sugar and almond, almost exactly like other sweet molar-killers I'd encountered at Greek and Middle Eastern bakeries.

Next up—we weren't being too fussy about Escoffier's rules of order—was an odd little pastry called *palummeddi* (little pigeons) if you came from Siracusa and *ossi di morti* (bones of the dead) if Messina was your hometown. They certainly looked like the dearly departed's no-longer-needed vertebrae, but in taste they were slightly more appealing—chewy and sweet from the mixture of sugar, flour and egg whites. The dead appeared again when a plate of *marmillata di cutugnu* was unveiled, moulds of quince paste decorated with flowers, birds, pinwheels and crosses. The next time you find yourself in possession of these gooey things, hand them out to your children and grandchildren on All Souls' Day with the words, "*I murticeddi tannu purtatu*" (The dead have brought you this; supply your own Handi Wipes). You don't hear that sort of thing very often in the more pretentious Southern Italian restaurants.

Now I know this isn't remotely like the brilliant everyday food that people who've travelled through Italy admire so much (partly because it's so easy on their digestive systems; you can always handle a sprint across a Roman intersection after a nourishing Italian lunch). It may even seem to be aspiring to the status of cuisine, if only because of the strange names and the old stories that go with them. But although these traditional foods are connected with special occasions, they're still things that ordinary folks eat without thinking themselves special. There's none of that self-consciousness about eating that can make the breathless North American food scene so hard to bear. At worst there's a nostalgia for the ancient foods, which need the enthusiastic efforts of a Sicilian Cultural Society to keep them alive in a forward-facing world.

The Church helps as well. Non-believers who are keen to see religion lose its grip should consider how few great atheist foods there are. Holy days are responsible for many traditional Sicilian specialties and as long as the faith is kept, the hunger for these foods will persist (unless of course it's the other way around). So on St. Martin's Day, November 11, you must try a puffy kind of fritter called *sfinci*, meaning sponge—a good description of its texture. The one I sampled was a delicious mixture of salty dough and sugar coating, but you can make them with raisins or anchovies or hot peppers—the Sicilians, as I said, are not a rigid people. In fact, the religious feast of St. Martin's Day also happens to mark the time when you want to taste your new wine and relax whatever rigidity you have left. These deep-fried puffs are the standard accompaniment.

Such delicacies aren't easy to track down, unless your favourite haunts include church suppers, multicultural celebrations and Sicilian weddings — you might find it worth marrying a Sicilian for the food alone. Once access is gained, be sure to search out *cuddureddi*, delicate little pastry wreaths filled with raisins, candied fruit, almonds and sesame seeds, looking something like a mincemeat tart. Or *vota vota*, which means turnover and refers to a pizza-like dough wrapped around something like tomatoes, parsley, capers and garlic, then baked and cut into sandwich-like slices. Or the salt cod and cauliflower stew that I never did get the Sicilian for, but which I know I'll never see under any name in a stylish Southern Italian restaurant.

And then there's *cunigghiu a la stimpirata*, which you may not recognize as marinated rabbit. But this rabbit is nothing like the more conventional rabbit stews of Northern Italy (which are still too unconventional to find their way onto stereotyped Northern Italian menus). It includes green olives, capers, onions, crinkly-cut potatoes, oregano, vinegar and the Middle Eastern taste of fresh mint. One bite and I was immediately taken back to the English mint sauces of my childhood, the product, no doubt, of some joint venture during the Crusades a few years back.

The confrontations between Christians and Arabs in the Middle Ages may not have been very efficient ways to advance the cause of religion, but they certainly did the world of food some lasting good. Not that you would know it when you sample the chef's creation du jour at a local hot-spot. There you're eating food that, whatever else it does, can tell no story — it didn't exist yesterday (unless it was ripped off from the current issue of Australian *Vogue*) and it won't be around tomorrow. One of the great pleasures that comes from searching for new foods in older cultures is that the food on your plate is not just food on your plate. It has a history quite separate from the thoughts of the person who made it and the appetites of the person consuming it. Bite into a breakfast pastry from Southern Italy, feel the pull of the past, and for a moment the cynical world of food fads disappears.

Our own grandiose historical quest started innocently enough. We were driving to the Niagara Peninsula to stare at the Falls, taste some wine, search for the elusive ripe plum and satisfy a yearly craving for vanilla fudge. But five minutes along the highway, the steamy summer turned into the rainy season and made driving even more of a death wish than usual. So we turned off at the first exit and found our way home on that quiet Sunday morning along leafy boulevards overrun by sodden joggers, through deserted industrial subdivisions hawking bed frames and diapers at factory-direct prices, past a public-housing development where gospel music resounded through the open windows and chased down Saturday night's lost souls.

And then, though it was only eight a.m., we came across a traffic jam outside a bakery. Recognizing a good thing—the rain was pouring down hard enough to reconcile anyone to the indoor life—we pulled over.

The place was buzzing—early-morning Mass nourishes the body less than the soul—and it became clear that the best way to get served was just to point whenever the sales clerk came within range. When we got home and made sure the coffee was well underway, I unpacked the plastic bags to see what I'd bought: several unadventurous glazed doughnuts, two objects that had looked like flaky almond croissants in the display case but now felt disturbingly firm and heavy, some crusty spiral-shaped rolls that would be delicious with raspberry jam—and one pastry that stood out from the rest. At the bakery, from a distance, it hadn't looked like anything too far out of the ordinary: an elongated diamond scored transversely with innumerable cuts, dusted with icing sugar to present a prim, delicate appearance.

But when I picked it up, it behaved quite unlike any sweet I'd ever come across. Each cut across the pastry was like a joint and wherever I applied pressure with my greedy hand, the thing would bend over and then slightly recoil. On close examination, it looked and behaved something like a Slinky, something like a Japanese fan, something like an armadillo, except that the over-lapping plates of the animal's armour were here replaced by loops of phyllo pastry.

I don't suppose I'm making it sound too appetizing. At this point it was more like a captured specimen, an exotic that had escaped from its natural habitat. But the taste, when I'd finished manhandling the creature, was almost as striking: a light curd-like filling, flavoured delicately with some sort of extract (orange? rosewater? prickly pear?), bits of festive candied peel and the crunchy, elastic pastry that unwound as you chewed it like a single noodle from a coil of tagliatelle. I called the bakery to find out what it was I was enjoying after all these years of ignorance. With a certain amount of give and take, and references to secret family recipes that must never be divulged, we agreed that I had bought something called *sfogliatelle*.

The word intrigued me. I could see the Italian for leaf, foglia, at the centre of it, and the combination of leaf and pastry sug-gested the Greek phyllo dough (from phyllon, a leaf) which in turn opened up centuries of Mediterranean possibilities before my befogged Sunday morning brain. Looking up sfogliatelle in Waverley Root's scholarly *Food of Italy* (I had time as well as icing sugar on my hands), I came across this cross-cultural explanation.

"You could draw a map of the limits of Muslim invasion," Root wrote, "by plotting the places where, during the Middle Ages, their fine, flaky pastry became established. It is the pastilla of Morocco; the rustic tourtière and the aristocratic mille-feuille of France (where they got as far as Poitiers); the strudel of Central Europe (where they reached the Adriatic and threatened

Vienna); and in Italy the mille-foglie of Sicily and the sfogliatelle of Naples."

Now maybe you've known about sfogliatelle for decades and find it no more exciting than an egg roll—the curse of the familiar—but to me there was something wonderful in this chance discovery. A singular little pastry found its way from the Arab world across the treacherous waters of the Mediterranean to the Bay of Naples. Then, after a decent interval, it passed through the Strait of Gibraltar, crossed the stormy Atlantic and ended up tempting the passing trade on a rainy morning a few blocks from my kitchen table. To me, that pastry's worth a puff.

While other cultures prepare for Christmas by stringing flashing lights along the eavestrough or parading oversized cartoon characters down main streets, the Italians I know like to stack boxes in food shops. Passageways in bakeries and delis that once allowed shoppers plenty of room to peer at the prosciutto or cross-examine the crostini are suddenly blocked, as November gives way to December, by elegantly elevated piles of goodies.

You leave your Maserati beneath the No Parking sign, confident that you can grab the crusty Calabrese loaf and be back in a flash. But because it's Christmas season, the crowds are gathered in voluble wonder around the cartons of seasonal treats. While you fight your way through with a polite "Permesso" and an insincere "Mi scusi" and a barely suppressed "Move it, sister," the ticket on the windshield is already acquiring the patina of age. Better to park legally—hire a neighbourhood kid to stand guard if you've got those gold-plated hubcaps—and linger a while. The Italian confectionery industry provides hours of entertainment with the packaging alone, drawing on the country's treasury of hill towns, Renaissance heraldry and sad-eyed madonnas to decorate the spare-no-expense containers that imported delicacies call home.

But it's the food inside that's of abiding interest to anyone out to acquire new tastes and make someone else's traditions their own. Stacks of torrone, the honey-and-almond nougat that has bankrupted Mediterranean dental plans for centuries, rise up over the rings of Smyrna figs from Turkey and California almonds in their bleached yellow shells. Propped up against them with a fine sense of sweet-shop masonry are biscuits and cakes from Sapori of Siena, melt-in-the-mouth ricciarelli tasting of bitter almond, and the dense compound of candied fruit and nuts called panforte.

Rising high above the rest are the oversized dainties that take pride of place (if only because they take up so much of the place), the angular boxes that contain the cakes and sweet breads. In the more deliberately cramped Italian stores, the sort that go in for the layered look in food display, these pointy boxes are hung on wires that stretch from wall to wall, creating seasonal hazards for visiting NBA players. From a distance the containers look very similar, and the standard reaction of the non-Italian on a flying visit is to wonder how the cognoscenti choose one over another. But on closer examination—don't worry, there's still money in the meter—considerable differences become clear.

The first thing to notice, if you plan to make use of these sweet breads and fluffy cakes and not just to stare at them, is the difference in styles. The most basic and traditional are the simplest pandoro and panettone. These foods spring almost directly from the Renaissance, tall, yeast-raised breads that are full of air and wonderfully light. Pandoro, literally bread of gold, has a higher egg-yolk content and perhaps a moister texture than panettone, which takes its flavour from the sultana raisins and bits of candied peel that saturate each slice. Both of these breads are made in a traditional toadstool shape, their round tops rising out of a band of (non-edible) parchment baking paper. They go best with a hot mug of dense coffee early in the day, and though you don't have to butter them they're certainly not hurt by a little excess fat.

A quick panettone joke: Puccini used to send his friend Toscanini a panettone every Christmas. One year, when they were on the outs, he decided not to send his gift. But the bakery where he had his standing order delivered one anyway. Mortified, Puccini fired off a telegram: "Panettone sent by mistake." Toscanini's reply was swift: "Panettone eaten by mistake."

Some people, in less of a hurry to devour their panettone, prefer it toasted, like raisin bread. Some use their leftover panettone to make an Italian bread pudding: Lightly toasted slices are brushed with butter, put to soak for 15 minutes in a baking dish with some vanilla custard, then baked for 40 minutes at 350°F or until just set. But since the moister panettones keep so well, how does anyone end up with leftovers?

One odd thing about these breads-cum-cakes, at least for those of us from thrifty cultures who mourn every quarter lost to the parking meter—there's an enormous range in price. Savvy shoppers will quickly realize that the high-cost brands are not five times better, but only five times better wrapped. The expensive versions—some packed in collect-and-save cookie tins, others in visions-of-the-Virgin cartons—are used as gifts. But the cheaper ones, packed in nasty plastic bags and kept hidden in the back, can taste much the same.

These relatively chaste sweet breads are the classics. Many of the other items filling up the room are the new, move-with-the-times models, from chocolate-covered panettone to white-chocolate crescent moons and more dubious combinations of cake and cream filling. One I saw, but refused to taste, was a chocolate-covered pandoro stuffed with a "champagne" cream filling. Best consumed, I think, at a low point on New Year's Eve when the homemade spumante's running low.

I should have been more open-minded, I suppose, in keeping with my own advice. Sfogliatelle was once a novelty in Naples, and how long would it have lasted if the locals had mocked its strange pastry? But it's funny how easy it is to laugh at other people's tastes. Funny, I mean, compared with how hard it is to joke about anything else that belongs to a different culture.

The public campaigns against bigotry and stereotyping that are so much a part of modern life have only succeeded so far. Most people keep their unkind thoughts about other ethnic groups to themselves. They may think they've detected a pattern in one race's driving habits or another nationality's love of pounding bass notes, but they're now much more careful about passing on these insights to the world at large. So it surprises me when people who are careful to appear free of bigotry in every other area think they can be as prejudiced as they want when it comes to food. The kind of slur you could never get away with if you said it about an ethnic group is perfectly acceptable when you say it about what they eat.

Now I'm not suggesting we mount a bus-shelter poster campaign against everyone who ever expressed doubts about Jamaican saltfish or Vietnamese drinks or English steamed puddings. Taste can't be enforced. Beyond that, there are some genuine cultural barriers—a predisposition toward salt, or well-done meat, or undercooked steamed vegetables—that take some overcoming. But I sometimes wish the people who are so confirmed in their own tastes could drop their culturally induced complacency just long enough to discover what they're missing.

Of all the kinds of foods that invite instant prejudice, other people's desserts and sweets seem to evoke the harshest response. Why the end of the meal should catch us at our least adventurous I'm not sure, though I expect it has something to do with the innately conservative tastes of childhood that dessert calls up.

I've known people who would eat Cantonese sea cucumber without trepidation and yet gasp at the thought of such traditional Chinese treats as lotus-nut dumplings or the steamed dessert square called chin jung go, which gets its squishy moistness from tiny cubes of pork fat. What is stranger still is the person who claims to enjoy parathas and pilaus but has no time for Indian sweets.

Now it may be you've never encountered Indian sweets, and what I should tell you is that you don't know what you're missing. But I won't say that, because experience tells me that you may be happier giving them a miss. The usual complaint, as I recall, is that "they're too sweet." Coming from a culture that brought us vanilla fudge, chocolate truffles and Hawaiian doughnuts with sprinkles on top, this is rich.

Indian sweets, I regret to say, are sweet. Some of them — not the kind I prefer, but never mind that — consist of cheese curd balls or deep-fried lentil-flour sausages soaked in rosewater syrup. These definitely take some getting used to, being nothing like apple pie or chocolate-mousse cake, but they are at the very least both delicate and exotic. The sweets that really make the world a richer place, though, are the Indian versions of fudge and halvah. The basis of many of these delicacies, odd as it may sound to anyone with a stereotypical view of South Asian culture, is milk. Reduced to a grainy, toffee-like consistency through long simmering, flavoured with the haunting taste of cardamom, enriched with ground almonds or cashews or pistachios, the plainest of North American drinks is transformed into a sweet of unrivalled richness. These confections were fed to Indian strongmen to keep up their strength, but they're also the sort of dainty you'll find at a wedding or religious feast.

Yes, I know, I'm getting carried away, and you neither wrestle under the name of Tiger Jeet Singh nor worship as a devotee of Vishnu. My only excuse is that Indian sweets exert a powerful hold on those who succumb to them. Sweet they are, but it seems far easier and less depraved to go through an assortment of carrot halvah and fudge-like almond barfi than a box of chocolates. As desserts go, they're relatively nutritious, allowing for the occasional lapses with food colouring and ornamental silver leaf. But it's really the unusual combination of aromatic spice, intense but complex sweetness and soft, melting texture that makes me drive off to my favourite sweet shops on a whim or, when I'm feeling very fit, try to make some carrot halvah myself. It takes several hours of constant stirring—reacquaint yourself with the Bach cello suites or the early work of The Temptations—but the result puts the dominant culture's carrot cake to shame.

"Try anything once" is the motto of people who are determined not to let life's possibilities go to waste. These heroic creatures think nothing of climbing a rock face one weekend, sampling a ménage à trois the next and starring at a comedy club's amateur night the following Tuesday. Fear does not enter the picture. Propriety is an unknown word.

Me, I worry too much about what the neighbours will say or who will clean up the mess. My motto is more restrained: taste anything once.

Being omnivorous has its hazards too, though when it comes to filleting a pig's head or biting into goat's testicles, most of the horror lies in the anticipation. It all tastes like chicken, more or less. But the rewards far outnumber the risks. If it weren't for this open-mouthed courage, this suicidal fascination with foods my mother never served, I'd never have come across the moon cake.

There it sat on the top shelf of the Chinese bakery where I'd been keeping a daily vigil for oddities. Through long and careful study, I'd grown used to the strange Chinese sweets with their fillings of black bean and green bean and winter melon. But this pastry, which had appeared out of nowhere to take over the shelves and attract a frenzied crowd, was on a different plane altogether. The palm-sized cakes were a shiny brown and embossed with Chinese characters that had been pressed into the intricate pastry. They looked a lot more serious than the "Happy Birthday, Grandma!" scribbles on the cakes of the West, and the cost confirmed that this was something out of the ordinary.

I handed over my $5, rushed out of the bakery, took a bite when no one was looking, and what was this? A hard orange egg yolk.

No one said adapting to the ways of others would be a piece of cake. I thought I was about to sample a luxury sweet. Instead I had bitten into a symbol.

At the time, I wasn't so understanding. I just thought it was one of those acquired tastes that I was in no hurry to acquire. Then I encountered a friend from Hong Kong and realized just how powerful an effect a tiny cake could have.

She'd found herself looking out the window from the fifty-fourth floor of an office tower one night in the fall. The moon was at its brightest and fullest. Staring at it across the city lights, she wished she were back in her homeland, where every September the citizenry climb the highest hills to greet the harvest moon. Its appearance marks the beginning of the Chinese mid-autumn festival, a time to celebrate the harvest of the crops and be reminded—by the moon's round shape, apparently—of the importance of family harmony and unity. Were she back in Hong Kong, my friend said, she could have looked out and seen ceremonial lanterns bobbing and weaving their way across the city, some in the shape of rabbits, others looking like fish or butterflies or even persimmons.

My friend had reason to be wistful. But if the lunar lanterns don't bob as merrily on the North American streets as one might like, at least there's the consolation of the moon cake.

The moon cake carries immense symbolic value, and the egg yolk is the reason why. It represents the harvest moon that lies low in the autumn sky, or a good likeness thereof, created from the yolk of a duck egg that has been placed in a jar, coated in a mixture of salt, wine, tea and clay (or grass and sawdust if your mud-merchant's short on clay), and left for a month to harden. Firm, crumbly and extremely salty, it's not what Westerners expect to find in a sweet.

But it's not our emotions and expectations that the salty orange cake-filling is meant to feed. The moon cake is to the Chinese expatriate what the plum pudding must have been to a Victorian Empire–builder compelled to celebrate Christmas in some hot and dusty corner of Her Britannic Majesty's realm. Food, yes, but not in any life-sustaining, seven-essential-nutrients way; rather, a collection of shapes and flavours and textures that together give a sense of occasion, a feeling of festivity, a compacted set of memories.

The power of symbolic food should not be underrated. Think of the American Olympian abroad sustained by the dubious nutrients of the Big Mac or the South African who will journey for hours to find boerewors for the barbecue. It's no use telling them that there are better-flavoured or more nourishing foods to be found at half the price and effort. The taste of what they're about to eat is already imprinted on their minds, and they simply need the thing itself to make their memories real again.

We who lack this particular bit of oral history may have trouble figuring out these alien tastes. But it's well worth persisting, to expand our cultural range by understanding that what we're eating isn't just what we're tasting. And yet if you can accept the unusual combinations of flavours in this Chinese sweet — and aren't unusual combinations of flavours what we claim to admire about so much modern cooking? — so much the better. The yolk (or yolks; more expensive cakes to impress your friends contain two or even four) is enclosed in a chewy, sugary pastry and a dense sweet filling made from lotus seed, mashed beans, rice flour or coconut. The various flavourings of the coconut pose a further challenge to the gastronomically impaired. Hip bakeries will offer coconut moon cakes blended with the savage perfume of the durian, the famous Asian fruit deemed so aromatic that it's banned by some airlines. Alongside the durian is my favourite, a variety that takes some of its flavour from sweet Yunnan ham and some of its moist texture from finely chopped fatback pork. I hope it isn't spoiling the sense of adventure to say that the ham moon cakes also include (and here I'm guessing somewhat) crystallized winter melon, melon seeds, sesame seeds, almonds, sugar lumps and candied orange. The egg, by the way, isn't just a stand-in for the harvest moon—no food should be just a symbol. Its saltiness cuts the sweetness and the effect ends up being something like an old-fashioned fruit cake; put that way, it sounds almost familiar and tame.

Maybe too familiar, at least for ever-restless Hong Kong tastes. This is a place where desserts now come topped with gold leaf, caviar is a standard seasoning, and the humble Italian dish of squid cooked in its own ink isn't complete without hunks of lobster. My friend tells me that even the ancient moon cake has been made to adapt to the city's urgent sense of modernity: three layers of sherbet, with yellow mango at the centre representing an icier, more sophisticated moon. Just as we acquire an ancient taste, it has to modernize. I'm feeling wistful already.

Timelessness is becoming a lost virtue in the food we eat. You don't have to be totally stratified in your tastes to regret the changes that have been forced on food for change's sake. You feel a need for barley soup? But that's so mid-'90s. You came to love brandade de morue while on a hockey scholarship at the University of Marseilles? Sorry, salt cod's as passé as the wrist shot—

this is the year of smoked quail. And how could you still be purée-ing parsnips when the arbiters of taste have moved on to scal-loped squash?

Or is it the other way around? As each year's menus labour to work their way into the national psyche, and we begin to de-velop an inexplicable fondness for pit-roast kohlrabi or tamale dumplings, I can't help but feel the urge to buck the trends and make a statement for timelessness.

Every New Year's Eve, as the old is symbolically giving way to the new, I take my stand. What I feast on is totally unfashion-able. For a start, it's wholly at odds with the prevailing health mania, consisting largely of fatty, salty meat with hardly any veg-etables. It doesn't address current worries about osteoporosis, nor does it make any attempt to solve the problem of insufficient folic-acid intake. Recipes from the emerging Latin and African cuisines are given short shrift in my favourite meal. Nor is my dinner quick to prepare in keeping with the needs of stressed-out, time-poor baby boomers. It took a full half-hour of driving, plus an extra four minutes of genial end-of-year chit-chat, to pick it up and bring it home. Putting it on a plate took up several more minutes of valuable time that might have been better used diver-sifying my client network or strengthening my power base.

But since I stubbornly resist annual invitations to join Geri Halliwell on the beaches of Barbados just so I can sit down to this New Year's Eve dinner, you can appreciate how good Chinese bar-becue must be.

There, I've given away my little secret. Yet somehow I know I'll still be the only non-Asian to be found ogling the meat in the no-nonsense Chinese barbecue shops on December 31. I can think of all kinds of reasons people might offer for keeping their dis-tance—nervousness around the lifelike carcasses, anxieties about hygiene, worries about the language barrier, concerns that the shops aren't as swish as Tiffany's. None of these is convincing enough to nullify one of life's enduring pleasures, yet each New Year's Eve I have the place to myself.

Every barbecue shop worthy of the name, it's true, does hang a whole crisp-skinned pig in the window. But in countries where food is enjoyed rather than feared, this is seen as a come-on. If the shop is well-stocked — in spite of the New Year's Eve rush — there should also be rows of whole barbecued duck and chicken hanging on hooks with their heads turned mutely to one side. Down below, there will be skewers of misshapen red meat, which are hunks of juicy pork loin that have been marinated in sugar, soy, garlic, red vinegar and such like. You may also find creamy chicken livers, tough orange-tinted cuttlefish and innards cooked to make them a little less innardy. At my local barbecue shop, which resembles a French charcuterie in its talent for using up the whole pig, there's also a steam table of tripe and intestines cooked in various improving ways to maximize the sauce and minimize the meat in that fine old Chinese tradition.

After several years of experimentation — while the rest of you were wearing funny hats and partying till dawn — I've decided I prefer to welcome the New Year with a combination of barbecued duck (half a bird is enough for two) and a sliced slab of pork loin. Nothing against the fattier pork hacked from the carcass — it's wonderful scattered across a bed of rice in a brown gravy with chunks of custardy tofu — but for prolonged nibbling, the leaner loin is more bearable. Especially when eaten with the barbecued duck, which is one of the great achievements of Cantonese cuisine. The barbecue chef hacks up the duck into manageable pieces so you can add them to a noodle soup or a heap of rice along with some quickly boiled greens. But on a contemplative night like New Year's Eve, with a glass of Veuve Clicquot in hand and *This Is Spinal Tap* on the VCR, duck is best consumed as finger food. Hand-held food rarely offers such a range of tastes: the anise-cinnamon spicing of the skin, the juicy lusciousness of fat beneath and the prolonged, rich flavour of the dense meat itself.

You should always buy enough Chinese barbecue to carry over into the next few meals, maybe popping the chopped pork into a dish of noodles with some shrimp and bean sprouts or making upscale fried rice with what's left of the duck. Being someone who sees the point of the cyclical feast (as long as it's not turkey for both Thanksgiving and Christmas), I mark each New Year's Day by chopping my pork and boned duck into a salad of watercress, arugula and radicchio, the bitterness of the leaves balancing the sweet richness of the meat, the leftovers from the old year being a reminder that the past is always with us in the present. Dressed with a simple vinaigrette, it doesn't stand a chance of becoming this year's trend.

The past is always with us, but sometimes the present refuses to reconcile itself to that fact. Which explains why things sometimes could get a little hairy down at Tolbert's original Chili Parlor and Museum of the Chili Culture in the unreformed Cedar Springs part of Dallas.

I married into Dallas. I didn't choose it. It wasn't a place I'd planned on seeing any time soon and certainly wasn't a priority when it came to picking up some new tastes in food. I've yet to go to Venice, for goodness' sake.

The first time I went down to visit my in-laws and swim in their pool — think Venice with chlorine — the newspapers were full of stories about the great Texas chili cook-off. The Canadian in me imagined a gathering of earnest middle-aged gentleladies weighing out minced beef at the hygienic test kitchens of a prim women's magazine. But the Texas idea of chili isn't quite like that. The cook-off took place in some godforsaken corner of the state called Terlingua that was full of snakes and ghost towns. It seemed to involve bikers on a bender, women who needed no encouragement to take off their tops and unshaven guys who used son-of-a-bitch as a cooking term. Suddenly I appreciated why the forward-thinking Dallas health department felt a bit queasy whenever it had to look in on the Museum of the Chili Culture.

It's said the department's inspectors used to grow increasingly anxious as the date approached for the meetings of the Chili Appreciation Society that was quartered at Tolbert's, and with good reason. Regulars at the monthly get-togethers back in the early eighties came to include not just a few feverish devotees of cowhand cuisine but—as the cult of chili con carne turned into an almost Proustian reverie for urbane Dallas' temps perdu —their horses, roosters, goats, burros and armadillos. Someone once brought a chimpanzee and sat him down in front of what plain-speaking Texans call a bowl of red. There are those who say this was going too far for a Museum of Chili Culture, chimps not being native-born Texans; but others say going too far is what chili culture, and the Wild West in general, is all about.

This coming together of chili and chimp was commemorated by a photograph that for many years adorned the walls at Tolbert's after it upgraded to a renovated warehouse in the city's West End. At the point when I first visited the restaurant, in an attempt to understand the place my transplanted in-laws now called home, the menagerie of weird animals was just a memory. There were no snakes or bikers, no topless women strutting their stuff for chili. Health concerns and financial opportunism had combined to push Tolbert's way upscale. The clientele, snakeskin cowboy boots notwithstanding, was more at home in skyscrapers than on the range.

But the appreciation of a simple bowl of red was still deep-felt at Tolbert's. No amount of change in every other aspect of Texan life could take away the hunger for something so basic and pure. Wherever I looked, there was chili—dense, beefy, bur-

nished red chili with all the smoky pungence of hot peppers—
being dispensed by the cup, by the bowl and, best of all, in Texas-
size tureens that kept hunger at bay until the cows came home.
As for the nouvelle Texas cuisine that stuffs ravioli with black
beans and mates goat's cheese with a cream of ancho peppers,
"We have," said an old Tolbert's hand, "a kind of philosophical
problem with that."

The restaurant traced its lineage and a few of its recipes to an
investigative journalist and chili theorist named Frank X. Tolbert,
whose investigations were concerned less with Lyndon Johnson's
peccadillos than with his tendency to overdo the tomatoes in his
Pedernales River Chili. Besides watching over the presidential skillet, Tolbert founded the Chili Appreciation Society, organized the
World Series of Chili cook-offs in Terlingua and devoted himself
to tracing the true origins of chili con carne. To call him single-
minded would be to underestimate the spiritual range of chili.

Souvenirs of his researches were scattered around the barn-
board and limestone surfaces of the restaurant that looked so different from the sleek marble malls where Dallas now spends
most of its free time. Pride of place went to an excerpt from The
Chili Prayer, words of devotion reported by Tolbert just as they
were spoken by a chuckwagon cook from the Texas Panhandle
named Bones Hooks. "Chili eaters is some of Your chosen people.
We don't know why You so doggone good to us. But, Lord God,
don't never think we ain't grateful for this chili we are about to
eat. Amen."

Anyone reared on that soupy mixture of kidney beans, tomato
paste and hamburger that passes itself off as chili in the rest of the
world will find it hard to believe that God was anywhere near the
kitchen. But real Texas chili con carne is a different breed. It starts
with the carne, lean pieces of inside round coarsely diced and
combined with beef suet. The choice of spices is important and
while powdered chili pepper can substitute for the flesh of puréed

pods if you're pressed, there's no leaving out the garlic, cumin and oregano. Tomatoes are tolerated in more liberal circles, so long as they don't take over. Beans are considered an abomination.

Tourists and urban cowboys sometimes like to turn chili into a test of strength and for them Tolbert's prepared a hellfire version that made its sufferers fall prostrate and utter prayers of deliverance. But down in Texas, real chili, that simple heartwarming bowl of red, makes its devotees say prayers of thanks.

Tolbert's Bowl of Red

To cook true Texas chili, set those beans aside and put faith in the power of beef and ancho peppers.

For a start, don't use ground meat. Take 3 pounds of lean beef (or venison), and cut into ½-inch cubes. Place ½ cup of beef suet (or ¾ cup of fat trimmed from the meat) in a large stewpot over medium low heat. Allow to melt as completely as possible, then remove any solid pieces remaining. Add the meat, ¾ cup of beer and 2 cups water. Simmer, covered, for 20 minutes, then add ⅓ cup of tomato paste. Stir and simmer until the tomato paste is well blended into the mixture, then add 1 finely chopped medium-sized onion, 2 tablespoons of ground cumin, 1 tablespoon of oregano, 1 tablespoon of salt and 3 cloves of crushed garlic. Stir, cover and let simmer over low heat until the pepper sauce is ready.

To prepare the pepper sauce, remove the stems and seeds from 6 to 9 dried long red ancho peppers, which produce a smooth and rather mild heat. (Anchos are available at specialty markets, or you can use the alternative pepper mixture below.) Place the peppers in 3 cups of boiling water. Cover and simmer for 1 minute, then remove from heat and let stand, still covered, for 15 minutes. Purée water and peppers in a blender until smooth and add to the meat mixture. Mix well, return to the stove and allow to simmer again, covered, for at least 4 hours. Remove cover and simmer for an extra 30 minutes to thicken sauce, then serve garnished Texas-style with onions and shredded cheddar cheese, with corn chips on the side. Adding beans or stewed tomatoes to this chili is a hanging offence down Texas way.

Alternative Pepper Mixture

Assemble in a small heatproof bowl 4 tablespoons of crushed chili pepper, 5 tablespoons of dark red chili pepper, 1 tablespoon of ground cayenne pepper and 2 teaspoons of Hungarian paprika. Bring 1½ cups of water to a boil. Pour the boiling water over the spice mixture. Stir well, then allow to steep for 5 minutes. (For more heat, add more cayenne.) Add to the meat mixture at the point where the pepper sauce above is added, then add 1 extra cup of hot water, mix well and cook as directed.

Panettone

First rule: Never make your own panettone. Unless you are an expert baker with an oven you trust implicitly, you will only be able to make the crudest parody of the puffy sweet breads you can buy with such a feeling of festivity in Italian grocery stores.

But when you have an excess of panettone on hand—post-Christmas or Easter when the stores clear out their stock at prices too cheap to resist—put this airy bread to work. Almost any sweet recipe that calls for stale bread (bread pudding or apple charlotte, for example) can be adapted to panettone. But for a simple and quick panettone dessert, slice the round panettone as you would a loaf of bread so that you get even pieces rather than uneven wedges. Then toast, or (better) grill the slices—make sure there aren't any loose shreds around the edges that could burn—and place on a plate. Top with stewed fruit such as peeled blood orange segments with a little chopped candied peel or apples with cinnamon or peaches cooked with a little ginger (though this assumes that you live in a place where peaches and panettone can be made to coincide; last summer's preserved peaches may have to do). Sliced fresh mango is also a good topping, but here you want to make sure the grilled panettone is warm, for contrast's sake. The simplest topping—very nice at breakfast—is good marmalade with lots of bitter peel.

Carrot Fudge

I call this fudge to make it sound more appealing, but there's no disguising the fact that this Indian sweet takes its brilliant orange colour from a humble vegetable. Vegetable sweets don't have much of a reputation in the West—they had a bad tendency to be created during the deprivations of war or pioneer homesteading. Even the carrot cake that turns up in unfashionable restaurants tastes mostly of sour cream icing and heavy-handed spicing—cinnamon, cloves and nutmeg in enough quantity to banish all thoughts of cooked veg.

But in Indian cooking, a vegetable sweet like this is the most powerful kind of food, the sort of snack you give a wrestler to build up strength or a god to build up a reservoir of good will. The long-cooked reduction of milk supplies a dense, grainy sweetness that is very satisfying (and fortifies the forearms for any after-dinner arm wrestling). The perfumed scent of cardamom is another reminder that this isn't your ordinary industrial carrot cake.

Clean, dry and grate as finely as you can 2 pounds of carrots (larger ones are less work). Set aside along with any juice that's accumulated. Warm 2½ quarts of whole-fat (homogenized) milk, then add the carrots and 1 small cinnamon stick and bring to a boil. Reduce to a simmer and cook, stirring frequently until the liquid is brought down to a quarter of the original (this will take some time — listen to the ball game or Texaco's broadcasts from the Met). Take the seeds from 5 cardamom pods and crush finely or grind in a spice mill. Add to the cooking carrots, together with a few saffron threads and a handful of raisins. Stir until the milk dries up, then enrich with 2 ounces of butter, 2 tablespoons of honey and 6 ounces of brown sugar. Add 2 ounces of coarsely chopped almonds, ½ teaspoon of rosewater if you like, pack into a glass baking dish, chill, slice and serve.

Peppers

THE SWEET RED peppers of darkest winter are precious things, perfectly shaped, uniformly red and embossed with an oval label that discreetly reveals their beginnings under glass in a faraway land. When you see such a beautiful specimen, half the product of nature, half the creation of tinkering, pottering, exacting humans, you try hard not to look up and confront a price that's punitive.

It's too much to pay compared to the sensible winter vegetables—carrots, potatoes, turnips—being sold at bearable prices. Still, you buy one, hope the cost will disappear on the long sales slip between the toothpaste and the oven cleaner, and try to plan a dish that will justify this fit of extravagance. A winter tomato is a pale, sickly excuse for a tomato, imported corn can taste starchy and dry, but that single crunchy, juicy, succulent red pepper—roasted and dressed with olive oil, perhaps, or doled out over a few days into omelettes, soups and salads—makes it seem like summer again. As you clean it, cutting out the core, stripping off the ribs and picking away at the last tenacious seeds, you find yourself nibbling at any discarded piece with the slightest hint of red—nothing can be wasted.

And then, praise be, it's pepper season. The time has finally come when bushel baskets of mottled, ungainly vegetables fill the tailgates of pickups at farmers' markets and block the sidewalk outside Italian greengrocers. What they lack in perfect, exquisite beauty, they make up for in sheer profusion, and with the cost of a basket of peppers about that of a February handful, it's hard to resist buying the lot.

Then what? Do we stand dumbly in our kitchens like bears in a salmon stream and simply eat and eat as if there were no tomorrow? Do we, like our ancestors — the Hungarian ones anyway — throw a fit of boiling and salting and pickling, reducing the lushness of nature to laboratory jars of preserved peppers? Do we try to imagine all these peppers as the treasures they were six months ago and hand them out as tributes to coloratura sopranos or honoraria to guest speakers or tokens of triumph to the winners of the Olympic 1500 metres?

Well, why not? Peppers are a universal pleasure, after all, and remarkably versatile. A laurel wreath of victory might flavour a beef stew rather nicely, but that's about it, and a bouquet of roses tossed on stage after a nicely turned mad scene can do little more than perfume a jam or tisane. But short of whitening teeth or scouring the oven, a sweet pepper has almost no end of uses.

You will need those uses if you give in and buy a basket. And if you find yourself lugging home an entire year's supply of vitamin A and C in vegetable form, the first thing you must do is reduce the demands on the cook by getting rid of half of them as gifts. Now I know Martha Stewart says you're supposed to mark special occasions with scallop-edged felt plate-liners or a watered-silk handbound guest book, but most eaters of my acquaintance would be just as happy with dinner's raw materials. If determined to impress, you could, I suppose, wrap them in marbleized wrapping paper (preferably handmade) or stuff them in a lace-trimmed Souleiado drawstring sac. But, really, it's not necessary. Even at the height of the late-summer overflow, sweet peppers are a luxury.

Botanists, when they're not trying to make tomatoes square or teach wheat germ to talk, like to pretend that sweet peppers and hot peppers are closely related. The palate knows better. Even in their spare time, these two solitudes stand apart. Sweet peppers—red, green, yellow, orange, black—are eager to please, as a decorative touch to a noodle dish, a succulent emulsion on an antipasto plate or a happy-face stuffing for green olives.

But hot peppers take the macho approach. The more wimpish among us give wide berth to Mexican serrano peppers, but to an aficionado these tiny morsels are known as green bullets from hell. What others call a bowl of chili is son-of-a-bitch stew to your average hothead. And don't forget that the active element in hot peppers is used by cops to subdue bad guys. What other vegetable doubles as a crime-fighting tool?

Well, *vive la différence*, as the French say when confronted by hopelessly irreconcilable conflicts. It takes all sorts, variety is the spice and, just as hellfire exists because not everyone wants to spend eternity warbling *The Best of Celine* in the heavenly chorus, so, when it comes to peppers, some like it hot.

The sweet pepper is actually the exception to the family rule. Peppers are hot by nature and have stayed that way in most parts of the world. It was selective breeding by delicate Europeans that rid the bell pepper of heat while increasing its sweetness and fleshiness.

Partisans of hot peppers (for whom every argument is heated) tend to dismiss the sweet pepper as insipid, as decorator's food. And when I trail my sleeve in a yellow-pepper purée, I'm tempted to agree. But at the best of times, a ripe red pepper is one of the great co-productions of nature and science. Supremely refreshing to munch on raw, it can withstand long cooking without an appreciable loss of flavour (just don't parboil your bell peppers before you stuff them). The antipasto dish for which peppers are grilled or baked, skinned, dressed with good olive oil and left to steep is the best argument for this vegetable's greatness.

Sweet peppers are immediately ingratiating. Hot peppers are more of a test, and not everyone can pass the initiation. I have to admit that hot foods—blister-raising, devil-worshipping hot foods, not a little bit of minced pepper in my chicken all'arrabiata—can leave me cold. This is partly because I don't think food should become some kind of extreme sport, a tough-guy competition where the last one standing earns the reputation as the most sophisticated eater. But it's also because, I hate to admit it, my body just can't stand it.

Once, in more innocent days, I talked my mother into planting hot-pepper plants in her garden. The harvest was amazing and, straining to keep up with the ripening crop, I cooked with peppers every night. But after a few weeks of gingerly seeding, deribbing and finely chopping the flesh of one-eighth of a pepper and adding it to beef stews where it had no apparent effect, I decided it was time to get serious. Doing my best Aztec imitation, I boiled a mess of whole-grain cornmeal mush with plenty of shrimp and handfuls of bright red, cheerful chilies. I invited round some friends under the pretense of watching *The Godfather*, served up a few bowls of this polenta-gone-mad and was amazed at the effect. Suddenly we were gasping like Brando's Don Corleone.

They say you get used to it, that you develop a tolerance. Not me. Over the years I've found that while I can enjoy the sting of Chinese chili oil dipped drop by drop on dim sum dumplings, my feeble carcass still balks at fresh hot peppers. The mouth opens and no sound comes out. The throat constricts and the nose starts to run. Ears ring, eyes water and sweat nestles in the furrowing brows.

I can see why some people might like these effects. There's a poem by the Roman writer Catullus in which he describes the symptoms of lovesickness. They're not so different. Hot peppers mirror the sensations of intense pleasure, if only because the very physical feelings they produce are so completely out of the ordinary. And if a near-death experience isn't the best selling point for the mass market, don't forget that they ooze vitamins c and a, are a natural preservative, may even prevent hair loss (finely chop five small bird peppers into two cups of oil; massage into scalp), and as a cash crop their only rival is marijuana. But what about their taste?

It's hard to think of fiery heat and subtle flavours going together, and most people don't like to sweat their way through a fancy dinner. But once you're able to isolate the painful part of the pepper experience and park it in some anaesthetized part of the brain, there's a surprisingly wide range of sensations in the tempestuous hot-pepper family. Bell peppers will taste like invalid food after you work your way from the almost sweet mulato and more-bitter-than-hot pasilla of Mexico through the tingly, snub-nosed jalapeño and Pakistan's seismic Dundicott pepper, to the ferocious Jamaican Scotch bonnet, which should be stamped with a skull-and-crossbones and stored somewhere between the fire and the brimstone. One bite and you can sing like Bob Marley. Two bites and you enter the Reggae Hall of Fame, posthumously.

These three simple pepper recipes, one each for breakfast, lunch and dinner, show the independence of a vegetable that deserves to be more than just a decorative backdrop to meat.

Pipérade

To bacon fat heated in a broad frying pan, add 1 pound of sliced onions. When these begin to soften, mix in three sweet peppers, cleaned and cut into strips. When these are cooked, add 1 pound of peeled, chopped tomatoes, season with salt and cook uncovered until the mixture blends together. Then pour in 6 beaten eggs and cook them as if you were making scrambled eggs. Or you can fry the eggs separately and serve them on top.

Gazpacho

Chop up the following: 2 medium-sized cleaned red (and/or green) bell peppers, 1 fresh hot pepper, 1 onion, 2 cloves garlic, 1 medium-sized English cucumber, 4 peeled tomatoes, a few parsley sprigs, a dozen or so mint leaves and a handful of almonds or hazelnuts. Blend into a rough purée with a few spoonfuls of olive oil, a dash of red wine vinegar and enough water to give the right consistency. Serve cold, garnished with chopped pepper or olives.

Roasted Peppers

Cut 4 sweet peppers in half, remove the seeds, ribs and stalk, then bake them skin-side-up at 400°F until the flesh softens and the skin darkens. Peel and slice, then dress with olive oil, lemon juice (or red wine vinegar), salt, pepper, a little minced garlic and chopped parsley.

KITCHEN DETAIL

THE STAR OF THE HIT TV COMEDY *Frasier* is a commanding figure named Kelsey Grammer, whose deep voice and probing intelligence are a magnet for viewers. But while Grammer is the centre of attention, the greater pleasure for me comes from watching David Hyde Pierce, who plays his prim brother Niles. With his flickering eyes, arched brow and refined leer, Hyde Pierce is the classic supporting actor. With him, you sense, there is none of the baggage that comes with being a megastar, no hints of contract disputes or snits in the trailer or unplanned sabbaticals in rehab. He gets on with his job, does it effortlessly, fades into the background and, paradoxically, draws the attention and affection of off-centred people like me.

Most people, I know, remain fixed on the stars. That, if anything, reassures me that the delights on the margins are more real and less affected by the need to play to the crowd. You can take this approach to almost any creative art if you are so inclined, and suddenly realize that you prefer the cathedral's comic gargoyles to the solemnly suffering saints praised by the reverential guidebooks. And when I turn to the techniques of cooking, it's not hard to appreciate the same kind of role reversal.

Traditional menus as composed in professional kitchens are focused on something called the main course, and the main part of the main course is almost always a big hunk of meat. A veal chop, a rack of lamb, a sirloin steak; these form the star system in restaurants and at the dinner table. But no matter how good they are, to me at least they're invariably less interesting than what's going on around the edges of the plate. If I order steak-frites, though I'm paying for the steak, it's the fries that give supreme pleasure with their crisp skins and creamy centres. Fries by themselves would not be as enjoyable, perversely enough. They're too plain to be suited for the star role, and maybe like character actors on TV they need to play off the food that gets its name in lights. I would never have basmati rice by itself, much as I enjoy its popcorn perfumes wafting through the house while it simmers away in the kitchen. But when my cellmate cooks her pecan-coated chicken in mustard-cream sauce, I insist on the basmati and find that I push the chicken to the side in my rush to feast on the sauce-soaked rice.

Many people, it's clear, like salmon for the hollandaise, mussels for the marinière, Big Macs for the secret sauce. Serve me a crustless quiche or liver without onions and I'll feel like I'm being asked to do penance. John Lanchester, in his cuisinartistic novel *The Debt to Pleasure*, points out how French menus highlight this inseparability by the use of the possessive pronoun: Ris de veau et sa petite salade de lentilles de Puy suggests an intimacy and interdependence that goes far beyond sweetbreads with lentil salad.

I was making—attempting to make would be more like it—a dessert of caramelized blood oranges one day, and the one part of the dish I was determined to recreate from some long-ago vacation was the special taste and texture of the peel. Paying closer attention to the crimson-flecked fruit and its aromatic syrup might have produced a better result overall, but for me the entire purpose of the dessert lay in separating the bittersweet peel from the pith just so, cutting it into identical matchstick slices and cooking it in the syrup until it was translucent and sodden with sweet juice.

Better cooks than I realize that the fringe elements are to be embellished and embroidered only after the main task at hand is looked after. A Yorkshire pudding will not taste nearly so good if its roast is burnt, nor will the mashed potatoes shine if their lamb shank's gravy is watery. But having made sure that the temperature of the oven matches the thickness of the swordfish or the pork chops have an affinity for their marinade, the cook can leave the serious part of the meal behind and have some fun. Roasted fennel, say, that hits the table wrapped in the smoky bacon it's cooked with, is a side vegetable in name alone.

And could a turkey be a turkey without the support of its stuffing? You'd think it would be possible for a roast bird to exist independently, and yet how often do you see it? Visualizing an unstuffed turkey being carved up at the dinner table is like trying to imagine champagne without bubbles or foie without gras. In my mind, the stuffing should get top billing, and we should all be jotting down the twenty-four-hour hotline of the Stuffing Advisory Board on the list of emergency numbers in case the chestnuts turn out to be mouldy and we have to switch stuffings in mid-farce. A turkey, after all, is much the same thing every year. Some are bigger than others and won't fit into the new oven, some are overcooked and taste dryer than usual, some are suspected of harbouring poisons injected by shady animal-rights organizations, some are frozen solid and won't be defrosted until Boxing Day. But in the end, most manage to be a predictable recreation of what they always have been and ever shall be.

Not stuffings, which are limited only by the imagination of the cook and the size of the viscera they displace. And yet for all I love the chestnut, cilantro and Italian sausage stuffing that wafts its fragrance over my particular holiday dinner, it wouldn't be the same without the turkey it comes with. The stuffing enriches the turkey no end, but the turkey also improves the stuffing, supplying not just the odd cooking medium—a slow form of steaming, I think you'd call it—but a layer of meaty flavours and fragrances as well. Like the steak that goes with the frites, separated by only the tiniest hyphen, stuffings and what they stuff need each other.

You can try to make stuffing by itself if you like, but you know quite well that it will never taste as good as what comes out of the turkey's backside. Stuffed foods are inseparably the sum of their parts, and the process of stuffing invariably creates a new kind of dish with its own peculiar charms. A mushroom omelette is something quite different from eggs and mushrooms served side by side, a crêpe filled with Gruyère arouses expectations that could never be met by pancakes surrounded by cheese, and the won ton floating in your Chinese soup opens up all kinds of possibilities that noodles and minced meat by themselves couldn't hope to duplicate.

Stuffed foods have a fun side that we overlook in our mad rush to make eating serious and sophisticated. Why else do the olives that turn up at cocktail parties come stuffed with red pepper? The artificial quality of stuffed foods may seem outmoded in these straightforward times when ingredients can be praised merely for looking and tasting like themselves. But the pleasure we take in stuffing and then unstuffing a turkey has at least a little to do with the magician's art of concealing and revealing. Our tastes have changed considerably from those of world-weary aristocrats who required their cooks to invent illusionary food to pass the time until the next meal—a big bird enclosing a smaller bird enclosing a smaller bird enclosing an even smaller bird with a very small songbird at the centre, alive and singing when the roast was opened if the cook got it right. But the charm of a stuffed food is still available for those open to it. They're a long way from stuffed turkey, to be sure, but the appeal of Cantonese dim sum dumplings to Western eaters has almost as much to do with the magic of eating them as with their taste: a quivering noodle pouch encloses a thick soup, a football-shaped fritter of mashed taro root hides a filling of minced pork and bamboo shoot at its centre, a neatly wrapped lotus leaf is opened up to reveal a steaming mass of rice and chicken, sweet sausage and egg.

Stuffed dishes take extra work—the fine chopping, the delicate seasoning, the careful timing—but the evidence of your work adds an extra layer of pleasure for those who see only the final result. The unusual method of cooking, the co-dependent relationship between the stuffing and the stuffed, also makes for a dish that catches attention. No one with pretensions cooks cabbage rolls or stuffed peppers these days, but if I were put in charge of a festive meal, that's what I'd serve. And you don't have to wait fifteen minutes for someone to carve them up.

Alas, the days of modest supporting foods may almost be over. Fashionable menus now describe every element of a dish with equal enthusiasm, and when even the buttermilk whipped potatoes or the minced jalapeños in the stuffing share star billing, your expectations rise. Kelsey Grammer, it's worth remembering, was once just a character actor on *Cheers*. He was so good, they gave him his own show.

And after a while we will tire of Kelsey Grammer, if we haven't already. The threat of overexposure increases dramatically the closer you get to the centre of the stage, and the more we see you, the less we notice you. It's the same with cooking: you can have too much of a good thing. Scientists, whose contributions to the techniques of good eating are few and far between, got it right when they hit on the idea of sense fatigue. The more sweet (or sour or salty or bitter) tastes you're exposed to as you eat, the less discerning your taste buds become in dealing with more of the same. Of course that's not how the scientists would express it. Their studies come from labs, not dining tables, and words like "discerning" have no part in their value-free vocabulary. But the application of their work in the real world is still clear—you have to vary your menu if you want to make an impression.

This is a basic principle for cooks, whether they're planning a multi-course meal or just feeding a difficult child. Of course, anyone who has watched children devour bags of Hickory Sticks knows that the basic animal instincts can be overridden. And having conducted my own experiments into the number of chocolates I can eat before sense fatigue sets in, I'm amazed at the persistence of the pleasure. How many years did *Seinfeld* run? And right up to the end, the gorged masses wanted more.

But with the chocolates, at least, the scientists are onto something. The geniuses who filled the box I'm busy emptying found a way around my sense fatigue by creating a mixed assortment, with the smoky bitterness of the hazelnut fillings taking over just as the fatigue from the boozy Grand Marnier cream and the intense chocolate truffle begins to take hold. It's just this kind of sly variation that needs to be brought to the rest of the foods we eat. I was tucking into a side order of the Italian green called rapini the other night, savouring the ancient bitterness of the long-cooked vegetable that had been tempered with a little garlic, olive oil and smoked bacon. And as I finished it and asked for more before even noticing the grilled pork, I suddenly realized how important the rapini's bitterness was in catching my attention. So much of the food we eat now is blandly sweet and uncomplicated and relentlessly healthy. After a while you stop appreciating the nuances of the roasted red peppers in olive oil or the chopped fresh low-acid tomatoes on the pasta or the endless expanse of dried-out low-fat meat. But throw in a bitter green and your taste buds take notice.

Bitterness, the most elusive of the basic tastes in the modern world, can also be found in nuts; when you make your agnolotti with sun-dried tomatoes, you will want to chop some bitter-skinned walnuts into the cream sauce. Fruit and vegetable skins are another good source of this complicating flavour, which is why it's worth avoiding recipes that call for peeling or (much the same effect) parboiling. Have you ever noticed how strangely sweet the peeled eggplant tastes in a Chinese cold-weather hot pot?

But it's not just bitterness that's disappearing: there's a narrowing of flavours going on in other parts of our diet. In the wine world, Chardonnay and Cabernet made in a standard international style are supplanting more obscure and unusual local varieties. As I was opening a bottle of white wine to pour into the pot of moules marinière, I realized that it was a gentle, oaky California Chardonnay. A nice wine for drinking, maybe, but the original recipe called for something harsher, greener and more acidic to undercut the richness of the shellfish—the kind of poor man's wine, like the forbiddingly named Gros Plant, that no one drinks any more.

Some cuisines, more respectful of tradition, less amenable to the ways of the world, have kept their full spectrum of flavours. In a good Chinese kitchen, for example, though the eggplant may be peeled, you can expect to find such arresting, even startling ingredients as dried shiitake mushrooms, fermented black beans, salted vegetables, bitter melons and dried shrimp. In bolder European cuisines, it might be tart unflavoured yogurt that wakes up the slumbering palate, or wild mountain herbs or bitter olives or sauerkraut or salty anchovies. In Latin American cuisine, the earthy smells and tastes of hot peppers rescue food in danger of becoming dull.

Of course any of these flavourings can taste like more of the same when used to excess. A daily diet of sauerkraut and sausages would be even worse than listening to an endless recital of *Seinfeld* catchphrases. The good chef, cooking for effect and not just for maintenance, practises an almost unbearable discretion. Something as invigorating as nutty, bitter, fragrant pesto only amazes when you have it rarely. And yet in the pretty magazines and fancy restaurants where the menus display linguine al pesto year-round, where it always seems like one long climate-controlled summer, the potential for boredom is unlimited.

When herbs like the basil that goes into pesto first took command of the modern menu, it didn't seem so bad. They summoned up exotic places, brightened our bland food and woke up jaded palates. Free of fat, full of vitamins and friendly fibre, they gave us all those lingering aromas guilt-free. And from the crafty cook's point of view, they achieved their instant effect with little effort or cost. Pasta with tomato sauce might once have seemed a dull, common thing, but with basil our dormant Mediterranean senses revived.

And then, in the overstated way of the fashionable cook, the herbs took over, and the new ingredients became old hat. It became hard to enter a restaurant that didn't smell of freshly chopped basil on the tomato salad, or oregano on the wood-fired pizza or rosemary on the freshly grilled lamb. Every dessert started appearing with a sprig of fresh mint, every soup floated cilantro leaf on top and just when you thought enough was enough, lovage and lemon balm began to muscle their way in. If you're anything like me, you longed for the pure and ancient taste of pasta with tomato sauce as it was before the herbivores took command.

And what is especially weird is that during this culinary revolution, when the herbs that were once no more than cameo performers suddenly took over the stage, we lost our taste for a much greater range of aromas and tastes. Allspice, anise, cardamom, fennel seed, nutmeg, mace, cloves, coriander seed, caraway, cumin, poppy seed—when was the last time you saw these spices listed with pride on a menu? When did you last look at a soup or a stew and say, "What this needs is a good dash of cassia"? While we pretend to be making culinary progress, we have been depriving our foods of the world's most intriguing and most important flavours. Five centuries ago, nutmeg and pepper were as important as ideology and technology in shaping history. Entire empires rose and fell over the spice trade, and the smell of food was at the heart of European imperialism.

That's not a great recommendation these days, I admit. But spices remain the most potent ingredient in the kitchen because they appeal to our highly developed sense of smell rather than to our relatively coarse and primitive sense of taste. Nothing against herbs—better than no flavour at all—but spices are far more complicated and volatile. Stews should carry a clove and a stick of cinnamon as automatically as a bay leaf, and every sausage should hint at the taste of coriander or fennel seeds. Fettuccine with basil is good enough if you have to live off your garden, but spices open up the world: lobster ravioli with vanilla bean sauce, spinach cannelloni scented with freshly grated nutmeg, cardamom ice cream, strawberries with black pepper, fried bananas in a cinnamon-rum sauce. There's a good reason why the phrase is spice up your life —do you really think that Herb Girls would have had quite the same effect on the people of the world?

It's one of the unstated premises of fashionable cooking that so many of the great advances end up being a rejection of something else. The ascendancy of fresh herbs may seem like a victory for the modern sensibility, but it can just as easily be seen as the loss both of spices and the kind of complex, long-cooked dishes that they called home. And by giving the grill pride of place in the up-to-date kitchen, we have traded away centuries of recipes for the taste-alike dishes of health-conscious, short-order cuisine.

Pretending to broaden our range of foods and flavours, we've actually managed to narrow them. Outside the placid Mediterranean biosphere inhabited by too many chefs and food writers, there's a more interesting world that still acknowledges the seasons, that can vary its recipes and techniques as the fresh herbs wither and the cold winds start to blow.

I hear the objections. The supermarkets are full of bright Mediterranean vegetables and fragrant herbs year-round. So who needs to boil turnips? It sounds all too much like the eighteenth-century aristocrats who used to amuse themselves by playing peasants for a day. The reality is that in our thermostat-controlled homes and offices, every waking moment is like a pleasant spring morning in Capri. So why pretend it's an endless night in Siberia? We have grills that can replicate the tastes of the summer barbecue and provide an instant fantasy to banish all thoughts of black ice and airport delays. So who wants to bring back those thoughts with a canned tuna casserole that might as well cry out, Sorry, suckers, you're stuck with it!

Then comes the loudest and most persistent complaint of all: cold-weather recipes are heavy and dull. And that's the hardest one to deal with, for it's so often the truth. Think back to those worthy New Zealand lamb casseroles that steamed up the windows while they shrivelled silently in the oven the whole day. They provided a certain kind of dependable comfort as they cooked away, and they were certainly good at holding onto their heat after dinner was served, cheering those who'd spent their days outdoors building obscene snowmen with a few choice root vegetables. But as food and food alone minus the nostalgia trip, they were—how did those words go again?—heavy and dull. I have a friend who, whenever things are going bad, reminds herself that she never has to eat a New England boiled dinner again.

And then she's cured, for who wouldn't feel the lifting of a weight at the thought of no more plates stacked with boiled corned beef, cabbage and carrots?

Some traditions are worth setting aside for a lifetime or two. The humble ingredients from which cold-weather dishes are composed—because slow cooking, humble ingredients and traditional winters seem to go together—lack the joie de vivre so attractive in times when vie is short on the readier forms of joie. Long-cooked, dried-out beef is certainly preferable to the tough, not-yet-dried-out beef it was eight hours before, but on the whole there aren't many foods you can improve by day-long boiling or baking.

You can see why so many cooks take evasive action and fall back on grilled meat with herbs year-round. And yet it's precisely by facing up to the seasonal obstacles that cooking is made creative. Those who persist in making cold-weather dishes have picked up a few life-enhancing tricks: they add orange peel to beef stews for a little warm-weather fragrance, or toss some deep-flavoured olives into the casserole toward the end of the cooking to provide a semblance of summer. Or, instead of boiling the vegetables to an early death, they sauté them separately and add them to the pot at the last minute. And maybe, at the same time—you wanted steamed windows, you got steamed windows—they ladle out some of the cooking liquid and reduce it to something more concentrated. Or perhaps they borrow Thai herbs and flavourings, and fool the palate with lime leaf and chili pepper into thinking that this boring old beef isn't so boring after all.

In the traditional repertoire of the tricky chef, sauces were the greatest salvation of foods that couldn't get by on their own taste. Haul out your handy copy of *Larousse Gastronomique*, and you will notice that an inordinate—no, a ridiculous—amount of space is devoted to the art of the sauce. But the old concoctions such as tournedos Périgord were thought to be too heavy and too rich for a more nimble and health-conscious age. And so the thick cream and butter and brandy sauces went away unmourned, to be replaced by yet another variation on the inescapable theme of fresh-market cuisine.

Hunks of meat that used to come enveloped in a dark and heady reduction of dairy and alcohol were suddenly transformed into mincing slivers of meat that floated on top of a brightly coloured fruit or vegetable sauce. Those raspberry and tomato purées, undeniably colourful but artistic only to the eye, have nothing to do with the meats sitting atop them. Contrast is everything. Rather than harmonizing with a meat, as the best of the old sauces did, these improved versions are designed to stand out on their own. The lengthy menu descriptions we now accept as normal began with this exotic layering. In the process, an amazing number of words have been inserted into the language as alternatives to the suspect word "sauce." One of the menus I keep around to understand the obsessions of my contemporaries describes its main ingredients as being partnered or flavoured by infused oils, vinaigrette, roasted eggplant and garlic confit, lobster nage, roasted pepper aioli, garlic cream, tomato-red wine glaze, crème fraîche, lingonberry coulis, Riesling jelly—and those are just for the appetizers.

For all the rich vocabulary, the refined sauces of today are often either too minimalist (who can taste the white truffle in the radicchio's truffle oil?) or too jarring (what does this tart boysenberry coulis add to my expensive foie gras?). Undoubtedly they are healthier, if health is really the kind of thing you can achieve in an elaborate meal. But there's still too strong a sense that these flavourings are designed for readers, prone to be attracted by the restraint in "glaze" or the lightness of "sabayon," than for the person who finally eats the dish. One sign of the modern sauce's refusal to adapt to the needs of the table—trendy chefs now like to serve their creations in bowls. Diners find it impossible to cut up their meat and vegetables, but at least the soupy coulis isn't oozing all over the plate.

If you're trying to liven up off-season food and make meals that aren't just a Californian imitation of the Mediterranean summer, a splash of raspberry goo or tomato water isn't going to do the trick. A smarter adjustment is to vary the traditional cold-climate cooking techniques: abandon boiling or baking and switch to braising instead. Braising, to my taste, seems to enhance the flavours of the foods it's applied to while still producing the rich, warming fare that is beyond the reach of the grill. Best of all, it's a style that magically generates its own sauce, one that's integrated with the dish because it takes its flavours from the cooking ingredients.

Braising is a mongrel kind of cooking. First you brown your basic ingredients in fat; not, as is often said, to seal in juices but to produce interesting changes on the surface of the food that create more complex flavours. From there, you add liquid, to provide a moist medium for the cooking. But only a little liquid, enough to flavour your meat, keep it moist and make it tender. Braising can be short (for tender meat like chops) or long (for bigger hunks of tough meat). Some say a braised dish should be covered, to let the steam from the liquid cook the browned meat on the top of the stove. Others prefer to uncover, partially cover or sporadically cover the meat while cooking in the oven, or start it uncovered on the top of the stove and then move it covered to the oven. A mongrel, as I said.

Osso buco, veal shank in tomato sauce, is a classic Italian braised dish, which just goes to show you that even people raised on the Mediterranean diet can make time for winter. But the best braised dish I've ever tasted was actually fast-cooked in the high heat of a wok: eel (a variant recipe for the faint-hearted uses oysters) is quickly stir-fried, then simmered in stock with barbecued pork, garlic, chopped green onion, ginger and a host of Cantonese kitchen potions. Rushed to the table and served to people whose cheeks are still thawing from the outdoors, it accomplishes the feat of making cold weather seem both necessary and desirable.

Knowing full well that salt is basic to survival, that animals throng salt licks and humans crave potato chips, that the ancients likened salt's role in a dish to wit in conversation, I still look at the tiny white grains with suspicion.

Friend or foe? It's hard to say. Having bought salt-free bread by mistake at the local Italian bakery, I know that the ancients were on to something. Being stuck on a no-sodium diet must be like listening to Disney love themes while driving through the flatter parts of Nebraska on cruise control.

But having become a part of modern society's great high-sodium experiment, I'm not sure that mass blandness isn't preferable. My descent into the salt-caked depths was a typical consequence of these hurried times: the adults in my house who once had hours to study cookbooks and compose menus were suddenly hard-pressed to set the table. The microwave acquired to make après-school popcorn and warm up last night's leftovers became the frazzled chef's refuge of first resort. It wasn't long before the freezer that formerly sheltered a lonely ice-cube tray and a crystallizing tub of ice cream was suddenly brimming with frozen spring rolls, microwaveable lasagna, breaded cheese sticks and Old El Paso burritos. And when it seemed too much trouble to open the freezer door or press the microwave buttons, the telephone beckoned with takeout pizza, Chinese food, barbecued chicken. If we'd been more efficient, we would have put them all on speed-dial.

Such foods are salvation for the tired, the weak and the hungry, but for anyone used to a steady diet of home cooking, they come as a sudden shock — there's simply too much salt. Heat up a supermarket's cheese and bacon quiche after work or nibble on a takeout pizza and halfway through the night your dehydrated tongue has turned into a pillar of salt. When historians come to write about the last fitful years of the twentieth century, they will do well to forget about global conflict for a moment and ask whether less salt would have made the world a happier, calmer place.

A heavy hand with the salt cellar isn't exactly a recent development, of course. The same ancients who took such pleasure in the witty style of Sophocles—the droll author of that jeu d'esprit about the guy who murdered his dad, slept with his mom and gouged out his own eyes as an afterthought—also went a bit overboard on the Kalamata olives and anchovies. Salt has long been a cheap, handy preservative, and what started off as necessity rapidly became the preferred taste.

Salt is an attractive sensation up to a point. French fries and steak alike seem to be given a lift by a dash or two or three. And if you find you're cooking for heavy smokers or drinkers—a bracing prospect for a Saturday night—you'll need to use more salt than usual to awaken their anaesthetized palates. Loud, smoky bistros and trattorias abide firmly by this rule, which is one reason why their menus are filled with high-sodium items such as olives, capers, anchovies, salami, grated cheese and frites. Light, simple food seems flavourless in such a frantic environment.

But as all lazy chefs know, salt dulls and tires the appetite when used to excess. Salt also provokes the thirst, which is fine if you're selling beer in a bar but not so good if you're taking responsibility for the well-being of your tablemates. Using wine to slake their thirst is like quenching a fire with lighter fluid or taking out a loan to pay off the VISA bill.

Cutting out salt altogether isn't possible or even desirable, but cutting back will lead to a more interesting and better balanced meal. We all know that pancetta and artichoke hearts and the like taste salty, but as cooks we sometimes forget that they're a form of seasoning as well as a food in their own right. It's simply careless to use too many of these cured or briny foods in combination and then add a few shakes of salt as you would for other dishes. This problem can be turned to advantage though: a soup that takes its saltiness from crumbled Stilton or grated Gruyère has a more interesting taste than one laced with table salt.

Obviously, with long-cooked dishes such as soups and stews, most of the salting should be left to the end (when you might consider replacing it with the acidic bite of lime juice or vinegar). The same delayed approach goes for sauces, keeping in mind that almost any reduction, but especially those made with meat juices, will taste salty even before the seasoning is added (remember how salty your blood tasted when you licked a cut as a child; meat has a similar sodium content). The most important thing, though, is to taste before you salt. It's surprising how many amateur cooks religiously follow the cookbook's instructions and from awe or a misplaced sense of hygiene refuse to let their own tongues be their guide. Watch a professional chef at work if you want to see how it's done — he sticks his finger right into an underling's sauce to make sure the taste is right.

It's all about finding a balance — "Moderation in all things," as the with-it minister at my childhood church used to preach when he was trying to persuade us kids that Christianity wasn't entirely nay-saying, "and all things in moderation." But a measured sense of restraint isn't going to get you very far in a culture where overkill is always seen as the preferable option. Consider the way we treat heat.

When the aproned waiter in a pretentious eatery sets your plate in front of you with the warning — too late — "Don't touch, it's hot," instead of screaming for ice water to soothe your melting flesh, you're supposed to thrill at a restaurant that can actually keep food scalding-hot in the twenty-metre dash between kitchen and table. This is heat for heat's sake, elevating and exaggerating one aspect of good food—warmth—to the level of abuse. If you sacrifice your customers, friends or family on the altar of hot cuisine, the most lasting impression you leave is likely to be a scar. But the incineration won't stop, because just as oversalting is somehow mistaken for flavour, and a herb dependency becomes a passion for healthy food, so overheating is equated with hospitality. Remember the case of the eighty-one-year-old New Mexican woman who was awarded $2.9 million after suffering burns to her thighs, groin and buttocks when she spilled a cup of McDonald's coffee? McDonald's required its coffee to be brewed at a temperature between 195° and 205°F and held at 180° to 190°. Such temperatures, the company believed, were necessary to produce the best cup of coffee.

There's certainly a scientific basis for this policy. Too low a heat in the brewing and you end up not just with weak coffee but with sour coffee, since the acids in the beans dissolve before the more appealing flavours have a chance to emerge. And high temperature also releases the aromatics that make coffee as much a room-filling fragrance as a head-clearing drink.

Yet at McDonald's, as at many restaurants that try to put the gloss of professionalism on everyday food, the role of heat is largely symbolic. Maybe their beans are only ordinary in quality and aren't roasted long enough or at a high enough heat; maybe they know that their middle-of-the-road customers aren't pining for the bitterness of double espresso but for heat and heat alone. In the end, the steam rising from the 190°F liquid becomes a smokescreen for insipid flavour, and if you insist on a drink that will cloud your glasses and numb your tongue, then you probably aren't overly sensitive to the subtleties of taste.

As a veteran drinker of my wife's tepid coffee—the Scavenger Gourmet, they call me, after the health inspector found sniffing the contents of the Fawlty Towers refrigerator—I've satisfied myself that good coffee retains flavour even at a temperature where only I and the cat will consume it. But quality is not uppermost in people's minds when it comes to heat. Those fancy restaurants with their dangerous plates and chafing dishes—very useful for impressing Michelin critics—must be concentrating on showmanship, because no properly cooked food is improved by being held at a high heat once it's ready. At least in the sizzling hot plates that are used to dazzle diners in Chinese restaurants, the kitchen has the good sense to add raw vegetables before setting the whole overpriced extravaganza alight.

Cultures that treat good food as the normal part of daily life don't feel the same urge to inflict pain. In many warm-weather countries where heat is recognized as a force of extremism, lukewarm is a standard serving temperature for roast meat, stews, casseroles, cooked vegetables and warm salads. If you take away the need to serve food hot, dinnertime is much less urgent an event and the dinner hour itself is less likely to proceed on a downhill course from ready to tepid to cold. All kinds of possibilities open up, from the simple potato, lentil and bean salads dressed and served while the vegetables are warm, to the inventive *salades tièdes* of bistro-style cooks: sautéed sesame chicken served on a radicchio and arugula vinaigrette; warm new potatoes mixed with smoked duck and mayonnaise; chicken livers and bacon glazed with raspberry vinegar and olive oil before being arranged on ripped spinach. And as a bonus, cultures that take a more relaxed attitude toward their eating don't feel the need to chill their food to death: no icebox brie that might as well be Velveeta, no leftover pizza eaten by the pale refrigerator light, no sub-zero beer you could play hockey on slushed into frosted glasses you can't hold.

There is, honesty and my by-now tepid sense of Christianity force me to admit, one glaring exception to this rule. Diehard coffee drinkers from hot-weather countries where you'd think they'd know better insist that their brew be torrid. "They drink it as hot as they can suffer it," wrote William Biddulph of the Turks he met in 1609. A few centuries later, when I saw an Italian friend down a just-brewed espresso in one quick gulp, I realized she had transcended suffering, like the early martyrs singing hymns as they boiled in oil, and moved on to a higher state of being. Coffee, I like to think for consistency's sake, had stopped being a pleasure for her. It had become a ritual, a habit, a quick hit, no longer something to be tasted and savoured.

A good cook knows how to find the balance between the warring claims of pleasure and ritual, fashion and tradition, health and happiness, herbs and spices. That doesn't sound very exciting, does it? Balance, moderation, common sense — all passé. Instead, the ideal is the genius chef, and the extremist positions he (no need to be gender-neutral here) stakes out with his showstopping creations. Good cooks like to pretend after a dinner where the garlic mashed potatoes had just the right degree of lightness that maybe they could open a restaurant and win good reviews. But it is not enough in fashionable food culture to have mastered techniques. To be proclaimed celebrity chef, I'm afraid, you have to be born to it. You have to have the aura of genius.

Let's see what you need to make your name with the fawning food writers. The starting point of genius, as far as I can tell after years of observing it in the kitchen, is good looks and male gender. But don't get me wrong. It's not enough to have bedroom eyes and a centre-court body. You need to be an artist. You must have visions. Where lesser beings simmer stocks or bind sauces, you make statements and issue manifestos. The more ordinary cook takes delivery of food from suppliers. You wander the markets on your environmentally sound bicycle, or prowl the ethnic neighbourhoods for as yet undiscovered strains of Thai basil, or restlessly search the forest and the seas for fungi and shellfish that have long sustained the aboriginal peoples. Lesser chefs are busy administering. You are free to create, and appear in the gossip columns.

But what about the restaurant, the kitchen, the customers? Ah, I was hoping you wouldn't ask that one. Geniuses don't seem to fit into restaurants very well, at least not the kind of places that you can depend on for a good meal. If ever you find yourself in a restaurant that harbours a superstar, you will recognize his somewhat unnerving presence in several ways. First of all, the serving staff will carry themselves with an air of supreme self-importance. If you dare ask whether the kha root can be left out of the soup or the half-raw fish could be cooked a tad more — well, you might as well ask Picasso's brush-scrubbers if he could be prevailed upon to make the portraits a teensy bit more lifelike.

Then there's the menu. Outlandish, of course, with no end of unfathomable ingredients crammed into the description of each book-length listing. Unless of course the chef is in one of his faux-rustic moods. Then you'll fork over a few hundred for roast chicken and potatoes. Having found the courage to order foods you have either never heard of or long since grown tired of, you must next set aside a few hours for the food to be cooked. This wait, without which genius becomes commonplace, is referred to as "service problems" in friendly restaurant reviews. But the time you spend aching for the ragout of sea urchin to appear has nothing to do with your server's footwork or the maître d's on-again off-again affair with the sous-chef. What it really comes down to is genius. The ego in the kitchen moves at his own speed. His menus are elaborate and involved, and shun preparation. He cooks from scratch, or at least claims to when anyone complains, because you can't hurry love or art.

I remember meeting one of these agonizing artists a few years ago. His restaurant was the hottest around, and as the representative of a trend-loving magazine I was admitted into the inner sanctum to observe the wunderkind at work. The underlings in the kitchen were hard at it when I arrived. The restaurant would be opening in a few minutes. The tall, dreamy chef stood contemplating a bushel basket of prune plums.

For a good half hour, the much-acclaimed master pitted plums. While his assistants cooked his famous soups and made ready his signature vegetables, he was transfixed by the summer bounty. As someone with a back-to-basics approach to food myself, I had to admire this passion for simple unfashionable fruit. But in the dining room, his distraction might not come across quite so honourably.

The genius chef lost interest in his plums and pulled out a few veal hearts he'd discovered. While the more laborious cooks at his side put together plates of salmon trout dotted with salmon roe atop a froth of lime, the wunderkind chopped up the heart with a few wild mushrooms and started frying. As the rest of the kitchen team worked frantically at the genius' innovations, he and I dined well and fast on heart. I now believe that his behaviour was a cry for help, and a message to good cooks everywhere: Don't be fooled by the glamour of the restaurant business, or lured in by all those exotic ingredients and magazine-ready platings of smoked-salmon curlicues. Home is where the heart is.

And still we summon up our ambitions and try to reproduce the recipes of the professionals, hoping to be told at meal's end that the food could pass muster with Michelin. But at home even more than in restaurants, it's an experience—lazy cooks will be happy to hear this—destined to end in frustration.

Even when the presiding geniuses in the best restaurants have gone intellectually AWOL, their kitchens still have better equipment, bigger budgets and a larger staff with more specialized training than anything you're going to find in the home. One gifted amateur hunched over the old four-burner all day Saturday can accomplish some pretty interesting things, but the limits become obvious just about the time the hollandaise starts curdling, the grilling salmon sets off the smoke detector and the cat knocks over a wineglass.

You want to scream, and in real professional kitchens they do scream when the mood moves (unless they got stuck with an open kitchen in the last redesign and have to make do with looks that could kill). But decorum rules at home, at least in front of the assembled guests for whom you are labouring so sweetly. And so you bottle up your frustrations, only to feel disappointment when the intricate dishes reach the table. For however much your dear friends praise your work, to you who have tested spoonful after spoonful in front of the burning oven and the seething pots, nothing seems very new or interesting.

Other people's cooking looks so much more attractive to the gifted amateur at this point. But the worst is still to come. When the meal is over and the brandy has been consumed and the guests stagger home, that's not quite the end, not even close. Somebody has to clean up.

Professional chefs don't worry too much about the number of pots and pans they use en route to creating a masterpiece. The more damage inflicted on the batterie de cuisine, the more obvious it is that they have crafted a complex work of art. Peasants cook one-pot casseroles, but a chef's reputation for genius is measured by how high the sink is filled, and how many menials it takes to restore the status quo.

At home, you are your own menial. Or if you manage to delegate responsibility, it is only to a partner or close friend who will silently curse your extravagance with the pots as the two-hour clean-up gets under way. When you take on a recipe from a professional chef, whatever claims the publisher makes that the dish has been adapted for home use, the chances are good that the chef will still mess up. The glorious illustrations never show the chaos created in the kitchen, and while the mouth-watering ingredients are itemized at length, nowhere does it state that both your back and your patience will break under the strain of washing thirteen different utensils afterward.

Look at the well-received book entitled *Simply French*, a collaboration of American food writer Patricia Wells with the highly regarded French chef Joël Robuchon (who retired prematurely from his busy Paris restaurant, presumably because he couldn't keep it simple). The recipes in this lavish volume may well be straightforward by the elaborate standards of a three-star Michelin joint, but when it comes time to reach for the dish detergent, they betray their true origins. Those who learn to read a recipe for the post-prandial drudgework it contains will quickly spot problems with Robuchon's simple Pheasant Roasted on a Bed of Braised Endive. Not only do the instructions consist of thirteen steps that go on for two full pages, but the recipe ominously begins with the words "Prepare the luting pastry." Steel yourself to clean a measuring cup, a heavy-duty electric mixer, a trussing needle, a skillet, a fine-mesh sieve, a casserole dish, a bowl, a carving board, a serving platter and various other victims of the chef's studied simplicity.

Robuchon, like so many careful chefs schooled in a profession that long valued delicacy of presentation, has a soft spot for his fine-mesh sieve, a kitchen aid I have never managed to get completely clean. For a simple dish of steamed mussels (in which, by the way, the indelicate parsley stems are bundled with cotton twine for easier removal), a fine sieve is even brought in to strain the cooking liquid — as if the gaping mussels would be diminished by bits of minced shallot. Likewise for his famous potato purée — just imagine what it takes to become famous for a potato purée — after you have simmered the potatoes, drained them, peeled them, heated up milk in a separate saucepan, passed the potatoes and milk through the finest grid of a food mill into a saucepan and stirred the mixture with a wooden spatula, the crowning touch comes when you press the purée through a flat fine-mesh drum sieve. Don't even think about what it is like to clean potato out of a fine sieve, especially if, distracted by your delightful guests, you let the gloppy stuff dry and harden.

And this is just a side order of harmless potato. Imagine what a whole meal would be like cooked with such disregard for the low-paid help. No, the more useful cookbooks, and the better cooks, are the ones that foresee the trouble lying in wait after dinner, and then manage to avoid it. But there's another kind of trouble that's harder to avoid in the average kitchen, one that takes a kind of talent rarely drawn on by the star chefs with their well-stocked cupboards. I'm talking of course about the improvised genius required at those times—stores are closed for the holiday, a guest is dragged home unexpectedly, the dollar has lost its purchasing power—when you have to live out of your larder. Which is to say, by your wits.

Unless you're that rare sort who always shops yesterday for today, keeps flank steak marinating just in case, and is probably putting together next year's birthday-gift lists at this very moment, ad hoc cooking is a pleasure best enjoyed in the abstract.

Which is a shame. All of modern society seems designed to counteract the slightest bit of extemporaneous creativity. Where's the need for the daring it takes to go boldly forth into the back of the cupboard when a quick phone call will bring a pizza? Our hardy ancestors, who knew what it was like to wield a can opener and build a meal with their bare hands, would be ashamed of what we've become: timid, unenterprising types who would rather Sunday-shop the microwave section at the supermarket than attempt a simple salade niçoise.

I should watch what I say about microwaves. They have, after all, elevated passivity to such an art that opening a can of tuna seems like an act of genius to rival Escoffier. But having ventured into the cupboard and discovered the tuna, what next? Well, first of all, never reject any bit of inspiration, however hackneyed. When you find yourself practising the art of la cuisine trouvée, it's important not to feel that you have to overreach. The faculty at Cordon Bleu may sneer at tuna salad, but for someone who hasn't eaten tuna sandwiches since childhood, the dish can have a certain nostalgic charm years later. Still, there are those who got their fill of tuna salad—and more to the point, Hellmann's mayonnaise—a long time ago. For them, we reach into the cupboard with one hand, into the fridge with the other and make—presto! —salade niçoise.

The great advantage of this improvised standby is that its recipe is highly flexible. Elizabeth David in *French Provincial Cooking* offers four variations, one for every nice person in Nice. What they seem to have in common is a willingness to use ingredients that even the most unprepared chef should have around the house: tuna, a dozen olives, 4 or 6 anchovy fillets, a couple of artichoke hearts, 2 hard-boiled eggs cut in half, 2 quartered tomatoes, roughly shredded lettuce and a garlicky, mustardy vinaigrette. Fresh herbs would be nice as well, but since we're already stretching the limits of improvisation—fresh tomatoes are a reach —we can't be too fussy.

This brings up the question of what kind of staples should be kept on hand for just such an occasion (which is entirely different from the things we actually have on hand, like year-old Girl Guide cookies and three varieties of slow-cooking lentils). A short list of basic necessities for the urban survivalist might include olive oil, vinegar, mustard, noodles, peanut butter (as the basis for noodle sauce and good cookies), bacon, a stick of Italian salami, eggs, tomato salsa (mild and hot), a choice of nuts (pistachios, almonds, cashews), garlic, those pricy bottled sauces that friends always give the chef who has everything (though unsubtle, they're good for transforming leftover meat or a dull salad), chili sauce, pickled things (dills, olives, beets, capers), beans, cheese and canned fish (tuna, sardines, anchovies and a tin with an atmospheric label of Poseidon riding the waves that you can look at for all those years it remains unopened).

Working within these limitations, you can produce roasted almonds, the olive and anchovy paste called tapénade to go with toast, scrambled eggs with grated cheese (Parmesan will do the job nicely), spaghetti with garlic and olive oil or—I'm sensing desperation here—a salsa omelette. If you've got some carrots at the bottom of the fridge—and who doesn't?—you can grate them, add chopped walnuts and dress them with a gentle vinaigrette to make an easy salad. Incredibly foresighted cooks, meanwhile, will reach to the back of the cupboard and pull out the sesame paste they bought three years ago for just such an occasion. Now if only they could find the canned chickpeas, they'd make hummus.

Having been made well aware of our appalling ignorance by sarcastic high-school teachers, most of us don't race home at the end of the day to perform chemistry or physics experiments. The safety of the civilized world, after all, not to mention the appraised value of our houses, depends on acknowledging certain scientific limitations.

And yet we happily wander into the kitchen almost every night and blithely take on the forces of science lurking there as if it were a battle between equals. Without quite knowing why or how, we merrily produce food that is edible and rarely toxic, confounding those teachers who told us we weren't even smart enough to boil water.

Okay, so occasionally the spaghetti pot does boil over because someone forgot to add a dash of salt (or is it a spoonful of olive oil?). And maybe the mashed potatoes taste gummier than the nice creamy purées you get in smart restaurants. And the beef in the stew is unfathomably tough, the hollandaise tends to separate, no amount of paprika can hide the grey tint of the hard-boiled eggs, and the chocolate soufflé looks as if it ran out of breath on the frantic race from the oven to the table. Becoming a world-class chef isn't quite as easy as it seems. Culinary ingenuity can be faked but there's no bluffing the basic laws of kitchen science.

So maybe we are still winging it just the way we did back in high school. But what do you expect from people who learned how to cook the way teenagers learn about sex: from books and magazines, word of mouth and trial by error.

It's with good reason that food and sex are often compared. But while schools have now given themselves over wholeheart-edly to sex education, ensuring that every eight-year-old in the land can make condom jokes and write script treatments for *South Park: The Next Generation*, the authorities lose interest when it comes to cooking. And so we have to figure it out for ourselves. Looking at my own rather patchy education (strong on theory, weak on practice, highly dangerous near pâtisserie), I recognize the problems. Cooking should be a natural thing—they used to say the same thing about sex—and yet the opportunity for failure is so great, and the display of knowledge by the experts so over-whelming, that we end up confining ourselves to a few dishes we know we have mastered.

These fears and hesitations have not gone unnoticed among cagier cookbook writers. Realizing that many people are unwill-ing to expose their weaknesses in cooking schools—which can be much like those aerobics classes you avoid until you're sure you're in good shape—they try to overcome insecurity by offer-ing readers the benefit of inside knowledge.

There is even a special name for these culinary tricks of the trade. In-the-know types, aware that calling them just plain tricks might devalue the shamanistic knowledge they're imparting, refer to them as "trucs." The word is French, like so much that is impressive and slightly superior in the world of food. But what it actually means, according to my dictionary, is thingamajig, thingummy, whatsit and, finally, trick.

It's comforting to know that the French will never be at a loss to translate the word "whatsit." And perhaps just as comforting to learn, from the trucs I find in my reference books, that you can flavour lentils by adding a teaspoon of vinegar and a sugar cube to the cooking water, or keep terrines fresh for a month by covering them with melted pork fat, or test eggs for freshness by seeing if they sink to the bottom of a bowl of cold salted water. And if they rise? Then I guess you check the calendar and see if the terrine is still edible.

Trucs / tricks can be annoyingly limiting if the information they provide doesn't happen to fit with your needs at the time. As much as you would enjoy flavourful lentils on some other occasion, right now you're wondering how to poach an egg. Old catch-all handbooks like *The Joy of Cooking* used to provide such info in quantity, though the quality of the advice varied widely, depending on the influence of the folk-wisdom lobby. Scientific manuals such as Harold McGee's magisterial *On Food and Cooking* are sounder on the natural forces at work in the kitchen — how sauces emulsify, why preliminary browning improves the meat in a stew. But they are practical only so far as the individual cook, whose attitude to the whole idea of molecules is probably adversarial, can apply scientific principles to the disaster at hand.

How do you get long pasta into a small pot, the innocent chef asks, as the water starts to boil and the guests are knocking at the door? Is there any way to avoid those onion crying jags, you wonder tearfully, as the the knife slides off the onion and into your finger? What's the best method of straining jelly? (Hint: think jelly bag, string and an upside-down stool.) How do you get rid of the strong flavour of garlic (and why would you want to?)?

Granted, we all have different needs as we try to repair our ignorance in the kitchen. But sometimes the answer isn't in books. Sometimes—wasn't it David Carradine who said this in his Kung Fu period?—the knowledge lies within. For years, I scanned cookbooks trying to figure out how to make the perfect poached egg. A tablespoon of vinegar in the water will do the trick, said one. Stir the water rapidly, said another, and then break the egg immediately into the resulting whirl before it has a chance to sub-side. Preheat the egg in hot water to set the white before cracking it open, said the third in a list of many. I'm sure there were some scientific principles being put into play, but for all the good it did it might as well have been hocus-pocus.

Eventually, through much trial and many errors in my kitchen laboratory, I discovered this truc: Heat water to simmering. Break egg into water. Reduce heat. Let rest until ready. Some trick!

Penne with Rapini

The smoky taste of the bacon, the fruitiness of the olive oil and the bitter edge of the rapini greens make this a favourite adults-only supper dish in our house.

Cut ½ pound of sliced bacon into ½-inch-wide pieces and gently sauté in a large, broad heavy skillet until the bacon is cooked through but not crisp. Use a slotted spoon to remove the cooked bacon and drain on a paper towel, then add 1 clove of minced garlic and 2 minced anchovy fillets to the pan and slowly cook until the garlic is tender and the anchovy bits have largely dissolved. Stir in ½ teaspoon of chili pepper flakes and 3 table-spoons of extra-virgin olive oil. Keep warm over low heat until you're ready to add the rapini to the pan.

While the bacon is cooking, wash the rapini. Discard any thick stalks, peel the thinner stems and cut into 2-inch pieces.

Roughly chop the tender sprouts and leaves. Bring to a boil 14 ounces of penne. While the pasta is cooking, add the prepared rapini to the skillet. Gently sauté, tossing the greens to coat them evenly. After a few minutes, loosely cover the pan and let the rapini continue to cook over moderate heat until the stalks are completely tender. When the pasta is ready, drain it well, then add to the cooked rapini and gently combine. Transfer to a heated serving platter or bowl, season with salt and pepper if desired, toss with a little more olive oil if you like, grate Parmesan over the top and serve immediately.

Braised Eels with Pork and Garlic

This warming and very filling Cantonese dish was more than enough to lure me to London in the cold-weather months when I was a student at Oxford. Given the choice between turning pages in an unheated study with my frozen fingers and passing the time eating in a steamy, noisy restaurant, I'm surprised I managed to read as much Greek history as I did. To balance things out, I did try to look in on the Elgin Marbles at the British Museum before I sauntered down to Soho for my dinner. In retrospect, I think more libraries and museums should have Cantonese restaurants on the premises to keep the scholars from wandering.

Laying your hands on the eel (the skinny anguilla, not the larger conger or moray) is the hardest part of making this dish. Fish stores in Chinese neighbourhoods, the kind that have big tanks crowded with water creatures, are the best bet year-round. Eels are also an Italian Christmas-Eve tradition, so you will stand a better chance of finding some in season at the neighbourhood pescheria. Eels, keep in mind, are sold live. If you're feeling squeamish, have the fishmonger dispatch them for you. They may still be moving as you carry them home.

When you get home, set to work. You'll want about 1½ pounds of eel. Slice them into 2-inch sections and marinate in 2 tablespoons of soy sauce. Deep-fry the eel in hot oil until brown, about 2 minutes. Take ½ pound of crisp-skinned barbecued pork belly (which can be bought from Chinese barbecue shops), and cut into about 20 pieces. Peel and crush 12 cloves of garlic and finely chop 1 small piece of ginger. Soak 5 or 6 medium-sized dried shiitake mushrooms in warm water until soft, then trim the tough stems and cut into small pieces. While they're soaking, trim 4 green onions and cut into sections about the size of the eel pieces.

Stir-fry the ginger and garlic cloves in 2 ounces of peanut oil until they soften, then add the eel, pork, mushrooms, 1 tablespoon of rice wine, 2 cups of chicken stock and 1 teaspoon of salt. Cover and simmer for 15 to 20 minutes, then add the green onions and 1 tablespoon of soy sauce. Cook another minute more, or until the green onion is cooked but still crunchy. Cornstarch paste, for thickening, is optional. Serve with rice, in bountiful quantities.

I've adapted this recipe from *The Techniques of Chinese Cooking*, put together by the staff of the Shih Chien Home Economics College in Taiwan, where eels and education go together.

Brasato al Barolo

This simple dish from the Piedmont region of Northern Italy shows the transforming power of slow braising.

Melt 1 ounce of unsalted butter and some fat from Italian prosciutto in a broad casserole dish. Add a 2-pound piece of rump steak and brown on both sides, then add ½ bottle of a concentrated red wine, Barolo if you're feeling traditional and prosperous (Barbaresco is a slightly cheaper equivalent). Cook covered on low heat for about 2 hours, or until tender. If the pot is getting too dry, add a little beef stock. Toward the end of the cooking, add 2 ounces of rum, simmer for a few minutes more, then slice the meat and serve. Serve on a snowy night with mashed potatoes or polenta.

Primitive Mashed Potato

The mashed-potato revival that's taken place over the last few years has been one of the stranger developments in modern cooking. I don't suppose there's anything wrong with turning this diner standby into a high-end luxury, and certainly you have to look at the potato with new respect when it's keeping company with seared scallops and plump beads of caviar instead of soaking up ersatz gravy. But I still have a fondness for the simpler, coarser technique I dreamt up as a student for improving the taste of my cut-rate mash. My inspiration came from the health-food cookbook writer Adelle Davis, who taught me that no cooking liquid should ever go to waste, as much for the flavour you're throwing away as the vitamins.

What that means with this humble recipe is that you don't peel or boil the potatoes that go into your mash. Leaving the skins on, dice 4–6 medium-sized, relatively thin-skinned potatoes. Slowly heat about 10 ounces of milk, keeping a careful watch on the pot. When the liquid starts to bubble, stir in your potato, coating every square with milk. Cook at a slow simmer with the lid ajar, stirring from time to time. Don't let the milk bubble over and don't let the potatoes stick to the bottom and scorch. (Boiling with water is obviously much easier.)

When the potatoes are very soft, take the pan off the stove, add some butter for extra richness, and mash in your usual way.

For the really primitive effect, hand-mash. A food mill, the sort that you use to make applesauce and purée berries, produces a smoother mash with less potato skin, though you will never attain the lily-white standard of a Joël Robuchon purée. Hand-mixers are fine, but food processors produce a gummy result that makes all your stove-tending a waste of time.

CINNAMON AND GINGER

IT IS THE SAD fate of fine foods to be turned into decor.

Instead of flavouring roast lamb or bringing to life a plate of pasta, garlic is braided and transformed into an evocative Mediterranean wall-hanging. Rows of cool glass canisters display sticks of spaghettini and clusters of tagliatelle for all to admire. Hardy McIntosh apples are set in a carved wooden bowl atop an oak harvest table, the better to suggest homespun tranquility. Or so the real-estate agent says.

Now to the growing list of endangered foods can be added cinnamon. Long taken for granted — though lovingly taken for granted, like an old spaniel or a subscription to *The New Yorker* — the standard ingredient of the spice cupboard is at risk of being transformed into a design accessory. The elegantly curled sticks of bark that once aspired only to mull the cider suddenly occupy centre stage at self-conscious Christmas celebrations. With an entire cottage industry claiming cinnamon as its favourite raw material, palisades of cinnamon sticks, robed in seasonal ribbons and protecting a fat, fragrant wax candle, turn into the centrepiece of holiday gatherings. Symbolizing the new austerity — fragrant, but doesn't look it — cinnamon also finds its way into the low-key flower arrangements and bowls of potpourri marshalled along the sideboards. Whatever happened to cheese balls?

As much as we overlook cinnamon, what with fresh Mediterranean herbs and newly landed Asian flavourings competing for the attention of our easily distracted palates, it's a spice to be loved and savoured. And not displayed.

The coffee boom of the past few years has at least kept cinnamon in the air and on the minds of those who like fragrant foods. Powdered cinnamon sprinkled on the foam of a cappuccino is, you might say if you're sick of watching latte-laden TV shows, nothing more than a sophisticated form of air freshener, Pine Sol for those who pine to be elsewhere. But the somewhere else that cinnamon supplies so readily is much more appealing than sanitary forests and synthetic orange groves. It's a smell that transports escapists to a dreamier, more ethereal state of perfumed vapours and takes the nostalgic back to a childhood of warm cinnamon buns and buttery toast dusted with shakes of cinnamon sugar (perhaps the easiest dish of all to cook and the first that a child should learn).

Some department stores pipe in cinnamon odours to create a sense of well-being and free-spending generosity. Perfume manufacturers blend in cinnamon (or its cousin cassia) to create a warm, inviting scent that seduces without seeming cheap or brassy. Manufacturers of toothpaste depend on cinnamon to make the three-times-a-day habit more welcoming.

But before we end up offering a real-estate agent's tips on using cinnamon to sell a house, it's time to get back to food. Cinnamon, for all the longings it awakens, is not used with much versatility in the average kitchen (average, in this instance, excludes Greek, Indian, Sri Lankan, Moroccan and Chinese cooks, as well as staunch medievalists). Whenever apples are cooking, whether as pie or strudel or applesauce, ground cinnamon is automatic, too much so, some would say. I couldn't imagine my rum-sautéed bananas without a dash of cinnamon at the end, and

I know that devotees of beaver tails — deep-fried dough dipped in cinnamon sugar and topped with jam or syrup — wouldn't dream of damning the spice.

But once we leave the dessert section of the cookbook and the country fair, the cinnamon jar retreats to the cupboard. Its association with sweet foods is almost too strong for most cooks to think of using it in a savoury dish — but that's precisely why we should do so. One of the most obvious tricks in cooking for a crowd is to capture attention with something that the palate instinctively considers out of place. While a devotion to this kind of trickery produces the confusions of fusion food, a subtler touch wins you a reputation as an alchemist, or at least an artist.

But where to start? As usual, the cuisines that have held fast to tradition supply the best hints. Speaking generally — that is, after a happy morning leafing through cookbooks without a care in the world or a mouth to feed — I'd say that cinnamon is a natural flavouring for grilled lamb, rice pilaf, chicken and duck in almost any form, ground-meat kebabs, rabbit, eggplant and chickpeas. Many Greeks, and not just those auditioning for jobs with Wolfgang Puck, like to add a stick of cinnamon to lamb stewed with tomatoes, grind the spice into their turkey stuffing, flavour spaghetti sauce with the stuff and — back to dessert again — let no cake or syrupy sweet come to the table without the requisite dash. Variety like this brings the spice to life. And, best of all, nobody's going to use a plate of baklava to sell a house.

• • •

The Chinese have been cooking with ginger for at least twenty-five hundred years, so it shouldn't be surprising that they take something of a ho-hum attitude to this head-turning spice. Those of us whose culinary traditions needed a few millennia longer to discover the charms of this gnarled root may still swoon when its fragrance fills the air. But the people who stir-fry beef with ginger for our open-mouthed delight are apparently a little more measured in their appreciation after all these years.

I draw this sad conclusion—sad for its suggestion that all pleasures fade over time—from some terse comments made in an unusual little book called *Chinese Gastronomy* (long out of print, alas; my wife brought it to the marriage as part of her dowry, and unless you find a way to marry her the chances of digging up the book are slight). Under the heading of Kitchen Arts—so far, so good—Hsiang Ju Lin and Tsui Feng Lin outline a list of ways that Chinese cooks can quickly vary tastes and texture. Tricks, the authors call them unpoetically, and I suppose they're not far off when you think of how a last-minute addition of fermented black beans can pick up the taste of a bland meat dish or how a shot of vinegar can neatly adjust the intensity of chicken with hot pepper and orange peel.

But it's when the writers get to ginger that they really establish the unbridgeable cultural divide. Instead of regaling us with stories about how slivers of the fabled spice lift steamed fish to ambrosial realms or how a small amount chopped into stir-fried watercress will astonish your guests, the Chinese gastronomes can only bring themselves to say this about ginger: "Suppresses offensive flavours."

Now I know that ginger, like cinnamon, has at least this in common with air fresheners, that it's fully capable of taking over a room. Time and time again I've found myself turning my head almost involuntarily in a Chinese restaurant, looking for the source of the beautiful smell that doesn't so much freshen the air as pick it up and transport it to a mysterious, far-off place. But suppressing offensive flavours? Ketchup, breath mints and government inspectors suppress flavours; ginger elevates everything in its company.

Yet for such a powerful, unmistakable spice, ginger is oddly capable of blending in. Those beef-with-ginger dishes I keep ordering in Chinese restaurants never taste so strongly of ginger that I can't taste the supple beef, and when the sushi is served in a Japanese meal there's never any danger that the shavings of pickled ginger will end up dwarfing the sea urchin. Ginger is a sneaky presence in the air and in the mouth and, like a dab of perfume or the effusions of a wood fire, it can drift in and out of our appreciative mind without much awareness that a transforming effect is taking place.

Clearly the Chinese, or at least a few of the more cold-hearted Chinese, have managed to get over ginger's more obvious charms. Perhaps they look at other cultures and wonder why they can't see the infinite allure of the Delicious apple or the corn flake. But as familiar as I have tried to become with ginger in the past few years, its exotic powers haven't diminished in the slightest. If you offered me a bowl of ginger ice cream at this very minute—assuming you're not reading this at three a.m., though I still might be receptive—I couldn't help but be tantalized by the smoky, floral, almost illicit scents and flavours.

Fresh ginger has not been a part of broader food culture for very long. These days you can find it, cheap, juicy and mercifully unshrivelled, in almost any metropolitan supermarket, but when I was learning about food it was hard to come by. Ginger then meant ground ginger and, as we all know now but perhaps didn't suspect back then when we—I—poured it on sautéed scallops and hoped for a miracle, it is a completely different kind of flavouring. Still, better ground ginger than candied ginger.

I will say nothing bad about ground ginger, even though it infiltrated Western cooking traditions several centuries ago and is therefore ripe to be looked down upon for being too familiar. Ground ginger, like most of the dried spices we use, has ended up being associated with sweet cooking and doesn't make the transfer to savoury very easily. This has confined its use to gingersnaps, gingerbread and other grandmotherly standbys, which are fine but a little austere to be held up for praise or emulation by dessert fans. But if you can search out a recipe for a Yorkshire cake called parkin, you will encounter a richer and more modulated use of the spice that adds a lusher taste to the luxurious fragrance. The recipe I have in front of me (found in Alison Uttley's *Recipes from an Old Farmhouse*) may give you an idea: Work ½ pound of butter into 2 pounds of fine oatmeal and ½ pound of flour, then add ½ pound of brown sugar. Pour in 1½ pounds of warmed golden syrup and treacle—a 3:1 combination of corn syrup and molasses might be an inadequate substitute—and then 2 ounces of candied peel, the grated rind of 1 lemon and 2 ounces of ground ginger. Lastly, add 1 teaspoon baking powder and a little hot water to mix. Bake for an hour and a half in a not too hot oven—whatever not too hot means in a farmhouse. Cool and cut in wedges.

It's not lobster with ginger and spring vegetables or sea scallops in a ginger sauce. But you just might notice the family resemblance if you shut your eyes and breathe deeply.

Lamb Stew with Okra and Cinnamon

Cinnamon is rightly considered a sweet spice, but its penetrating scent adds a tantalizing complexity to cooked lamb.

Trim the fat from 3 pounds of stewing lamb and cut into 1-inch cubes. Heat 4 ounces of butter in a large pot, add the meat and brown it on all sides. Add 6 large tomatoes that have been peeled and chopped up, or drain and chop up the tomatoes from a 28-ounce tin and cook until soft. Salt and pepper to taste, then add a stick of cinnamon. Cover and cook for about 2 hours or until the lamb is tender. Add a little water if the stew threatens to dry out. About 40 minutes before the end of the cooking, add 1½ pounds of whole okra from which the stems have been trimmed. If you're having trouble figuring out tenderness-minus-40— stewing lamb being notoriously fickle in its willingness to soften —simply sauté the okra on its own until almost tender, then add to the stew for 10 or 15 minutes of familiarizing.

Ginger Custard

As exotic as it is in fragrance, ginger is a surprisingly appropriate ingredient in rich and simple desserts such as crème brûlée, ice cream and this inspired custard developed by my former colleague Nancy Enright for her book, *The Canadian Herb Cookbook*.

Mix together 3 tablespoons of brown sugar with 1 tablespoon of finely grated, freshly peeled ginger and then divide evenly among 6 buttered custard cups. Mix together 3 large beaten eggs with 2½ cups of cold milk, ⅓ cup of granulated sugar, 1 teaspoon of vanilla extract and a pinch each of cinnamon, nutmeg and salt. Pour this mixture into the custard cups. Put the cups in a large pan, then add enough water to the pan to come halfway up the sides of the cups. Bake in a 350°F oven for 35 to 40 minutes, or until a knife inserted around the edge of the cup comes out clean. Serve in the cups, or run a knife around the edge to loosen, place a plate over the cup, and invert.

REAL LIFE

IT SAYS SOMETHING ABOUT THE VALUES modern society holds dear that we willingly endure the hours lost commuting to and from work but begrudge every minute spent in the kitchen beyond the bare minimum.

How bare that minimum is depends quite obviously on the individual. Are you determined to eat homemade food every day; do you define store-bought mini-quiches heated up in the oven as homemade food; are you willing to shop seven days a week or is your larder stocked to allow for quick improvisation; are you the one person in a million organized enough to put up a duck confit the night before; are your housemates inclined to dis the duck and lobby for Taco Bell?

For some people, the time it takes for the toast to pop up — "Hurry, damn you, I've got *Headline Sports* coming on in 10 seconds"—is time wasted. For others, those who insist on pickling their own olives or farming their personal trout, an hour is not nearly enough to do the job properly. For both groups at the end of a long day, after a hard hour spent reading Elmore Leonard on the train or picking up hipness credits by listening to Wu-Tang

Clan in the car, the waiting stove can look like an impatient and implacable enemy.

The timetable of real life does not leave much space for complicated cooking. And why should it? When we make the choice to be busy during the better part of the day, we automatically make sacrifices: there just won't be a long-cooked Provençal daube of beef wafting its scents of red wine and orange peel through the kitchen when we return home. So park those gracious-living fantasies at the door—some limitations must be accepted.

Yet we still have to eat, and so many of us want to turn that obligation into a pleasure that the cookbook industry can't keep up. It's almost compulsory now for the dust jacket of a fashionable cookbook to boast how quick and easy are the fabulous recipes contained inside, and the competition's fierce to see who can create the most resonant recipes that take the least amount of time.

"Designed for the way we are cooking and eating today," says one such time-challenged volume, "Patricia Wells' *Trattoria* offers readers more than 30 recipes for pasta, most of which can be prepared in half an hour."

"Plan meals for family or guests quickly, efficiently and easily," commands the blurb for *Classic Home Cooking*, despite the fact that classic home cooking, almost by definition, was neither quick, nor efficient, nor easy. Such modern concerns as time management are almost antagonistic to the classic recipes (and values) of our grandmothers' day. But never mind. It's not the place of the modern cookbook to engage in a ruthless self-examination of our edgy lifestyle, not when we can be encouraged to take pride in making do. "If you have fifteen minutes," promises Sam Gugino's *Cooking to Beat the Clock*, "you can put a delicious dinner on the table."

Modern Western cultures like to make the connection between a shortage of time and a sense of importance. Anyone who has the leisure to cook a four-hour dish in the classic way is seen as either underemployed or underachieving. Real men (and women) eat takeout quiche. But takeout quickly palls—the salt, the sameness, the sense of guilt—and so we strive for that impossible balance, the great meal cooked instantly.

Time has been of the essence in the kitchen ever since women entered the workplace. But the difference with the modern obsession over time is this aspiration to consume show-off food every night of the week. I don't know how long it takes you to cook a great meal—I know it takes me an hour just to vacuum and set the table, and that's not even allowing for the inevitable battles with cats who insist the table belongs to them. But cooking-school headmistress Anne Willan has raised the qualifying standards for greatness considerably with her contribution to the art of stopwatch cuisine, *In and Out of the Kitchen*. While Patricia Wells thought she was doing pretty well in *Trattoria* by offering pasta recipes that could be accomplished in half an hour, Willan has cut that time in half.

Fifteen minutes of kitchen drudgery is the maximum she permits herself, but many of her recipes take even less time, allowing the determined workaholic an extra $\frac{1}{12}$ of an hour at the office. Chicken in chili coconut sauce and smoked salmon rillettes demand a mere nine minutes of kitchen work. Scallop salad with cumin dressing and tuna marchand de vin (featuring a borrowed steak sauce of shallots, red wine, butter and tarragon) demand a little more effort, a full ten minutes. For those with too much time on their hands, she offers such fifteen-minute extravaganzas as minestrone (with apologies for the canned beans) or a beef and scallop fire pot that's a little too accelerated to be described as Mongolian. But then the Mongolians, being nomadic, didn't have to work twelve-hour days downtown to pay the mortgage.

Willan's book is a beauty, a reassurance that you don't have to lower your standards to produce a dish in the time it takes to walk the dog or run a bath. It also reminds me of the speedreading course I took at the very credulous age of fifteen, where we were told we could read Steinbeck's *The Red Pony* in ten minutes just by trolling our forefinger down the centre of each page. Speed-cooking requires the same disregard for the limitations of reality. If you intend to master the instant salad of fig-stuffed chicken with blue cheese or make a sudden meal of pork chop with confit of onions, it's important to note the hurdles that will block your claims to such personal plats du jour. First, to beat the fifteen-minute limit, Willan requires you to define time in the kitchen separately from cooking time. Confident cooks, having put in their preliminary six minutes at the stove, may be content to march out of the kitchen and work up the latest focus-group report on the computer, but not all of us will want to take our eyes off the simmering confit for the half an hour it actually takes to cook. Add a few minutes.

Second, Willan is a professional and is used to doing three things at once (or getting others to do them for her). Rank amateurs may find they work better in series than in parallel. They may also discover that, unlike Willan, they do not always have oyster sauce, vanilla bean, couscous and peeled hazelnuts in their well-stocked pantries. Add a few more minutes for frenzied hazelnut-peeling.

Third, a single course does not always make a meal. If it takes fourteen minutes to produce a dessert of orange salad with caramel—and that includes peeling and slicing oranges at the same time you're monitoring a caramelizing sugar syrup and doling out essence of quality time to the kids—how do you apportion the remaining sixty seconds to make an appetizer and a main course? At a guess, I'd say thirty-five seconds to dress the unrinsed salad greens—what's a little grit between friends?—and twenty-five seconds to pay off the pizza delivery man. There may even be time—check your stopwatch—to say thank you.

Gratitude for the food that others cook for us is never misplaced, and adapting to the rhythm of modern life means taking advantage of the simple gifts the world offers those who want to eat well and fast. You can try to cook great meals yourself every night, and completely lose it in the longing to have it all. Or you can do what is done in older cultures that have a less adversarial relationship with their nightly meals — pick up a crusty loaf of bread and some oozing brie, stop by the Chinese barbecue shop for half a crisp-skinned duck, prepare a place in the microwave for the ready-made schnitzel from the Hungarian deli. Or study your collection of menus that take pride of place by the phone and fall back on takeout.

In the overall hierarchy of food — which resembles the Vatican in its subtlety of gradation between superior and inferior — anything carried home in a takeout bag ranks somewhere near Satan. Serious eaters (who have done so much to inflict their unrelenting seriousness on the rest of us) insist that their dishes be cooked to order and served *à point*, which is a fancy French term for perfection. When they go to restaurants, they like to sit at the chef's table right in the heart of the kitchen, so that no precious nanoseconds can be lost between the instant the rognons de veau sauce moutarde leaves the pan and the second it arrives on the plate. For them, even the moment a dish spends under a heat lamp waiting to catch the server's eye is an eternity of torment. Frantic thoughts race through the anxious mind — "The meat is getting cold, the vegetables are losing their crispness, the sauce is congealing, won't someone do something!" — and strip away whatever pleasure is left in the consummate dining experience.

Takeout food lacks this kind of urgency, which is one of the reasons it's so appealing. There is no food, quite clearly, that's enhanced by being cooked to doneness, forced into a covered container, stacked on top of other seething containers in a confined plastic bag, jammed onto the floor of a car and then taken on a rollicking ride through the urban jungle. And still, freed from the cares of self-conscious dining, appearing almost magically on the table out of bags emanating strange and wonderful fragrances, takeout food is a gift. Limp french fries notwithstanding, the range of available takeout extends well beyond the mediocre. After prodding a Japanese restaurant into producing a platter of sushi and sashimi on half an hour's notice—with no danger of overcooking either—I now realize that it's always worth interrogating any kind of restaurant about its to-go policies. (An added bonus: your own wine or beer is going to be a lot cheaper with takeout; and you can afford to leave yourself a generous tip.)

Sushi and chicken korma and penne all'arrabiata are always welcome at the last-minute table. But the best bet remains Chinese. It would be a very unusual Chinese restaurant that was unwilling or unable to send food home on a moment's notice, which is one of the reasons why Chinese cuisine inspires such devotion. An essential of modern urban life, as far as I can tell, is having a Chinese takeout restaurant to call one's own. The joint you dial up on a Sunday night, when you don't feel like the sameness of your own cooking, should have a place in your heart—or at least a menu under your fridge magnet. When you buy a house, it's essential to check out the local Chinese catering before you close the deal. You scoff—but think back to the amount of pleasure your local has given you in the past versus, say, the complete lack of joy provided by easy highway access or convenience to an airport.

Not just any takeout will do. The menu is the big challenge: is the cooking something real or is it completely fake? Most, of course, lie somewhere in between, trying to please all comers by mixing the heavily battered dishes loved by takeout traditionalists with the more downtown items (moo shu pork, beef with ginger and green onion, sautéed cuttlefish) favoured by lazy sophisticates. Oddly enough—is it nostalgia for the Polynesian bobo balls of our frittered-away youth, or just some lingering honesty poking through the accumulated layers of pretension?—

the deep-fried dishes I avoid in smarter Chinese restaurants are often what I like best in the neighbourhood. I'm thinking in particular of the breaded jumbo shrimp that one long-gone local thoughtfully coated in sesame seeds, but feel free to substitute won ton, chicken soo gai or that great compromise between the naive and the sophisticated, deep-fried squid with finely chopped hot pepper.

You've found a menu you like and after much trial and error, you've isolated the dishes you prefer. Then, if your neighbourhood is anything like mine, and your Chinese-takeout real-estate market is just as volatile, funny things start happening. I remember calling the usual number and placing the usual order and only then being directed to a different restaurant two miles away in a sleazier part of town where good bok choy would never venture. My local had call-forwarded for reasons I never quite figured out —landlord disputes, emergency vacation plans, reassignment of crankier customers? Another time, the name Wok Express at my favoured place was subtly transformed by new owners into Wok Experts—they'll never notice—and the sesame shrimp disappeared from our lives.

Then there was the night when the people behind the counter were complete strangers, didn't share a common language with the customers, fell an hour behind in the order process, said they didn't have any shrimp—you call yourself a takeout!—cooked us all the wrong dishes and were slipping out the back door of a darkened restaurant at nine p.m. when I came back to complain. I now think this was a robbery gone terribly wrong.

We still order takeout. It's just that out of frustration we now drive the extra twenty minutes downtown to Chinatown and think dark thoughts about the vegetables overcooking as we race back home. And not wanting to seem like hicks, we eat braised chicken with taro root, snails in black bean sauce, green beans with sautéed garlic and other such refinements instead of the breaded shrimp and egg fried rice we came to love. On the other hand, because we've spent twenty minutes in stop-and-go traffic ferrying our low-stress dinner home, the car smells like Chinese food for days afterward. Which is really what takeout food is all about.

Still, the neighbourhood connection remains important for anyone who wants to find a fit between real life and real food. Pressed for time, you can't always be making that fifty-kilometre trek to the cheese factory that produces world-class bocconcini or lining up forever at the only poultry shop in the Metroplex to smoke its own goose. If food is going to become a natural part of our existence, and not some exotic thrill obtained at huge cost to our bank accounts and our sanity, it has to be fitted into the daily routine.

And once that idea—if I may be allowed to elevate the activity of shopping for food with the word "idea"—is accepted, and you can make peace with the notion that a good-enough dinner can start on your doorstep, then the routine stands a better chance of becoming something special. It will, I hope, speak volumes about the comforting trends in modern merchandising when I tell you that the most exciting event my locale has witnessed in ages was the opening of a flashy new supermarket.

I encountered the neighbourhood philosopher just by the front door, looking exceptionally miffed by the direction the human experience was tending. "It's all such mindless consumerism," he said, setting down his basket full of ready-to-heat cannelloni and casting a despairing hand toward the exotic-fruit display. "What would Christopher Lasch make of it?"

Christopher Lasch, for the benefit of those who chose a life of pleasure-seeking frivolity, is a deceased critic of North America's more self-centred options.

"Christopher Lasch is dead," I said, attempting to point out a helpful distinction between political theory and practice.

But what I should have said, casting a somewhat less despairing hand toward the folks studying the exotic fruit—watch the spikes on that kiwano melon—was this: "These people are alive!" For there was something invigorating in the air of the new neighbourhood supermarket as the crowds surged toward the free samples of freshly squeezed orange juice and deep-fried chicken fingers. While no fan of the ultrahygienic Muzak-riven stores that drove Christopher Lasch to distraction—why are we fashionable political thinkers so predictable?—I sensed something different at work here. Every new supermarket that comes along is hailed—at least in those circles where supermarkets are hailed—as the store of the future. What this actually means depends on whatever is seen as futuristic at any particular time, be it mesmerizing bake ovens or cathedral ceilings or bar-code scanners that can supply marketing executives with your lifelong shopping patterns.

What made this particular store much more interesting, and explained why it was thronged with people who suddenly saw a greater potential for the nightly meal, was its vision—and no more apologies to all those abstracted thinkers who can't bear to see such a grandiose, life-altering term applied to mere shopping. Instead of looking to the wonders of the future, the new supermarket tried to make sense of more pressing present-day conflicts. We have no time? The solution is to pack as many shopping stops as possible under one supermarket roof, offering conflicted visitors a photo lab, a flower market, a travel shop, a wine store, a dry cleaner, a print shop (where you can rent your own postal box), a greeting-card stall, book and CD racks, an Internet playland for the children and a newsstand.

The supermarket proper is not really a supermarket proper but is itself divided up into niches and specialties. There's a drugstore side by side with a case-lot wholesale area (so you can buy your Nutella in bulk), a multicultural in-house bakery turning out focaccia and iced cupcakes alike, a meat area where you can actually make human contact with the butchers and a fish counter displaying salmon, stickleback and conger eel out in the open — because a real seafood fragrance is here considered part of the modern shopping experience and not a sensation to be denied, or confined only to expensive Mediterranean vacations.

Supermarkets are an all-in-one convenience, and convenience has traditionally been seen as the enemy of good eating. The easier it is to buy your apples and pears, goes this elitist thinking, and the closer the rib-eye is to piles of toilet paper and racks of hair conditioner, the less chance you have of blending real life with real food. But the modern supermarket no longer looks like a joyless compromise. If it's to be criticized for anything, it's that it has too successfully turned shopping into a form of entertainment, an end in itself rather than a stage on the way to a better meal. Spend time in the supermarket greengrocery, and you can't help but be captivated by the way it has become a microcosm of ethnic tastes (plantain, yams, papaya, green mango and taro) and a showcase of the esoterica (cherimoya, Cape gooseberries, golden raspberries) demanded by more fashion-conscious shoppers. Even Christopher Lasch might have appreciated this vivid demonstration of the short distance in a consumerist democracy between ethnic traditions and upscale fashion. The only way to tell which is which is to look at the price.

But after all those time-challenged shoppers use up even more precious time by meditating on the societal implications of the serrano pepper display, it becomes harder to contemplate actually cooking dinner, even one of those fifteen-minute wonders dreamt up by Anne Willan. Instead, the takeout gene kicks in, as the supermarket planners knew it would. These kumquats and rambutans, those persimmons and mangosteens, are they here just for show? Because after the astonished shoppers stare at them with rapture, and try to imagine how to fit them into their lives —kumquat-stuffed veal chop with a plantain and persimmon reduction?—they all too easily glide over to the in-store chefs who are hard at work turning fantasy into reality. Here you can buy salmon quiche, smoked chicken rösti, Caesar salad and brie sandwiches in a ciabatta pouch to take home for an instant dinner or eat straightaway in the store, making your neighbourhood supermarket your dining room as well.

Have you started marinating the salmon? Is the turkey breast hanging in the home smokehouse? Don't you think it's time to get out the mortar and grind those chili spices? There are school lunches to be made and every child wants to make a good impression at mealtime.

As if. For all the best intentions of finicky parents, children have their own agenda. The debate at home may centre on the comparative nutritional values of alfalfa sprouts and mustard cress. At school, it's who can eat the fastest or burp the loudest. Set against peer pressure, the pull of advertising and the heady taste of rebellion that comes from eating at a safe distance from authority figures, a well-meaning parent doesn't stand a chance.

You don't have children? You will never know what kind of gastronomic compromises you've been spared. Children don't just bring a jolt of reality to adult appetites. They remake reality, turning a sophisticated cook who used to smoke her own duck sausages into a desperado who will stop at nothing—not even packaged luncheon meat—to silence the complaints of the young.

It's a process that takes time, of course. At first, naive adults like to believe that their children are created in their own image and will take to dim sum or sushi instinctively. But once the offspring head off to school and escape the parental sphere of influence, their truly demented tastes come out in the open. Children go their own way when the lunch bell rings. And the funny thing is that anyone who was ever young—and hasn't yet undergone one of those mental makeovers that make you believe you were always as perfect and PBS-loving as you are now—should be able to remember the long-ago lapses from perfection.

I used to quote chapter and verse from nutrition books when I'd catch my children comparing notes on their school-lunch sequence of eating—Oreos first, chips second, sandwich here and there, apple almost never. I'd have been better off thinking back to the blissful barbarities of my own childhood. And memorable it was: the peanut butter-and-jam sandwiches thrown at the cafeteria ceiling to see if they'd stick, the milk money saved up and spent on a box of Three Musketeers bars (to be consumed in one sitting), the bug-infested locker where a classmate named Piggy left his nutritionally sound lunches to moulder while he dined out on french fries and gravy at the Varsity restaurant across the road. We once got kicked out of the Varsity for devising a drink we named the Varsity Special, a glass of water filled with wadded-up bits of hamburger bun, the contents of the chrome-plated serviette dispenser, lashings of pepper and red worms squeezed out of the plastic ketchup container. I now find myself carrying on about the tastes of old-vine Zinfandels. Could this really be the same person?

School-lunch reality may bite, but there are ways of biting back. Tolerance is still the best approach, since few juvenile passions last long unopposed. This too shall pass, I used to tell myself as I miserably slathered margarine on pre-sliced white bread for my young masters. And it did, in its own weird way. My children are now old enough that they have moved on to their own set of perfectionist ideals, antagonistic diets that don't allow you to eat meat or cheese or refined sugar. They now sneer at my too-uncritical tastes in food and, someday, when they finally acknowledge with the help of their therapists that they once had no interest whatsoever in healthy food, they will talk themselves into believing that their conformist father forced such a miserable diet on them.

But back then—it feels like another century in adult time but it was only a few years ago—the standard school lunch was baloney on white with the saving grace of lettuce, and I believe that it was customary to throw out the lettuce, or at least throw it at someone. Here is some wisdom learned from hard experience: send all the green leaves you like, all the grilled vegetables and grated carrot salads, but if no one eats them, you have satisfied only your conscience.

Having delivered that dark thought, I should amend it a little. There's a curious phenomenon that occurs at school—at least in the ten minutes of eating allowed by the lunchroom czars—called vicarious desire, better known as "What you got?" Children who would never be caught lugging an egg-salad sandwich out the front door in the morning return home at night full of praise for Sarah's mom's way with Hellmann's. Knowing this, you realize that whatever lunch you make, the result will still be mix 'n' match. When your son demands you send all the leftovers from your homemade onion, garlic and pepperoni pizza, it's not because he's suddenly been made ravenous for Italian cooking by a morning of long division, or because he's trying to hint that he craves Sicilian rabbit and anchovy stew for his birthday dinner. No, it's just that his best friends have fallen in love with your thin crust, thanks to his lunchtime giveaway program, and he now means to turn the art of the deal to his personal advantage.

Apart from teaching children how to share (or failing that, how to drive hard bargains), this communitarian approach to lunch has two useful spinoffs: by tasting other kids' food without the prejudice they bring to the products of their own kitchen, your children discover new pleasures (garlic bagel chips, spicy Jamaican beef patties, tacos). And more important, by seeing the admiration other children show for your food, your children learn to respect home cooking. That's the theory anyway.

Real life produces this longing for a theory that makes sense of the senseless. Our day-to-day existence is always going to come up short when measured against the exacting standards of the all-knowing Martha Stewarts. But even accepting that our flower arrangements will never furnish a room so authoritatively, that the borscht spilled on the tablecloth doesn't officially qualify as a homemade dye, we can't accept a routine that features so little order and so many compromises.

Mealtime is bound to be a mess if you add children to the mix? Put up with it, cut corners, take twenty years off the good life? Nonsense! Make them bend to you, not the other way around. All they need is some manners, I keep telling myself, and everything else will fall into place. On one of those mornings when the unfinished peanut butter on toast had ended up crunchy-side down on the carpet, and the arguments over who had left the freezer door open the night before drowned out the shock-jock tremors from the radio, I found yet another form of instant salvation: an ad in the newspaper for a book called *Tiffany's Table Manners for Teenagers*.

If Tiffany's can do breakfast, I thought, looking around at the chaos my own laissez-faire parenting had produced, why not lunch and dinner too? For $20 plus shipping, I could turn unruly children whose idea of etiquette was facing the other way when they burped into those high-boned creatures who stride confidently through charity galas and *New Yorker* cartoons.

But what arrived a few days later in a ribboned turquoise box wasn't quite the instant cure-all I'd hoped for. For a start, it dated all the way back to 1961, when most of the civilized world thought it had more to fear from Khrushchev than teenagers. The jewellery company's chairman, Walter Hoving, was smart enough to see the confrontation that was looming, but he failed to recognize where the final battle would be fought. For the patrician New Yorker, the most pressing concerns were the pretentiousness of corn handles and the proper way to hold cutlery ("Don't keep shifting the fork from the left to the right hand"). The worst behaviour in his day consisted of slicing your roll with a butter knife or leaving a spoon in the coffee cup. The ante has been upped considerably.

An amiable teenager of my immediate acquaintance, looking nothing like the Kennedyesque socialites in Hoving's book, slouches toward the table and slumps into his chair. He is wearing a T-shirt emblazoned with the phrase "Eww ... You're a Girl, and Girls Suck," the name of his friends' punk band. No one dares suggest he take it off, not least because of what may lurk beneath.

He sees a bowl of microwaved penne in front of him and says he isn't hungry. He has already eaten three falafel sandwiches downtown while looking for a cheap paperback copy of *Das Kapital*. He fills his mouth with penne anyway and simultaneously razzes his sister (thereby violating a number of Hoving rules, including "Don't talk with your mouth full" and "Don't air your views in a loud voice").

The phone rings and he jumps up to answer it ("Don't get up from the table until your hostess rises ..."), settling into the daily argument about best lines from *The Simpsons*—"Me fail English? That's unpossible" vies with "I mean, what's attempted murder? Do they give a Nobel Prize for attempted chemistry?"—until the rest of the table decide they've had enough and leave. The cat, who could also use a course in manners, tucks into the leftovers.

Hoving's guide to the intricacies of Manhattan social life seems wonderfully dated in an era when saying "Oops" after spilling your water glass is not the gravest offence of the young. But for anyone who breaks bread with teenagers on a regular basis, it isn't easy to dismiss his advice as completely inane. "Training in table manners must be started early enough to make them automatic," he says, and you're tempted to think, as you watch your own teenagers burp and badger their way through a meal, that maybe you should have intervened along Tiffany lines when the elbows were first thrust onto Sesame Street placemats years ago.

Back then, the idea of placing limits on your child's self-expression seemed artificial, not to say unpossible. Now what you crave is more artifice, less reality. And then suddenly, just as real life starts to do a victory dance on your defeated soul, you see a glimmer of hope. Life may no longer be one exquisite debutante ball, but Hoving actually has a few good ideas that make you think there's some sense in turning the clock back. "If you have to blow your nose," he advises, offering advice in a realm the modern teenager can actually relate to, "don't be embarrassed. Just blow it." He cautions against using the linen napkin for this purpose, but unfortunately doesn't go on to rule out shirt sleeves, cat's fur and the all-too-frequent combination of hands and trousers.

His argument against talking with a full mouth is undoubtedly timeless: "Some of your lunch may fall out." But Hoving, a veteran of New York dinner parties (and the father of a teenager who went on to run the Metropolitan Museum of Art) isn't entirely an old-school tyrant: he improves on the usual blanket prohibition against full-mouth discourse by suggesting some flexibility in the rule's application. "You must learn, however, to talk with a little in your mouth, simply because you can't always wait until you have swallowed everything before answering a question. So if you take a little at a time, you will always be ready to join in the conversation."

Seeing as there is no such thing as a little bite of a Bigfoot pizza, this idea may be hard to get across to a teenager who rarely, in any case, cares about joining in the conversation or even making himself understood. Of course, if he suddenly takes up with a girl whose father belongs to the Harvard Club or gets invited to the British embassy as a representative of inarticulate youth, he may regret not knowing which way the silverware works or how to knock back asparagus spears without looking like a trained seal. Unfortunately, most teenagers admire trained seals more than ambassadors and would do anything to avoid stuffed shirts. They may regret their ignorance the first time they're faced with a finger bowl or a fish knife somewhere well down the road, and yet it's hard to believe they will be crushed. In their social whirl, it's more important to know which brand of sneakers is acceptable or what kind of calcium goes best with a vegan diet.

No, the most likely readers of *Tiffany's Table Manners for Teenagers* are the modern teenager's insecure parents, the very diners-out who still know just enough about manners to know that they don't know enough. For them — for us — there is no little joy in learning how the politely repressed manipulate their knives and forks. Mr. Hoving, please — how do you eat tall food?

Manners matter, for they are all that keep us from savagery now that the Royals have proved to be feeble role models. But when the discussion of manners devolves into etiquette — how silverware should be monogrammed, what titles belong on a calling card, how many pillowcases should go into a bride's trousseau — the codes that govern the intricate details of human behaviour can suddenly seem both trivial and archaic.

In this pluralistic and occasionally democratic society, it's tempting to throw out the fussy old rules that were designed less to make life better — which is what manners should do — than to make it harder. No matter how good a person you are, the etiquette guides said, no matter how much you give to charity or how much respect you show to the elderly or how carefully you signal your lane changes, you will not be admitted into the inner circle until you have mastered the arcane details of upper-class American wedding ceremonies.

The priorities of the old etiquette books, designed to speed the ascent of the upwardly mobile and give them the couth that new money couldn't buy, seem hopelessly misplaced these days. If there still exist aristocrats whose waking hours are consumed with passing judgment on those who don't know how to treat servants on country-house weekends, they are more scorned than admired. Various wars and recessions and liberations of peoples over the century have changed the value we attach to getting unimportant things just right.

And undoubtedly the world is a better place for it—if you still have doubts, read a traditional book of etiquette on the rules of a formal dinner party, and then try to act accordingly, minus the servants who were deemed to be a part of every good household.

But while much has been made better, some things have certainly become worse in the new social disorder. It's not just that faux pas are so much easier in a multicultural society, though the hazards lurk everywhere—how do I eat the bread in an Ethiopian restaurant, are there strict Islamic rules on meat and dairy, which cultures want me to leave some food on my plate at the end of a meal and which insist that I finish everything, ask for seconds and drink toasts long into the night (while considering me rude when I yield to their insistence)?

No, the worst offences are the blindly intentional ones that come from living in a rough world where good manners have come to be seen as a sign of weakness. Parents, to take the most glaring example, refrain from knocking politeness into their children because there are so many more loving things to do at the end of a busy day. Then, presto, the little miscreants eat the trattoria's spaghetti alla carbonara with their fingers, or rock their chairs backward into the family at the next table, and civilization collapses a little bit more.

We can ignore it all, and pretend that it never happened or just doesn't matter. But for anyone with a social conscience—not the universal kind that worries about the injustices in East Timor, but the more intimate version that wonders if you're going to get punched in the nose by the patriarch at the next table—there's the salvation offered by *Emily Post's Etiquette*. As recently updated for these insecure times by Peggy Post, who's married to Emily's great-grandson, it's still very much a handbook of interactivity in the traditional vein—wedding minutiae occupy several hundred pages—but it also tries to steer straight modern diners who've lost their way. And as often with such guides, the advice proffered from on high seems to combine the sensible with the arbitrary, the thoughtful with the just plain weird.

You may eat french fries with your fingers, says Post, which is good news. But only when they accompany finger food. "At other times they should be cut into reasonable lengths and eaten with a fork," which doesn't sound like the delicate approach I'd want to be seen taking with my local bistro's steak-frites. Similarly, the bread you may use to soak up your snail juices or mussel broth must be attached to the end of a fork before you start your mopping—which is hardly in the rustic spirit of escargots bourguignonne or moules marinière.

Post is very good at illustrating table settings for formal dinners, but while her advice can be timely in other sections (the etiquette of voice mail, child-bearing by single parents, responses to sexual harassment) the food department is still conservative. It would be nice to hear some thoughts on eating Indian vegetarian dishes (by hand? which one?), or confronting tall food in a smart restaurant (knock it over?) or dealing with the homemade wine that a friend has brought to dinner (pour it into a decanter that you deftly switch with another decanter of Lafite when no one's looking?).

She offers some sensible suggestions that are worth stating for those of us who make up our behaviour as we go along: let your companion have the outward-looking seat at a restaurant, never accept your dinner guests' offer to do the dishes, don't smoke in your host's house even when he says it's fine. Post also permits the "American" method of dealing with meat: spearing the chop with the fork in the left hand while cutting, then switching the fork to the right for eating. Manner monitors have traditionally despised this method, but it strikes me as a calmer, less ravenous way to eat. Of course, it's the way I was taught—man makes manners, not the other way around.

Everyday eating distances itself from the formalities of a more mannered world. Sometimes we prefer to eat Portuguese cod croquettes out of a wax-paper wrapper while walking down the crowded street, and no one's going to tell us that this experience is in any way inferior to soup served on white linen and guarded by a massed phalanx of cutlery. Sometimes, giving in to the yearnings that developed from a rule-breaking meal in one of the more spontaneous parts of France, we start believing that bread tastes better when you rip it roughly on the tablecloth rather than sawing it up prissily and serving it in basketed formation.

But it would be a mistake to create too much of a divide between something called real life and the more elaborate rituals of the formal meal. Because if there's anything that needs a sprinkling of reality and a pinch of common sense, it's that strange occasion known as the dinner party. For some reason, what should be a natural extension of our day-to-day practice—only more and better—turns all too easily into a tension-filled gathering that's hard to stomach. Nobody minds a free meal, unless it's followed by a three-hour sales pitch on seafront condos. But just because we invite guests into our home and distribute food gratis does not mean we reserve the right to experiment upon them in the interests of culinary science.

Guests are funny, fragile creatures. As a hard-working host, you might think they should be eager to try out your four-course all-vinegar menu or the post-Hitlerian developments in German vegetarian cuisine. But all too often they fall short of their statutory obligation to be appreciative, and instead demand menus that are sensible. For anyone infatuated with his or her own dinner-party extravaganzas, this can seem like an imposition. But it also has its advantages. Even good cooks fall into ruts, using lemon with a heavy hand because they like the fragrance, softening too many pasta sauces with cream, adding the rosemary automatically to the lamb (it was good the first time in Rome, but not forever after), turning out the signature chocolate cake again and again because everyone said they adored it the first three times. Cooking with others in mind can be a way of fighting these habits before they turn into faults.

The most important rule in menu-building is to find a balance. You may be a dab hand at pastry-making, but no one except a hardworking Amish farmer with a secret weakness for butter crusts could bear a tarte tatin after a quiche after a bouchée à la reine. And even varying the starch is not much better. You wouldn't serve pasta after a risotto, but you might be tempted to try sweet crêpes after pasta. Think twice: most people lead terribly inert lives, and need all the encouragement you can offer to keep their appetites alive.

The effect of lightness can be achieved in several ways. The less-is-more school of cooks think smaller servings are the answer, but they conveniently ignore the consequences of their cutbacks:

- Guests are more likely to accept the offer of seconds when the servings are mingy, thus defeating the purpose;
- Hosts no sooner sit down to start a new, microscopic course than they have to jump up and clear the dishes;
- Small servings invariably seem precious and invite a silent, reverential gaze. The best and loosest conversation comes when there is plenty of food on the plate.

Some preferable ways to create a lighter effect: serve caviar as a first course, either on its own or sushi-style; watch out for the proliferation of heavy or fatty foods (sausages, rillettes, meat gravies, anything deep-fried, olive oil dressings, butter and cream); cut back on dessert if the main course is substantial (no pecan pie after the cassoulet; sherbet and amaretti fit the equation better).

Lightness of food can be self-regulating at least. Guests can ask for small helpings, leave a bit of meat hidden under a lettuce leaf, or do as Mr. Bean does and spit their unwanted steak tartare into a neighbour's handbag when no one's looking. But other balancing tricks are in the control of the host. To keep up interest, a meal should provide wide variations in flavour and in texture. This rule was widely ignored when the Cuisinart first came out and everyone had to reduce otherwise fine foods to processed mush: quenelles of smoked salmon, capon breast stuffed with shrimp mousse and, finally, strawberry mousse. A good meal has texture, whether it's the rubbery succulence of unmoussed smoked salmon, the crispness of radicchio, the dense meatiness of grilled tuna or the seedy crunch of fresh strawberries in a pastry tart, a Marsala froth or a light syrup. A real-life approach to cooking means respecting the integrity of these ingredients and not letting them be transformed into something unpleasant just to serve the whims of fashion or the new product lines at the kitchen-supply store.

But you can't be so taken by the low-key comforts of everyday eating that you cook without imagination. The fresh Tuscan olive oil and sweet balsamic vinegar that seem so bracing on your daily salad wear out their appeal quickly when used as a universal dressing and flavouring. Likewise attention-grabbing greens such as arugula and cilantro can reduce everything to a sameness precisely because of their look-at-me style. With a big spread, over a number of courses, garnishes and dressings must be varied to have any effect. Try chopped chives, Thai basil, mint, capers, minced black and green olives, pickled Japanese vegetables, little bits of hot red pepper, lime instead of lemon, hazelnut oil instead of olive oil, sherry vinegar in place of balsamic. No matter how much you like mayonnaise and its relatives, no more than once in a meal. And remember, if you're trying out a by-the-book themed meal — all Thai, or Southwest France or pre-Columbian

— watch out for the overlap you too often get by sticking to one ethnic style or one cookbook author.

A uniform tint to food should be as tedious as any other kind of imbalance. Imagine a white meal of cream of cucumber soup, tarragon chicken with rice and oeufs à la neige. But the problem here may be less the uniformity of colour than the general blandness of white foods. And here's my problem, which makes me question all these sensible prescriptions for special-occasion eating. One of the best meals I ever ate, served by a cook from Modena, where they make sports cars, vinegar and Pavarotti, consisted of pasta envelopes stuffed with sweet potato and bathed in meat juices; rump roast in a reduction of Barolo wine and rum; and a baked apple stuffed with crisp almond cookie bits. Only when I finished this feast did I realize that it was entirely a monochrome of dull, delicious brown.

So we can fuss too much over dinner-party cuisine even when we tell ourselves not to fuss — one part of common sense, at least when it comes to cooking, is to refrain from being too sensible. Calculating the desired effect may only make a meal end up seeming calculated — and I have yet to enjoy a dinner when I could actually hear the wheels turning.

It's like sex. The less you worry about it, the better it is. Which brings me to another one of those mealtime adventures that could profit from a bit of realism: the romantic dinner. Anyone who loves food has to look at romance with a jaundiced eye. Time and time again we are told that dinner is an effective agent of seduction, that the route to passion's seat somehow passes through the gastro-intestinal system. Fine cooking is merely a means to an end in this distorted world view, and the taste of lobster ravioli in vanilla-bean sauce is good only so far as it causes two cholesterol-laden hearts to beat as one.

How food got loaded with this subordinate role in life is hard to understand. Sure, there's a sensual side to both eating and sex.

But why should the old bump and grind be automatically proclaimed best of breed when eating is so much more enticing? Think about its advantages: stretch marks don't show; no complaints when you fall asleep afterward; you can do it for two or three hours well into your fifties; Madonna videos don't put you off the whole idea; no arguments over who finished first; no need to sneak in secret meals to spice up a tired relationship. The spice is always there.

Food can undoubtedly be linked to affection. But the most successful meals are bound to be the ones that are treated as an end in themselves. The truth of this point can be seen by looking in the opposite direction, since the worst meals of all time have to be those where the post-prandial possibility exists. The cook dithers long and hard over the menu and ends up an unbeddable wreck by worrying whether the spaghettini with fennel sausage was too heavy or the oyster stew too obvious. The poor victim of this gastronomic fan dance is left to fret over the polite way to refuse a second helping of asparagus hollandaise — can't look too easy — while wondering how much of the evening's progress should be left to kismet, and how much to alcohol.

Whether you're dining with someone for the first time or sitting down with the lump who long ago staked a claim to the other two-thirds of the bed, the point is much the same. Interesting food will lead to interesting possibilities. That isn't "interesting" in the intentionally weird sense of spitted meadowlarks or hare cooked in its own blood. Nor does it mean those show-off, cooking-school extravaganzas that take up three pages of a cookbook and three days of your life. It simply means arousing your partner's interest, and there are many, many ways to do that at the table.

Spending money is the easiest way to make an impression, less because of the huge bill you may feel tempted to wave around as a token of true affection than because the rarity that says you're one of a kind costs money. It's no coincidence that sales of champagne and caviar pick up just before Valentine's Day. But it's not enough that a food be expensive. Out-of-season strawberries and store-bought chicken chasseur don't come cheap, but neither can be depended on to win back the initial investment.

The best foods for making an impression have qualities that mark them out as special to eat: a heady aroma, an earthy lingering flavour, a sensual charm in the mouth. Think of the fragrance of saffron in a pilaf, the musky scent of a good Gewürztraminer, the pop of salty-sweet caviar eggs, the melting richness of foie gras, the tingle of champagne bubbles on the tongue, the woody aromas of wild mushrooms rising up out of a dark risotto, the lush bitterness of a chocolate truffle. And because they're all so expensive, they're more likely to be given the attention that well-made food deserves.

Anyone with money can buy pleasure up to a point, with food as with sex. But though the man who gives his partner champagne and chocolates on every special occasion may feel he's done his bit, he forgets that the novelty of the unexpected can be far more arousing than what comes to be seen as tried and true. Turning out a plate of sushi for a friend or friend-to-be undoubtedly demands work — tracking down good tuna and salmon, figuring out how long to cook the sticky rice, filling up the seaweed wrappers just so, coming up with a good self-deprecating joke when the wrappers fall apart at the touch of the chopstick — but the pleasure it brings is disproportionately high. The invigorating powers of Japanese horseradish, by the way, cannot be overrated.

A meal that inspires contentment and devotion and stimulation should be enough in itself. Those who insist on using food as a modus operandi should first ask themselves what good can come from violent contortions on a full stomach — make that two full stomachs. Better to go straight to sleep, turn out a Gorgonzola or salmon roe omelette the next morning, wash it down with a luscious sweet wine—a Coteaux du Layon from the Loire is nice —and only then get down to business.

But what you must avoid, wherever you choose to position the moment of reckoning, is a boring breakfast. Why go to all the trouble of arranging a fine romantic dinner only to follow it the morning after with Pop-Tarts or good old faithful Skippy on toast? A little realism is a much-needed thing at the table, but this reality is way too harsh. Though the eyes are the window to the soul, the breakfast you choose to eat is far more transparent. Do you really want to be revealed in the cold light of day as dull, deliberate and childish? Do you really want to kiss someone with the taste of peanut butter on your tongue and the crunchy bits caught in your teeth?

The problem lies with the traditional breakfast, and the role that we make it play in our daily lives. In contrast with the salmon-roe omelette initiative, the everyday morning meal is less about the flavour of foods than about the peculiar way they rouse the senses. Progressing from sleep to wakefulness, we pass through a transition period called morning that would be a long hard slog without a menu that brought us back to life. We do not taste the day's first meal so much as respond to its stimuli.

This vision of the early a.m. makes some sense, especially when you think about the traditional standbys of the breakfast table. On the one hand, the gentle, predictable foods that are like a warm bath or the clock radio that plays fifteen minutes of Mozart before the buzzer kicks in: soothing caffe latte, a sinuous croissant that is more texture than flavour, bland breakfast sausages, stodgy porridge. On the other hand, the shock treatment that is the edible equivalent of reveille: torrid black coffee designed to peel skin off the roof of the mouth, grapefruit so tart it would bring a dead man to life (which is the idea), orange marmalade that exorcises the late-night spirits with its intense combination of sweetness and bitterness, bacon functioning like a salt tablet in strip form, even the cayenne pepper that is the active ingredient in spicy hangover cures of the Jeeves and Wooster school.

But to think of breakfast as a remedy for the excesses or infirmities that beset us is to limit its appeal to the senses. Yes, it is a different kind of meal, but it definitely is a meal, not an over-the-counter form of therapy. Because breakfast is usually consumed by people not yet conscious enough to make a choice, it invites habitual behaviour—two eggs sunny side up, crunchy peanut butter on toasted whole wheat, a heaping bowl of Lucky Charms. And maybe there is something to be said for cautious conservatism at an hour when the Teletubbies can be an assault on the system. But my question then becomes, if we're trying to rouse ourselves into life, why do we consume the same old breakfast with such numbing regularity?

I realize it's nice to have at least one meal, competitive eating being the cutthroat pleasure it is these days, where no thought need be given for the latest fashions. The giddy institution of brunch, as we all know, was invented largely to provide an outlet for those who couldn't stomach the boredom of the breakfast table. But since we are going to break our fast anyway, why can't we do it as if we mean it, like people who haven't tasted precious food since at least the night before?

Actually, this might explain the enthusiasm people have for a mid-morning brunch, the zest brought to a pleasure because you've postponed it. That, and the fact that (I think we're getting to the heart of the matter here) you've got someone else doing the cooking. One doesn't want to go through life always eating someone else's food—witness Orson Welles—but there's much to be said for eating the day's first meal somewhere else. While self-important chefs are not necessarily practising their mystical arts early in the day, the morning palate used to low-fat granola and boiled eggs in a Mickey Mouse cup will feel uplifted by anything out of the ordinary. Cantonese dim sum served late in the dinner hour might well seem greasy or bland or just too simple —I don't know, since I've never been able to wait that long. But when I sit down in the morning light to eat steamed shrimp dumplings tinged with chili oil or fried bean-curd rolls stuffed with sprouts and laved with Lea & Perrins, my love for food, and for the world that came up with such pleasures, is boundless.

The waiting world offers many such joys: mixed grills presented in alarming quantities at farmhouse bed and breakfasts, odds and ends collected around the market square in a French provincial town in the early-morning light and served on the hotel floor, break-of-dawn trout cooked over the campfire at a northern lake (but don't ask what you eat while you wait for the trout to nibble). You can even, if you're feeling particularly perverse, go into one of those deluxe hotels that lure Asian visitors and salute the rising sun with a Japanese breakfast of miso soup, pickled vegetables, grilled salmon and green tea.

But the most stimulating breakfast I ever ate was at a small restaurant called the Indian Rice Factory in Toronto. The owner, Amar Patel, decided that the city's would-be sophisticates were ready for an opulent Indian breakfast. The menu that I saved— stole, I suppose, but for a good cause—still comes in handy when I want to think about how creative a.m. cooking can be. The best dish, for the way it took a traditional breakfast ingredient and went to town with it, was uppama, cream of wheat cooked in butter with chili peppers and ginger, garnished with cashews and raisins and served with yogurt. Make use of that one for your next early-morning tryst. But there were a dozen other dishes that were just as arresting, including lamb with saffron, scrambled eggs blended with chicken, ginger and coriander, rice kedgeree with coconut and mung beans, and cracked wheat cooked in milk, then flavoured with cinnamon, cloves and rich date-palm sugar.

It didn't catch on, which may be just as well. After a meal like that, everyday fare would forever seem disappointing. Dull, ordinary breakfasts are designed to keep such dangerous feelings in check.

As much a part of winter as splashed slush and slippery streets, the common cold descends. All thoughts of seductive dinners and romantic breakfasts dissipate in the fog of sickness. This is real life at its most real, which is to say completely unreal. The brain that used to dream up interesting things to do with turnips and cabbage is suddenly enveloped by primordial ooze. Nostrils that could sense the grated nutmeg in the gnocchi a block away from home are dulled to an almost inert nothingness. Taste buds that once sorted and savoured the dense layers of autumnal flavours in a mushroom and red wine risotto now languish unresponsive in the wintry bleakness.

And, worst of all, the will to cook is gone. "What's the point?" the body whimpers when asked to shuffle kitchenward and whip up something tasty. I don't have the strength to make dinner. I wouldn't be able to taste it if I did. And I don't feel hungry anyway.

Those fancy fifteen-minute recipes aren't much help now. A shortage of time is hardly the worst of your problems when your unresponsive body feels like so much dead weight. Still, unless Grandma's around to make chicken soup and blancmange, you have to do something for breakfast, lunch and dinner. But what? Getting away from the scene of your sickness is a good thing, though not one Martha would ever stoop to. But money spent on a fancy restaurant meal is money wasted when a virus takes charge. Labouring to breathe, you've long since lost the power to endure the recital of daily specials, the mental acuity needed to make between-courses small talk or the politeness expected of those who attempt to function in a public place.

Cheaper restaurants have the virtue of speed as well as price. If you can't taste the food, you've at least nourished your wreck of a body cheaply and quickly, leaving yourself that much more time to get home, stare at the wall vacantly and try to inhale. And because fuller flavours often go together with cheaper food— we're talking Chinese, Indian, Sri Lankan, Vietnamese and Middle Eastern, not Middle American—you may also find something that will clear the passages and come to the rescue of the senses. Off the top, I'd recommend ma po bean curd, a Chinese dish that doesn't have a huge amount of flavour even for well people, but what it does have it delivers with a nicely numbing chili wallop. Some alternatives for the discerningly infirm: throat-scorching Indian pork vindaloo, the aromatic Vietnamese beef broth called pho, Middle Eastern chicken kebabs with garlic sauce (preceded where possible by pickled hot peppers) and an array of tuna sushi, heavy on the wasabe dipping sauce. In fact, you might as well just order the wasabe straight up.

This presupposes that you are able and willing to go out into the cold, dark night. But when sickness clouds the mind, it's all too tempting to steer clear of the outside world and believe that home is some kind of refuge. This is fine, I suppose, if you're the sort of person who can lie in bed drinking herbal tea and reading Inspector Morse novels for hour upon hour. Such people get well fast and regard their illness as a sort of blessing, a chance to catch up on the latest fiction while shedding unwanted pounds by skipping a few meals.

But the rest of us may be better off prowling the frigid streets of the city in our wasted state, forgetting our woes for a moment by staring at the coils of paprika sausage hanging in the Hungarian butcher's window or enumerating and ranking the French pastries we will eat if we ever get well. This at least is a distraction, taking our minds off the troubles that torture us while putting queasy

stomachs at a safe distance from the foods that would upset them.
But when we lock ourselves in the home, it's all too easy to give
in to the impulses of a muddled brain.

There was the night I found myself dining off a bowl of
peanuts and a few bottles of dark beer. It all made sense at the
time. Though I couldn't taste them, the peanuts were salty and
oily and squished pleasantly in the mouth in a repetitive and
undemanding way. They generated a thirst that the strong, dark
winter beer (more placebo than cure) seemed to slake, and it
was not until the next morning—around three a.m., four a.m.
and five a.m., to be precise—that the peanut-and-beer dinner
model suddenly seemed imperfect.

It's easy, when you recover that flimsy thing called health, to
know what is best for the sick: soft scrambled eggs on brown
toast, flavoured only with chives and grated Parmesan; crab salad
made from that canned crab you providentially bought while you
were still well; chicken broth scented with ginger and flecked
with chopped green onions that comfort the rheumy eye with
their vibrant colour.

It's easy, when you're healthy, to go on and suggest that
making chicken soup—think of the steam rising up from the
pot and clearing the sinuses, think of the mind-numbing labour
involved in chopping up the onions and carrots, think of the
wafting ginger aroma in the Thai version that says you are still
alive—may be the best kind of distraction when you're sick.

When you really are sick, it will all seem like too much.
Gnaw on the peanuts if you must—better a pleasure you will
later regret than no pleasure at all—but at the same time pull out
a favourite cookbook full of comforting recipes that will offer
hope in time of affliction. With my last reserves of strength, I pick
up *The Lutèce Cookbook* by Andre Soltner and just by skimming the
pages—poached eggs on a bed of sorrel with a Gewürztraminer

sauce, terrine of guinea hen with wild mushrooms, sea urchin soufflé with shallots, roast pigeon with figs — I feel better.

Salmon Roe Omelette

This aphrodisiac recipe is inspired by Norman Douglas' *Venus in the Kitchen*, a wonderful and outlandish book of recipes by a novelist whose behaviour (though not his cooking) scandalized between-wars Capri. The free-spirited, free-spending Douglas used caviar in his post-seduction breakfast dish. On the assumption that no one today would cook with real caviar, certainly not after the fact, I prefer to use bright orange salmon eggs. They're a little harder to find, but try gourmet shops that sell regular caviar or Japanese grocery stores (since salmon roe is a favoured ingredient in sushi).

Beat together 4 eggs, then gently blend in a small spoonful of fresh bread crumbs, 2 tablespoons of salmon eggs, a pinch of chopped fresh chives, the same of chopped fresh parsley and a little grated lemon peel. Melt 1 ounce of butter in a large frying pan, and when it starts to bubble, pour in the egg mixture, making sure it spreads out over the bottom of the pan. When it's cooked on one side, turn and cook on the other. Serves 2 the morning after.

Seafood Salad

You talk about having friends round for dinner. You set a date weeks in advance when schedules are still clear. And then, if you're as oblivious to the outside world as I am, you forget about it. Suddenly on the day of, they politely call to ask when they should turn up, and you realize you've got to act fast. This simple but nicely varied salad is the one we always fall back on when time is short and deadlines cramp the imagination. Often we'll serve it as part of a main-course antipasto spread, a dinner that basically consists of whatever appetizers we can pull together in the time available, served at whatever temperatures they happen to have reached when the guests make their entrance. Though the kitchen can feel like a sweatshop as the hour of reckoning approaches, there's a great sense of relaxation when we sit down to eat: all the work's done and you can just nibble away on whatever catches your interest.

But first the work: rush out to the fish store and stock up on a variety of frutti di mare: 1 pound each of shrimps, mussels, scallops, clams and squid should do it. You may also want to stop by your closest Italian or Greek deli and pick up some pickled octopus. Clean the squid by separating the tentacles from the bodies, being sure to remove the ink sac, the stiff cellophane-like spine and the hard round "beak," or anus, along with the rest of the head. Cut the bodies into ¾-inch rings. Shell the shrimp. Clean the mussel and clam shells, discarding any that are broken or won't close when tapped. Pat dry the shrimp, scallops and squid, then quickly sauté each one by one in a little olive oil. Steam the mussels and clams in white wine and then shell them. Chop the octopus into small pieces so its pickled taste doesn't dominate. Mix the seafood together with a dressing of olive oil, lemon juice, salt, black pepper and hot pepper flakes to taste, then add 1 tablespoon of capers and 1 finely chopped onion. (Some people like to throw in a clove of finely minced garlic. I'm not one of them.) Taste before serving: sometimes the dressing can turn watery, and may need a little more olive oil and salt. If serving as a first course, place on cupped leaves of lightly dressed Boston lettuce and offer round lemon slices.

Penne all'Arrabbiata

This fiery dish is my wife's first resort when the houseful of young males playing video games and penning punk-rock tunes doesn't seem to be in any hurry to leave. It's also a standard menu item whenever the bands my concert-promoter son brings to town stop by for a pre-concert feed. One of my wife's proudest moments came when she was thanked from the stage of the El Mocambo club for her great pasta.

Heat a couple of ounces of olive oil in a large pan, then add 1 finely chopped onion, 2 finely chopped cloves of garlic, and 1 or 2 thinly sliced hot red or green peppers (dried peppers will do). As the vegetables start to soften, pour in a 28-ounce tin of peeled plum tomatoes that you have coarsely chopped, and 2 to 4 chopped anchovy fillets if the punk rockers you're feeding aren't also vegans. Cook for about 10 minutes. While the sauce is cooking, boil up a 14-ounce box of penne, which is the classic noodle for this sauce. When the penne is cooked, drain it and add it to the pan, throw in a good amount of chopped parsley, give it a stir and cook for another minute. The caper-loving members of our household add a tablespoon or two of the salty little buds at this point. Serve with energetic red wine or soy milk or whatever.

GARLIC

HERE'S THE BAD NEWS. Garlic is good for you. Not for your job prospects necessarily, not the morning after a bowl of that refreshing cucumber, yogurt and raw garlic salad. But eminent garlic researchers tell us that it's good for the blood, the digestive system and points south. And that is enough to make a hedonist cry.

You know what happens to do-gooding foods. First they're eaten for an ulterior motive. Then the ulterior motive becomes the real motive. And suddenly the food that tasted so good before the faddists took control has become just another medication, to be stomached with distaste. The Japanese perfected the smell-free garlic in tablet form and it won't be long before deodorized garlic soup is prescribed for the infirm and the impotent. Unless the garlic underground moves fast, the world's favourite flavouring will be made to fall into line with calcium-rich milk, lean pork chops and bowel-loosening, life-enhancing, fibre-rich bread.

Immortality is bought at a high price. Good taste always seems to disappear when food is tampered with for a higher purpose. But where the fragrance of garlic still fills the kitchen, there is hope. If Fate has dealt you a bad hand, you can still eat one of the most glorious meals in the world, thanks to garlic. Finely chop 4 or 5 peeled garlic cloves, throw in the pan with a little salt and 1 cup of oil (olive oil, if Fate can be distracted), heat and cook slowly until the garlic has browned, then toss the garlic oil with not too much freshly boiled spaghetti. A dash of chili pepper is also encouraged by the poor Neapolitans who gave this dish the singsong name of spaghetti con aglio e olio.

Garlic makes poverty bearable. Its emanations might even rescue the ozone layer as well as our insides. But these are ulterior motives, beside-the-fact afterthoughts. The main thing is that garlic, for all its forcefulness, is also capable of astonishing range. There aren't many condiments that can flavour their own soup the way garlic does, and then turn around and be the main ingredient in a pasta dish, give an aromatic edge to a roast leg of lamb, provide rubbery escargots with a taste to call their own, and make mashed potatoes seem sophisticated under the name of garlic mash.

Garlic stands a fighting chance of eluding do-gooders because it is so widely used and so deeply appreciated. And it will never be just a foodies' plaything, tossed aside when the next season's fashions arrive: where extra-virgin olive oil has a coterie, garlic has a power base. You can't order even a spring roll in a humble Vietnamese restaurant without falling prey to a garlic-flavoured dipping sauce and garlic is always within easy reach in a Chinese kitchen—anyone who really wants to find inner peace should order eggplant with garlic sauce or stir-fried string beans with crisp garlic.

Although it rarely turns up on menus, spaghetti con aglio e olio can be ordered with confidence at any authentic, tradition-affirming Italian restaurant. If the kitchen can't or won't perform this act of homage, it is not an Italian kitchen. Garlic is indispensable in Indian cooking, in Portuguese cooking, in Spanish cooking and as for Romanian, don't remind me of the effect it had on my nearest and not so dearest after a lunch of eggplant pâté—a Balkanized baba ghannoush.

The one cuisine that never accepted garlic is Anglo-Saxon. Some people would take that as proof that Anglo-Saxon cuisine is no cuisine at all. For its edginess with garlic, note the feeble attempts to introduce garlic through garlic salt, garlic juice and garlic cream, or through the clove of garlic the more daring Anglo-Saxon cooks of my formative years kept in the freezer to wipe the surface of the salad bowl. Garlic has to be used with confidence or not at all.

Garlic in the raw (which is how French working men prefer it as a morning tonic, washed down with the French equivalent of moonshine) is fierce to taste and potent in its after-effects. But cooked garlic is not necessarily a destroyer of beautiful relationships. A whole garlic clove, peeled but otherwise intact, tastes sweet and creamy after prolonged stewing, as in the paradisiacal Cantonese stew that combines fat barbecued pork, chopped eel (oysters may be substituted), green onions and a few dozen whole cloves of garlic. While the digestive system may never be the same, good taste outweighs any worry about bad breath.

It's the same with the garlic soups of France and Spain and the roasted garlic bulbs that lie in wait for fashionable eaters in search of a thrill. Uncut garlic is no stronger than onion or leek. But take the knife to garlic and the bulb takes on airs. Only a dedicated garlic fancier should mince garlic because the residual smell on the hands is pungent enough to wake a sleeping body three days later. Scientists, taking a break from more apocalyptic research, tell us that the contact of a chemical, allicin, and an enzyme, allinase, is what gives garlic its pronounced character. In the uncut clove, the two are separated by a cell membrane. Cutting allows the enzyme to break down the chemical, producing a sulphur compound that immediately finds its way to easily offended noses.

Cut less, cook more, or enjoy the consequences. The strongest garlic taste that's also appetizing to normal human beings is the

Greek tzatziki salad, made with finely chopped raw garlic. Raw garlic is also the starting point of the garlic sauce that's such an important part of Mediterranean cooking. The French mayonnaises aioli and rouille are often added to hot soups and stews, but in these cases the garlic softens in strength as the raw sauces are partly cooked by the heat. Still, they're not to be trifled with by those whose rank in the world depends on sweet exhalations.

Such sauces are the essence of garlic, but the bulbous perennial is more than just a strong scent in a mayonnaise. It's a supremely versatile and comforting flavouring to be used with indiscretion year-round. Garlic warms winter stews and brightens the seasonal malaise of cold-climate cooking. In the Mediterranean, it is considered as much a part of summer as the cicada's song. The Provençal feast of le grand aioli, when entire villages gather to dip vegetables and meat in garlic mayonnaise, is a warm-weather fixture. Aioli, by the way, is also known as le beurre de Provence, which tells you something about their priorities.

Quick Garlic Soup

More a broth really, but a good and easy restorative if sickness has sapped the energy to cook.

Crush 2 cloves of garlic beneath the blade of a knife. Put in a saucepan and add 1 bay leaf, 1 tablespoon of olive oil, 2 cups of hot water and some salt and pepper. Let boil for 8 to 10 minutes. Take the pan off the heat. Put the yolks of 2 eggs into a soup tureen, then add half a ladle of the garlic broth. Mix well and pour in the rest of the broth, stirring all the time. Add 4 chopped-up slices of stale bread (or croutons crisped in olive oil if you've recovered some of your energy).

This recipe comes from Edouard de Pomiane's wonderfully serene book for people in a hurry, *French Cooking in Ten Minutes, Or*

Adapting to the Rhythm of Modern Life. Most cookbooks today that try to come to terms with the accelerated pace of modern life have a frantic feel, as if cooking were just another item to be cleared from an overfilled agenda. De Pomiane, writing over five decades ago, was much wiser and more humane. He knew that when time is short, it's better to feel relaxed than to watch the clock. You get a good sense of his patient approach to modernity from the book's dedication: "My book is meant for the student, for the shop-assistant, for the clerk, for the artist, for lazy people, poets, men of action, dreamers and scientists, for everyone who has only an hour for lunch or dinner and yet wants half an hour of peace to watch the smoke of a cigarette while they sip a cup of coffee which has not even time to get cold."

Green Beans with Garlic and Soy

Reproducing Chinese-restaurant food in the home isn't easy—small flat skillets on a tiny gas burner just don't behave like huge rounded woks on a raging fire. But allowing for the differences, this dish approximates one an understanding restaurant devised after our increasingly vegetarian children shunned more and more of the standard items on the menu. It follows a two-stage process of steaming and frying here, but a Chinese chef would combine both methods in the wok. He would also cook the beans in more fat, effectively deep-frying them. In either case, it's important not to leave the beans too crunchy—they must soften, to take on the powerful flavours of the garlic and soy.

Some people like the ritual of hand-trimming the ends of their green beans—topping and tailing as it's known, one of the most cheerful kitchen expressions I can think of. But beans that are going to be cooked at a high heat, as these are, look much better trimmed more tediously and methodically with a sharp knife. So take 1 pound of fresh beans, make them presentable, steam until tender and dry them thoroughly (this is very important—otherwise you will be covered with fat when the wet beans start sputtering). Heat 3 tablespoons of peanut oil in a large heavy skillet just to the point where it's hot and begins to spit. Add the beans carefully and cook for 3 to 5 minutes, moving them around occasionally so they don't burn, until the beans begin to take on colour and shrivel slightly at the edges. Add 2 cloves of finely chopped garlic, ½ teaspoon of pepper flakes and 2 tablespoons of soy sauce. Stir, and then reduce the heat so that the garlic doesn't burn. Cook for another minute to let the garlic soften and the beans soak up the soy juices. Serve immediately.

A Year without Turkey

It wasn't winter as our hardy ances-tors knew it. Snow-shovelling muscles atro-phied through lack of use. The ice rink in the schoolyard made only a brief appearance, before turning into the splash pool in the schoolyard. The huskies got tired of doing nothing and went off to look for work in dog-food commercials. Believers in the relent-lessness of global warming once again had their faith affirmed.

Whatever happened to the cold, we moaned, as we studied the menu in a pricey restaurant and waited for the polar ice caps to melt. All around was a tepid squishiness of climate that could have been mistaken for the first week at Wimbledon or my base-ment in rainy season, but had no business passing itself off as a season of cold.

The only evidence that winter still existed was on the menu itself. Like a Dallas matron who faithfully puts on her fur coat come November, though the Texas autumn cries out for sun-screen, the resourceful kitchen paid the calendar its due and cooked up cold-weather food. Seasonal cooking is so much more stimulating than the one-size-fits-all approach of those endless-summer chefs who can't stop chopping fresh tarragon into the grilled chicken's yellow pepper purée. To do battle with the blustery winds and the bone-cracking cold that existed only in theory, there was baked garlic with warmed goat's cheese, roast chicken surrounded by garlicky creamed potatoes and braised lamb shank big enough to satisfy an outdoor appetite. Hardy bitter leaves like endive, rapini and radicchio signified that it was a time of survival, of strong, almost medicinal flavours and tough plants that could outlast the frost long after the delicate lamb's lettuce had gone south for the season. Best of all were the root vegetables that came up from the cellar when the more fashionable and fragile Cal-Ital veggies suddenly seemed out of place: deep-fried beet chips, a sweet-potato pancake, carrot purée, circles of Jerusalem artichokes and spears of parsnip in all its humble modesty.

It was a time when overlooked winter vegetables finally came into their own, and became a more satisfying taste for having been forgotten. But in the poor excuse for bad weather, it all seemed an academic exercise in nostalgia, like putting pediments on skyscrapers or trompe l'oeil in your jardin d'hiver.

And then winter came for real. Families huddled round the VCR for heat, prophets of global-warming idled their cars for twenty minutes every morning to avoid a cold steering wheel, imported cauliflower took on that sickly browned look and icicles formed on the eyelashes of anyone foolish enough to go shopping.

And when the cold descended, the hunger for winter food became just as real. The quality of the supermarket's trucked-in tomatoes, green peppers and eggplants looked dubious, the bright California colours were an assault on the sun-starved eye, and the prices made it seem like Martha Stewart had made them herself. When a cold front set up camp like the siege of Stalingrad, it was time to swear off the Mediterranean diet and answer that fundamental longing for primeval pleasures: split-pea soup simmered with a smoky ham bone, steak and kidneys steaming under a flaky shortcrust pastry, long-cooked casseroles that imbue the woodwork with the smells of garlic and red wine (and heat up a drafty house in the bargain).

Winter cooking comes but once a year, and then only if El Niño's in the mood. Almost all the trends we finicky eaters devour so slavishly come from warm climates. Italy, Provence, California and a co-operative highway network make it possible to eat a facsimile of summer cooking year-round, if you're so inclined. Dieticians successfully lobbied by the International Olive Oil Council tell us that the Mediterranean diet is healthier, which makes sense when you think about the scurvyish fare traditionally available to the sunless Northerner in the depths of a real winter: salted fish, smoked pig fat and mouldering rutabagas, with grain alcohol for warmth.

We've come a long way since then, those of us whose ancestors survived, but we've also lost something in switching to the universal meal plan. Light food may prolong lives and divert the jaded palate but it could never be said to warm the cockles, always assuming we still have cockles. For that you need—now what would do the trick?—barley soup prepared in the Swiss style, made with a chicken stock rather than a lamb base, not so thick that you can stand your spoon up in it, because that would leave a feeling of heaviness in this too inert age, but full of barley all the same. If you're going to cook by the outdoor thermometer and not the indoor thermostat, there's no point in going the cuisine minceur route and turning a hearty soup into a faux-frigid consommé with three perfect nuggets of barley.

Grains are ideal nourishment in cold weather for all the usual rib-sticking reasons and especially because they seem to have a remarkable ability to hold the heat. There's nothing worse in winter than welcoming guests from the cold, setting down a first course that came hot from the stove and discovering that it has cooled off by the third bite. Lumpy, glutinous grains that stick together in the cooking may have their decorative faults, but in soups or risottos they are wonderfully warming. (Be sure to heat the bowls first.)

You're tempted to pile heaviness on heartiness, and have chili or choucroute garni and apple brown betty after your barley soup, but that menu may better be saved for the next Ice Age. Go easy during this transitional period from all-weather fare to more elemental cuisine. Start with barley or lentil soup, then move on to a perfumed rice pilaf or a piece of good beef in mustard sauce. That should leave space for a valedictory winter dessert before you chase your guests out into the cold, perhaps bread pudding or pears simmered in port. The Acadian seal-fat cookies we can put off till Hell freezes over.

There are the ideal seasonal meals we dream of and then there are the compulsory ones inflicted on us. Millions of people sit down every Christmas (and every Thanksgiving if they're really unlucky) and find themselves staring at an ungainly, mahogany-coloured bird whose chief assets are three: cheap, easy to cook, feeds a crowd.

Perhaps half of those millions will welcome the sight of the Christmas turkey and take pleasure in the annual ritual of choosing white meat or dark. They will be content to believe that everyone around the dinner table feels the same way they do about ingrained holiday traditions. They will be wrong. For all the people who can't imagine Christmas without the big bird, there are almost as many who approach the day of days with a sense of dread.

These poor souls keep silent for the most part, not wanting to make a dull meal worse by starting an argument. They nurse a drink (having made sure there's good wine available to soothe the pain), or plot the ridiculously lucrative film script that's part of the coming New Year's resolution, or study the art on the wall and wonder what the Renaissance would have been like had someone told Michelangelo not to go to any trouble, just decorate the ceiling in a way that's cheap, easy to paint and satisfies everyone.

Attempting to satisfy everyone is the turkey's lot in life, but the role is not one for which it is well suited. Vegetarians obviously have their objections—especially given the humdrum vegetables (mashed turnips, for example) that aid and abet this Christmas travesty—and even dependable carnivores may have their doubts. Once, in its wild state, a turkey must have been a prized centrepiece to a celebration, with the intense gamey taste that came from having the run of North America. But the pumped-up domestic animal, confined to barracks through its uneventful life and nourished on the drab rations of scientific ntrition, has a lot less flavour to fill a lot more bird.

No wonder that when we pass around the dry, bland slices at the Christmas table, we make sure the gravy and stuffing quickly follow. Without the headier flavour of giblets and the concentrated essence of pan juices and the myriad weird ingredients that go into a conventional stuffing, there isn't much to taste in a turkey. Overworked traditions are the staple of Christmas, and the roast turkey is the most overworked of all. But Christmas dinner, to capture the spirit of the season, should be a stimulating meal and not just a dull habit. For the millions in search of release from turkey's tyranny, the options are endless.

Since we already know from our turkey experience that it's hard to find one food that will satisfy everyone, it's important to offer variety in the reconstructed Christmas meal. One obvious way to do this is to lay out a spread of dishes and let people pick and choose. Start with the cold dishes that can be prepared well in advance—smoked fish pâté, a shrimp salad, green lentils and chopped onions in a vinaigrette, steamed cauliflower in a parsley-anchovy sauce, a garlicky purée of salt cod, Thai-spiced strips of rare beef with strips of tart underripe tropical fruit in a sweet-sour dressing.

While the appetizers are being nibbled, heat up something substantial, such as cannelloni done three different ways, with crab meat, tomato and spinach-cheese fillings. Chase this with a crisp, slightly bitter salad of endive and chopped walnuts, which induces a healthy feeling that makes it easier to move on to the hazelnut torte, marzipan fruitcake and—sop to the traditionalists—apple pie with cheddar. Those stiff-backed traditionalists will still object that this approach is far too casual, that it's better suited to a New Year's Day gathering for like-minded friends than to the yoking of opposites that is a family Christmas.

They have a point. For those who see the modern world as an unregulated free-for-all, an all-you-can-eat smorgasbord, Christmas dinner is the last bastion of formality and self-sacrifice. You sit down at a table together and eat turkey and turnips off Grandma's chipped Royal Doulton not because it gives you pleasure but because it's a part of the human continuum that makes you who you are, God help you. Go your own way and you have lost out on the meaning of the occasion, and possibly the meaning of God (at least the Protestant one that demands self-sacrifice).

Fine, let's be more formal. Just not with turkey and the trimmings. This overinflated fowl, the Pamela Anderson of the poultry world, will get another chance to subdue a festive occasion when Thanksgiving comes round (memo to self: start planning alternative Thanksgiving menu now). A more dignified greeting-card kind of Christmas dinner could begin with a tureen of soup being placed in the middle of the lovingly decorated table. As the lid is lifted—Mind the sharp edges of the holly bush! Careful, your sleeve's brushing the candle! Help, the cat's licking the bûche de Noël!—the rich fragrance of a seasonal broth fills the room. It could be lobster bisque on the spare-no-expense-at-Christmas principle, or chestnut soup on the spare-no-effort principle (the chestnut peelers can show off their wounds at this point), or a warm cream of potato and leek on the principle that everyone likes potato and leek, especially if you crumble some Christmassy Stilton into the adults' servings. (Fresh bread would be good at this point: if you live in an area that's home to Italian or Portuguese bakeries, there's a good chance they'll be open for a few hours on the 25th, baking Christmas Day's daily bread.)

Follow the soup, after an appropriate interval devoted to singing carols in four-part harmony, with a dish for the masses: a Spanish stew of beef cooked in Rioja wine, osso buco, coq au vin, blanquette de veau or, perhaps best of all, if you're prepared for it, paella. Being prepared for paella is almost impossible, but then this is the season for taking on impossibilities. Make strong chicken stock in advance and search out a wide pan (or pans) big enough to hold a family-sized order (you may have to winnow down the family at this point) of saffron rice with several chickens, chorizo sausage, pork, ham, a pound of shrimp, two lobsters and a few dozen clams and mussels. You will also have to deal with the various allergies and antagonisms that arise in any large gathering, in which case it's wise to set aside some unadulterated rice for the festively uncompromising.

Vegetable garnishes are overdone at traditional Christmases, taking up space better used for dessert. A paella dinner, in any case, requires nothing more than a green salad afterward. Stews tend to be weighty enough to need little more than a nearby starch—rice, creamed potatoes, very simple pasta with just oil, cheese, parsley—and a simple, earthy vegetable, perhaps roast fennel, whole cooked lentils, sautéed Chinese greens or a purée of celery root.

Let guests bring desserts in the best Christmas tradition, hoping even at this late stage in the history of civilization that someone in the crowd has a talent for baking (shortbreads, amaretti, peanut butter cookies) and that others will contribute something expensive (chocolate truffles, panforte, marrons glacés) and something exotic (try the fudgelike barfi from a good Indian sweet shop). Anyone who volunteers to make crème brûlée or petits pots au chocolat should be canonized immediately. The host should not have to do anything at this stage, but it never hurts to have rich ice cream and traditional fruitcake on hand.

Traditional, that word again. For those who after all this jogging of the culinary imagination still can't get the thought of turkey out of their minds, there is an alternative that has been saved to the last. No, not the bourbon and mustard glazes or the inspired stuffings of oysters or anise-scented sausages, but a revolutionary tactic employed by good Italian chefs. Instead of roasting the whole bird into oblivion, bone the two sides of the breast and cut them into fillets. Cook as you would veal escalopes—in a white-wine sauce, with marsala or, for that festive occasion, filetti di tacchino bolognese: turkey breasts fried with ham, cheese and white truffles. With luck you won't even taste the turkey.

Yet what is it I see staring balefully back at me whenever I open the refrigerator in search of something to eat in the post-Christmas season? A plate of cold turkey recently separated from the mammoth carcass that dominated Christmas dinner. We wimped out after all, but then we always do. You can have your dreams to sustain you through the rest of the year, but cruel reality still wins out. And now the indolence of Christmas has turned into the paralyzing passivity of the week after Christmas. Ghastly chocolate-bar-flavoured milk drinks force their way to the front of the rack, pushing aside the cartons of orange juice and cider that have probably gone off. Lettuce lies withering in the crisper, the cream cheese is taking on the appearance of a holy relic and the cats' water looks like you could walk on it.

It's a time of year when not much cooking of consequence gets done, unless you count thawing out the frozen shrimp ring for the New Year's Day levee or trying out the old family recipes for curried turkey and bread pudding made from chestnut stuffing. In our house, normally the scene of frantic sabayon-whipping and frenzied spinach-wilting, the biggest culinary accomplishment in the ennui-rich post-Christmas period would be the decorating of a gingerbread house (made from modular parts precision-milled at a gingerbread plant in Sweden, where they still know a thing or two about traditional holiday observance).

The fact that this rare cooking-like activity doesn't get accomplished until December 27 probably counts against us — always assuming you don't accept the argument that we're on the early side for Ukrainian Christmas. On the other hand, we were able, post-holiday, to utilize gifts of marzipan fruits and vegetables that made a stunning gingerbread-house kitchen garden, with monster pumpkins and mutant oranges rising dramatically out of the snow-white icing-sugar ground.

To eat well in this lethargic time means depending on others, the Chinese barbecue house that roasts its ducks every day of the year, the Belgian pâtisserie that has the pain au chocolat ready at eight-thirty on a cold and quiet Sunday morning, the Italian deli that offers all the makings of a wonderful meal at a moment's notice. I went to the deli after a few too many days of cold turkey trying to think of something that would instantly lift our meals out of the holiday doldrums. As strongly as I believe in the virtues of winter food — see above — there are times in the long grey season when one gets tired of feeling virtuous. In the tradition-bound holiday period, as the lumpiest and least imaginative forms of seasonal fare force themselves on the table unbidden, those times tend to be mealtimes.

The best antidote I could think of for making an instant transformation from the world of mashed turnips and fruitcake paperweights was prosciutto, partly because it still retains the image of a luxury food, which can elevate a spirit laid low by the diminishing returns of leftovers, but mostly because of its subtle and lingering taste. Prosciutto is unsmoked ham, and much as I like the smell and flavour of smoke its strength is its one weakness: smoke overwhelms everything else around. In the late stages of the holiday season, being overwhelmed is not on the top of anyone's must-do list.

Salt-cured, seasoned and air-dried, good prosciutto has a more nuanced flavour than your average smoked ham. Sliced very thin and eaten very slowly, it offers up a sweet, nutty taste that lingers in the mouth for minutes after you've finished chewing —although the best prosciutto is so smooth and succulent that you barely need to move your jaws. It just melts gently away in the mouth. Some people, blessed with a vivid imagination or just prodded into hallucinating by the dreary post-Christmas menus, insist they can taste the acorns and peaches that the fattening prosciutto pigs have munched on over the course of their well-nourished lives.

I'm already thinking these happy thoughts when I place my order—memo to self: stop drooling—and as the young woman behind the counter pulls out an entire ham and begins the painstaking process of delivering to me my 250 grams, I let my dinner-menu mind wander even more aimlessly, admiring the fresh bocconcini cheeses floating in water, sizing up the solid low-rise ciabatta loaves of bread, calculating whether there's room in the cupboard for another atmospheric tin of salted Sicilian anchovies. In a ritualized series of tasks that elevate food into something beyond a quick-fix meal, the keeper of the prosciutto cuts away at the skin, trims off some off the fat—but not too much—sets the slicer to a thinness prized by the most difficult customers and slices very carefully, making sure to shear off the prosciutto in perfect even lengths. These she lays out in an overlapping pattern on the thick transparent butcher wrap that is so neatly and symmetrically arranged it provides its own small pleasure. On a good day. We'll conveniently forget the bad holiday dinners when the untrained counter girl called into work because of a Christmas staff shortage butchered the poor prosciutto and left us to celebrate the season with ripped rags of unskinned meat.

I could go to the supermarket and buy my precision-cut prosciutto in a hygienic vacuum-wrapped pack. But then again, if I'd wanted convenience, I could have stayed home and stared back at the turkey for another day.

Eventually the holiday inertia will wear off and you'll be drawn back to the chopping board and the stove. In summer, it would be enough to throw some sautéed vegetables and olive oil into a bowl of steaming spaghetti and call it dinner. But in the sterile grey months of the dead season, you'll need to counter the effects of the cold with something more creative.

There are many ways to create a good recipe, if your artistic tendencies are so inclined. Plagiarism is the most common— most of the recipes we claim as our own started off as someone else's, and someone else's again before that. But some few, rare people are true originals: they pick up inspiration on their travels or study old cookbooks for new ideas, seize on the possibilities offered by seed catalogues or haunt the weird-and-interesting section of ethnic groceries, pondering how tamarind would go best with lamb or fresh dates with chicken.

The end of winter is the best time to pursue these researches, not just because the kitchen has finally had its fill of all those variations on barley soup, but because Easter is imminent. As a feast of rebirth, drawing on the pagan celebration of spring and building upon the jubilation of Passover, Easter should be synonymous with good eating and productive of appetizing recipes. But somehow, in the mainstream of North American food culture anyway, the religious feast has never quite managed to turn into a real feast. So low have we sunk that the food most closely identified with Easter in my part of the world is a chocolate egg produced by a bunny that clucks like a chicken.

Religious differences stand in the way, of course. Non-Christians don't rush to embrace meals with a symbolic tie to the resurrection of Christ, and those Christians whose Easter traditions are confined to overcooked New Zealand lamb and vinegary mint sauce won't be in any hurry to proselytize. And yet as any adventurous eater knows—I'm thinking of my Indian-sweet rampages, which bear only a very slight resemblance to the Hindu veneration of the elephant god Ganesh—the most stimulating foods often start with traditions far from our own. With two thousand years of Easter culinary tradition to draw on, very little of which is connected with overdone lamb and bottled sauce, I think we can do better.

But where to start? Well, I see no harm in reaching back beyond Christianity, drawing on some of the pagan symbols of rebirth, such as the egg. Stracciatelle, egg-drop soup, would be simple and pure. For less simple and reverential tastes, the definition of egg can be expanded to include caviar on lacy pancakes and salmon roe sushi. But anyone seeking inspiration will want to start by studying the Greeks, who take Easter very seriously. They do some amazing things with the innards of the lamb that they will spit-roast on Easter Sunday, not the least of which is a midnight soup called mayiritsa made with liver, heart, spleen, stomach, intestines and lots of herbs to cover up the flavour. For those not coming off forty days of Lenten fasting, a less daunting version may be a quick sauté of lamb's kidneys with a revivifying measure of garlic, fresh fennel or dill and Greek rigani.

For the main course, there's always pasta—Lord, how there's always pasta—symbolizing the early Christian attempts to get a quick light Northern Italian dish in a Rome still dominated by the heavy old-fashioned Southern specialties. I don't think I've ever come across lamb pasta, but what's stopping us in this creative season? Chunks of lamb sausage or shavings of smoked lamb would be more in keeping with tradition, or maybe a bolognese sauce made with minced lamb instead of beef (and sheep's-milk Pecorino Romano instead of Parmesan). But I would rather stick to received wisdom and dine off a garlicky leg of lamb pan-roasted in the old Umbrian style with sprigs of rosemary and white wine.

But wait, cries the creative cook with the culinary genius' sense of perfect timing: isn't the sap rising up through the arteries of the maple trees at this time of year, bringing a sense of renewal to sweet-toothed people everywhere? Isn't maple syrup a necessary part of the seasonal menu?

Well, yes it is, and it may now seem surprising that the early Christians who put roast lamb on the first Easter menus omitted the pancake breakfast. Still, omit it they did, and now it's up to us to update Easter by putting a cold-climate contribution to seasonal food back on the festive menu. But how? Certainly there's no good way to work maple syrup into the main course, despite the efforts of all those Culinary Olympians who try desperately to invent a full-fledged local cuisine by sautéeing salmon steaks in maple liqueur. The only main-course maple-syrup traditions I can see drawing on are with baked beans (not very exciting as a welcome-to-spring dish) and as a glaze for baked ham, which I seem to remember my grandmother serving at Easter dinner with miniature-marshmallow squash and mashed potatoes (except that she usually replaced the maple syrup with brown sugar for economy's sake).

No, if we're going to work in maple syrup, better to use it in a dessert. It's a part of the Easter menu where we have to start afresh anyway, since there's a marked shortage of traditional Easter sweets that aren't heavy breads or cakes decorated with whole eggs dyed to represent the blood of Christ. (Sometimes religion does assert itself a little too forcefully into the meal.) I'd like to recommend maple sugar fashioned in the shapes of triumphant lambs, but the market not providing, my second choice is maple crème brûlée. You could serve it scooped into the leftover shells of the eggs it's made from if you were determined to capture the spirit of the season. A certain leap of faith may be required.

It's easy enough to recognize Easter season in time to get out the old recipes or figure out some new and improved ones. That's what calendars and statutory holidays are for. But knowing when the new crop of fresh maple syrup is coming due so that you can make feast-worthy maple crème brûlée—now that requires the seasonal cook to be more cunning.

The old farmers used to say that you'd know it was maple syrup time when the first crow took flight. Being a city boy and more accustomed to seagulls hovering over the landfill site year-round, I've had to come up with a more useful measurement. I call it the discomfort index.

You know that time of year when the sun comes out and the snow, should you be privileged enough to have it, melts away and you truly believe that spring has arrived? You throw open the windows and turn down the thermostat and strip the winter blankets off the bed before falling asleep. And then you freeze all night because the temperature has dropped. So you wise up and pull your long underwear back out of the cedar chest and dress for winter's last icy gasp. Only the sun comes out and the temperature shoots up and you collapse from heat exhaustion on the way to lunch.

Toes frozen at night? Deodorant ineffective by day? Feeling out of sorts with the wacky ways of Mother Earth? The discomfort index is sending a message: it's maple syrup time. When the weather seems impossible, the sap starts running. You may be lucky enough to live in a place where the March-April weather isn't so indecisive, where the warm days that announce it's spring don't suddenly turn around and become the cold nights of winter.

But in that case you're unlucky enough to live in a forlorn place where they can't make something as glorious as maple syrup.

Cold nights and warm days are what you need if you're going to get the sap to start flowing from your sugar maple. But once the thin, sugary juice is collected and boiled down into rich, concentrated, unmatchable syrup, does anyone in the wider and more temperate world really care? Somehow we have managed to produce one of the world's greatest seasonal delicacies without winning the acclaim such greatness deserves.

Oh, sure, you can go to Harrods in London or Fauchon in Paris and pay top dollar for concentrated tree juice from Quebec or Vermont. But they'll also charge you big bucks—excessive Euros, I mean—for imported Skippy peanut butter, and that doesn't mean they think it's right up there with caviar as a food for the gods. Rare and unusual our maple syrup may be to the cultivated European taste but it's not sufficiently exotic—like mangos, say, or candied ginger—to be allowed into the gourmet club. It's from the North American mainstream, after all, where we so esteem maple syrup that we drizzle it on our doughy pancakes and pour it into the pot of pork and beans if we're feeling flush. It's like ladling your best Château d'Yquem into the Jell-O mix. How can anyone respect a food like that?

If I asked for a show of hands—How many of you have had maple syrup recently?—I think the only reaction would come from parents who felt compelled to finish off the kids' leftover pancakes because they know the cost of what's going to waste. So let me say that there are better ways to sample maple syrup than the old traditional. If you can make a good thin buckwheat pancake, then by all means pour on the syrup. The sour, wild taste of buckwheat mixes nicely with the woody aromatics of the sugar maple. But spare me the bland pancake mixes or the frozen waffles that are largely responsible for the innocent maple's decline and mutation into grotesque artificial syrups.

The best way for a cook to get a sense of maple syrup's potential in the kitchen is to taste it on its own. Go to a farmer's market somewhere in maple country—I'm sorry, Texas, that sorghum syrup just isn't the same—and buy a few bottles of different colours, light, amber and dark. One by one, pour out a spoonful of each and sip it like wine. I'd be surprised if you didn't think the rich, dark stuff was far and away the best and certainly the most complex—like stone-ground whole-wheat loaf beside the light syrup's sliced white, or an inky old-vine Zinfandel matched against a neutral house wine. But the syrup industry is still caught up in old-fashioned ideas of refinement and gentility, and downgrades the opaque dark syrup.

Now what to do with this precious liquid? I'll confess up front to drinking it on its own when no one's looking, as if it were a dessert wine (though one better savoured by the spoonful than by the glass). But because it's so sweet (98 per cent sucrose) and lacks the kind of acidity that makes the best sweet wines so bracing, straight-up syrup doesn't work for very long. So then I dilute it, knowing the powerful flavour will win out in any combination. Maple syrup on buttered whole-wheat toast is delicious, as is the creamy maple butter that some dealers produce. Fried bananas with rum aren't complete until you add a shot of maple. A bowl of milk is a dull thing, fit only for complacent cats, but trickle in some syrup and it becomes the lightest of nursery desserts—don't completely stir up the syrup but allow the thick swirls of maple a little unhomogenized independence.

The best way to make maple-walnut ice cream is to pour maple syrup on chopped walnuts over vanilla ice cream. A superior crème brûlée, as I've suggested, comes flavoured with maple. Before the repetition becomes unbearable, I should mention maple mousse, maple syrup cookies, maple-and-cider-vinegar dressing for salads made with crisped bacon (compare raspberry vinegar), real maple fudge, maple-and-butter sauce on a baked cake of coarse cornmeal—johnnycake, if you want to be traditional—and mapled pear pie in a ground-almond crust. But not mapled wieners and beans—enthusiasm can go too far.

The nicest treat of all, the perfect accompaniment to your cappuccino at the end of the evening meal, are those maple-sugar maple leaves forever associated with tourist traps in the maple regions. Buy some all the same—they're cheaper, though never cheap, at farmers' markets—but don't chew them up like common candy: just put one on your tongue and let it melt forever.

The warmth, almost miraculously, has returned. Birds sing, air conditioners hum, and it becomes easier to believe that somewhere the earth is sending forth fruit and vegetables that will soon find their way to our table.

Spring, as in primavera, as in pasta primavera, barely exists in my part of the world. The Italian spring (as well as the French and Californian and almost anywhere else currently influencing our cooking) is my summer. While fiddleheads and morels and the first tender dandelion greens may get to the local markets well before Midsummer's Night, I don't see the classic spring vegetables of pasta fame—peas, carrots, peppers—until late June or July. You'd almost think the good earth has the good sense to wait until the winter game of hockey has concluded, which now doesn't happen until a week before the summer solstice.

We're late bloomers in these parts. When peas are ready for market in southern Italy, we're still huddled around the maple tree in our long johns wondering when the sap is going to start running. That's not an image you see in Botticelli's *Primavera*, nor is there slush pooling around the feet of Ms. Primavera or road-salt despoiling the pastoral landscape. When the English—in England, please note, not some semi-tropical Mediterranean piece of paradise—start chopping spring onions into their salads, we're still counting the months until we can finally dare to plant our green onions (same as the English spring onion, with one obvious difference) in the frost-free garden.

Greenhouse owners will challenge me and say that they've turned the whole year into one eternal primavera (though again not quite like the version that draws crowds to the Botticelli corner of the Uffizi museum). I'm sure greenhouses are a blessing in these northern latitudes, particularly if The Big One sinks California beneath the waves and we have to become self-sufficient in pasta ingredients. If we were willing to bring baseball indoors, why not our vegetables? But all we really need to do is be patient and endure a little longer, on the principle that all good things come to those who wait, and they taste even better when your expectations are postponed. For if spring in these parts is just a malicious afterthought to winter, summer is glorious.

That's an eater's perspective, of course, to praise a time when the things we want to eat can actually grow. Other seasons are just passages through the year, artificial constructs that try to fool us into believing autumn lasts until late December or spaghetti primavera can make its debut on March 21. But when summer appears, we turn all credulous and play along, desperate for a season that will finally live up to expectations.

I know there are city people who find it all too oppressive, the sweltering heat, the inevitable confrontations as the housebound move outdoors, the tour-bus exhaust fumes choking sippers of warm wine as they try to recreate a Mediterranean experience at sidewalk cafés. Through all these agonies (why did we long for summer?) it's worth remembering that the strawberries will start to taste sweet again, the red peppers will be cheap and abundant, the fragrance of the melons will fill a room, and the lettuce will come with dirt and bugs—and flavour.

I've often wondered—the eater's perspective again—how people can bear to leave all this behind and fly away on exotic summer vacations. Go to Greece in April, when its tomatoes have plenty of taste and ours don't. But don't go in the summer when you can make just as good a Greek salad here, not to mention mashed eggplant with garlic or stuffed red pepper, while having to march through far fewer sun-dried Mycenaean sites.

Even more incredible to me are the people who flee at the first sign of ripe vegetables and head north for canoe trips and freeze-dried dinners reconstituted over an open flame. It's as if they were trying to evade the summer harvest because it was in conflict with some fundamental law of cold-climate austerity. Still, anyone who can find happiness eating dehydrated carrots in July deserves to be somewhere else.

It makes sense for people who suffer the extremes of cold to idealize summer. But this pursuit of the summery ideal in the hopeful kitchen has a dangerous side as well. Just let the sun shine for a few days, the drab lawns turn green, the cafés put out their sidewalk tables, and otherwise rational cooks are transformed into lifestyle-magazine addicts who can't wait to fit the seasonal stereotype. The moment they spot a cover story on Sorbets That Sizzle or Warm Salad Days (and Nights), they lose all sense of proportion. Intoxicated by the mere suggestion of heat, they make the kinds of errors in judgment that would never happen on a brisk, alert autumn day. The Tex-Mex recipe published mid-June calls for corn, and just because the local crops don't come in for two months is no excuse for postponing immediate gratification. Tired old imported ears or frozen kernels are substituted so an illusion can be achieved. With luck, the table napkins have an authentic Hopi design to turn conversation away from the food.

Jumping the gun on summer ingredients is one of the first mistakes made by the sunstruck. In a marketplace where so many fruits and vegetables are imported for so much of the year, that may not seem the worst sin, but it goes against the very values that summer-worshippers claim to be promoting. Local produce isn't always riper, fresher and more nutritious, but it should be. And it's worth waiting for: when abundant, it's also cheap, spurring the cook to buy bushel baskets instead of plastic pints and then come up with inspired recipes for disposing of the overflow.

Here's where we misjudge the seasons yet again. Those recipes need a thoughtful few minutes indoors around the bookshelf to pass on their inspiration. But they don't stand much of a chance in a household that likes to summer on the terrace and sacrifice burnt offerings on the barbecue. When barbecue-selling season is in full swing, the lifestyle magazines are once again filled with close-up shots of sweating vegetables and scorched hunks of meat to please the advertisers. Resistance is useless and escape impossible. It's only June, but the smells of blackened flesh and vegetables pervade the June air, mingling with the chemical scent of lighter fluid and the anguished shouts of parents warning children — too late — to get away from the open flame.

Burning food in the backyard is a time-honoured summer ritual that will not go away because of a few cranky complaints and carcinogenic scares. I have to admit to enjoying the results when the marinated mushroom caps or chicken kebabs are seared without being charred and turn out juicy and succulent. But the obvious tastes of barbecue food — smoke, burnt flesh, salty seasonings, hot and sugary sauces — weary the palate just as the distractions of outdoor eating take away from the subtlety of flavouring.

Barbecuing really isn't about eating good food, but about celebrating life outside the walls and beyond the boundaries that cold weather imposes. If I think of summer cooking I've enjoyed, barbecues rarely come to mind, but the outdoors almost always does: picnicking off farmhouse cheeses in a Loire Valley meadow, say, or standing on the edge of an English village green, watching a cricket match with fish and chips in one hand and a pint of

Fuller's bitter in the other. The setting is incomparable, the mood relaxed and the food simple and unhurried. People who are infatuated with their barbecues always seem to be worrying about time.

If you're cooking for friends in the summertime, and can't afford to hire the Concorde for a quick hop to the European outdoors, you probably have to prepare something slightly more complex. Complex, however, shouldn't mean long hours in front of the hot stove—that's for winter—unless you can put in the hard labour well in advance, the day before for terrines, soups and stewed apricots or pears; the morning of for quiches, marinades and roasts to be served warm but not hot. But even the most catty and spiteful of friends will forgive you if on a hot summer day you follow the hallowed *faites-simple* dictum: clams cooked in white wine, boiled lobster salad with just enough mayonnaise, new potatoes with chives, sautéed chicken on tart mixed greens, a salad of raw mushrooms soaked in olive oil, peanut noodles with sautéed shrimp, and—if you can hold out till July, when the raspberries and redcurrants come in, and summer really gets going—a tart summer pudding.

It's a peaceful and rewarding season. But the very abundance of produce after so many lean months also makes it risky. You may not realize it, as you sit seraphically in your lawn chair listening to the cicada's buzz and waiting for the ice cubes to harden, but this is a dangerous time. Danger No. 1: with summer temperatures at their peak, all kinds of ripe fruits are thronging the market at prices that tempt shoppers to buy in bulk. Danger No. 2: with summer temperatures at their peak, all kinds of people who can't stand the heat are getting out of the kitchen. Combine No. 1 with No. 2 and the result is disastrous.

Perched on their lawn chairs well away from the flames of the barbecue, they turn the ever-engaging pages of *Vanity Fair*— Is Cameron Diaz really the next Katharine Hepburn?—and congratulate themselves for avoiding the oven. There will be no roast chicken to add its 375°F to this hellish summer, no baked Gruyère on toast with fresh tomato and garlic sauce.

Everyone will stay cool. But as the pages turn and the issues of the day get their airing under the relentless August sun — Is Brad Pitt ready to play *Lear*? Aren't the Bush boys presidential? How could we have ignored Kate Moss's cries for help? — another question, even more pressing, intrudes: What will we do for dinner? And then the inquiring mind takes a turn that is fraught with more hazards than the career path of Cameron Diaz: How about making a meal out of all that fruit?

The idea of cooking with fruit — if it can be called cooking, if indeed it can be called an idea — becomes the rage every summer. This madness has turned into an annual event for several good reasons:

- The moment when fruit is at its best is also the time when there's the most of it and prices have dropped. A glut of perishables like cherries and plums produces a desire to use them up fast.

- Marketing boards, government bureaus, public-relations agencies and food columnists at a loss for something to write about seize on the idea and drive it home. With recipes for pickerel in blueberry foam and watermelon-yogurt soup showing up wherever you turn — well maybe not in *Vanity Fair*, not yet — one starts to get that inescapable North American urge to go with the flow.

- Promoters of healthy, low-fat food see fruit as the ideal propaganda tool. While not everyone, even in this enlightened age, can honestly admit to a love of green vegetables, sweet, non-threatening fruit has immediate appeal.

Fruit is a good thing and we should all eat more of it. But that doesn't mean that we should be making appetizers and main courses out of it, especially along the lines recommended by this era's experts. The traditional ways to include fruit in cooking are nothing like what's being proposed these days. Modern recipes make use of soft, ripe produce—cream of mango soup, say, from *The Silver Palate Cookbook*—but older recipes prized fruit for its sharp acidity. There was once much greater use made of unripe or sour fruit to cut the fat in a dish or simply add a welcome note of tartness.

You can still get a sense of this kind of cooking in the cuisines of ancient cultures that haven't yet been conquered by lifestyle magazines. Thai cooks, for example, like to make a salad from peeled, thinly sliced green-skinned mango and fried ground pork, though much of the flavouring, it must be admitted, comes from the surrounding garlic, green onion, shrimp powder, fish sauce, peanut butter, brown sugar, black pepper, chili flakes and lime (another aromatic fruit long admired for its beguiling tartness). A few mushy cherries wouldn't stand a chance in such company. But then cooking with sweet cherries was almost unthinkable until recently. For centuries, cooks rightly preferred sour varieties of cherries to balance the fat of roast duck. Now at a time when every health-centred cookbook trumpets the virtues of fruit, producers of sour cherries have trouble finding buyers. Tart cooking apples—substitutes for green mango in Thai recipes—are in much the same position. Trees will be torn up and replaced, leaving the few people who remember how to cook with fruit at a loss. Tart up your red cabbage with mushy Golden Delicious and you're making a mockery of the recipe.

It's not all bad. We now have fruit vinegars to give us tartness and fruit spirits to supply concentrated aromas. Certain fruits— fresh pineapple being the most obvious—can play a useful role in modern salads while retaining some of the attention-getting sourness. But at the risk of going back to the stove in a sultry season, it's worth rediscovering some of the older ways with fruit: mackerel with gooseberries, smoked sausage sautéed with apples, pork stewed with tough old prunes and the fermented grape drink from Vouvray.

The warmth of summer is a glorious thing. And then it's not. In kitchens filled with steaming dishwashers, heaving refrigerators, overheated track lighting and bodies on the boil, even central air can't cope. So why do we make the home fires even more hellish in summer's inferno by continuing to cook for a more temperate climate? Habit mostly. The seasons and the supermarkets now impose few of their old limitations on the food we can eat. If you like roasted red peppers in January, you're going to like them in July. Only when you're cranking up the oven to sear the pepper skins do you begin to think of the numbing consequences.

And even though you appreciate Vivaldi enough to remember that languid summer invariably follows life-giving spring, you can't always scale down your culinary energies from allegro to andante. Suppose you're entertaining friends and, being a thoughtful host, you issued the invitations several weeks before, back on a rainy Wimbledonish June day when gathering round the blazing hearth seemed like a friendly and humane thing to do. But now the humidex is excessive, the mercury's mercurial and the slow-cooked cassoulet de Toulouse looks like a lousy idea. What do you do?

Make sandwiches? Nibble carrot sticks? Order pizza? Hardly. Guests who are passing up a day at the ballpark or a night with *Armageddon III* deserve better and, according to the traditional rules governing hospitality, must be able to see that considerable energy has been expended on them.

There's always the barbecue, of course. When the summer sun enters the torrid zone, even anti-BBQ crusaders recognize its power to draw the heat from the kitchen. But just because it's a machine that causes grown men to apply sauces with a paintbrush doesn't mean it can't do with a bit of subtlety: shrimps charred in the shell, peeled and dipped in a cayenne mayonnaise, thin slices of eggplant desiccated on the grill and then dressed with olive oil and mint, chunks of chicken marinated in yogurt and Indian tikka paste, barbecued on skewers and served on pilaf rice or couscous. And don't forget the cucumber-and-yogurt salad, raita, that should accompany the chicken. The aggressive flavours of barbecued food need a tart, cooling contrast on a hot summer's day.

As much as we pretend to be immune to the seasons in our controlled climate, they still get to us. No one wants casseroled pork hocks or a glass of vintage port in scorching weather, even if the air conditioner simulates spring. That's why the ideal hot-weather menu, even better from the diner's point of view than chancing it at the barbecue, is a selection of antipasti, better served at lunch when you can get away with seeming casual. Because they're served cold—though cold is a misnomer since they're best offered at a range of temperatures—antipasti can be prepared in advance, sparing the guests, if not the poor cook, the sweat-shop ambience.

Antipasto is the greatest culinary understatement of all. It translates from the Italian as "before the meal," which is a little like saying that Leonardo da Vinci drew pictures. The possibilities for an antipasto feast—or tapas or hors d'oeuvres or meze, depending on your particular Mediterranean inspiration—are almost endless. A small selection on a summer's day could include steamed cauliflower dressed while still warm with a green sauce of olive oil, lemon juice, parsley and finely chopped anchovy, served tepid with capers on top; those inescapable roasted red peppers; a salad of tomatoes and fresh bocconcini cheese; bean or lentil salad with olive oil and chopped sweet onions; caponata, a ratatouille-like stew of eggplant, celery, onions, tomatoes and olives, served tepid; marinated salmon; pork tonnato, made by covering slices of plainly roasted pork (or veal in the deluxe version) with a sauce of puréed canned tuna and mayo; shrimp and squid, soaked in more olive oil and lemon juice if you can stand it; the aforementioned barbecued eggplant; salami, spiced olives, thinly sliced prosciutto to bring back those memories of the Christmas season and crusty bread. But no butter. Use the bread to mop up the juices left on your plate. And make sure that your red wines are chilled—none of this room-temperature nonsense.

What other foods keep the heat at bay? Cold soups are tricky. The best are the old favourites—gazpacho, vichyssoise, borscht—and the worst are the fruit soups that taste like sugared water and are prone to ferment at room temperature. Middle Eastern dips such as baba ghannoush and hummus (relax, use the canned chickpeas) go well with warmed pita or raw vegetables. Smoked fish pâté (trout or mackerel) needs nothing more than toast, as does the earthy black olive spread called tapénade. And here's that chance you've been waiting for to work fruit into the menu: chicken salad—granted, you have to cook the chicken at some point, or cheat and buy from a Portuguese churrasqueira—can outdo any hot dish when made with fresh pineapple as well as celery, walnuts and mayonnaise.

And for dessert? Forget that the word chocoholic was ever invented and revert to fruit salad, which will be taken more seriously if you add a splash of sherry vinegar to the simmering syrup or a dash of eau-de-vie to the end product. Ice cream is nice, even if it's long since lost its seasonal properties, but for the most summery cooler find your way to the closest Italian bar dispensing lemon or coffee granita—an adult version of a Slurpee.

Smoked Mackerel Pâté

This is the simplest of dips, something to put out at a stand-up gathering or use as part of a spreads-on-toast crostini appetizer alongside tapénade, artichoke paste, puréed eggplant, creamed beans and so on. Smoked mackerel is usually cheaper than smoked trout, though it can get pricier if you start buying some of the packaged spiced-mackerel gourmet versions. The fish's higher fat content makes it a good candidate for smoking, but it can get mushy a little too easily. Look for drier versions if you like a pâté with more texture.

Separate the meat from four smoked mackerel fillets or two whole fish, keeping an eye out for tiny bones. Blend with about ½ pound unsalted butter and the juice from 1 lemon. Add a vigorous amount of fresh pepper. Serve on baguette toasts or fresh crusty brown bread. (Do not feed leftovers to cats.)

Chestnut Soup

Vegetable stocks come in handy when you have to feed vegetarians, but otherwise I don't think they produce very interesting soups (and even worse risotto, for that matter) — they're either too thin or, when they're concentrated, taste too much of the vegetables they're made from. But here's an exception, a hearty winter potage based on Elizabeth David's recipe in *French Provincial Cooking*.

You'll need 3 pounds of chestnuts in good condition (firm and tight to their skins, not soft or moldy), 4 carrots, 4 leeks, 1 large head of celery or 2 small ones, 2 onions, a handful of parsley, 3 ounces of butter and 1 cup of milk. To skin the chestnuts, score an x through the surface of the rounded side of the nuts, place on a baking sheet and heat in a 325°F oven for 15 to 20 minutes. Remove and shell while warm, making ample use of kitchen helpers to save your fingers and get the job done before the nuts cool. Squeeze each chestnut between your fingers so the shell cracks; use a sharp knife to pry off the sticky bits that cling to the surprisingly intricate folds of the chestnut's flesh. Set the nuts aside. Clean, slice and gently sauté the vegetables in butter. When they soften, add 5 cups of cold water, season with salt, cover the pan and simmer for 1 hour or more. Pour off half the liquid (but save it for later) and stew the shelled, skinned chestnuts in the remainder until they are soft. Purée, then thin to taste with the reserved strained broth. To serve, heat up the soup with a cup of warm whole milk and check the seasoning.

Umbrian Roast Lamb

Fresh young Easter lamb is always tender but sometimes a little too mild in taste for the price you're asked to pay. This recipe from Le Tre Vaselle restaurant in Torgiano, Umbria, just down the road from Assisi, makes sure there's no shortage of flavour in the religious feast. Marinate a small leg or rack of fresh lamb for a few hours, then make some incisions in the top side and spread on a paste made from 5 garlic cloves, 6 or 7 rosemary sprigs and 2 tablespoons of lard (no nouvelle cuisine here). Blend together in a roasting pan 1 cup of meat stock, 3 tablespoons of olive oil, 1 chopped lemon and 1 cup of white wine, then add the lamb, cooking it for an hour in a 300°F oven, basting often.

This dish is part of an Easter menu in the Tre Vaselle cookbook *Il Piacere della Tavola* that also includes Pecorino and Gruyère cheese bread with dry-cured capicollo ham, chicken soup with tagliolini egg noodles, a salad of radicchio and wild greens, and vino santo ("holy wine") ice cream.

Brown Sugar Shortbreads

This recipe comes from Mary Macleod, who, when the world went mad a few years ago and fell for oversized cookies with dumb messages written on them, opened a shop dedicated to shortbreads and restored a measure of old-fashioned sanity.

Preheat the oven to 300°F. In a mixing bowl, combine 2½ cups of sifted cake and pastry flour and ⅔ cup of dark brown sugar. Using knives or a pastry blender, cut in ¾ cup of butter until the mixture resembles coarse crumbs. Melt ¼ cup butter and work into the flour mixture.

Transfer to an unfloured board and knead for 2 to 3 minutes until a soft dough is formed. Cut the dough into two sections and shape each into a circle 7 inches in diameter. Place these on a baking sheet and bake until lightly browned. Sprinkle with fine white granulated sugar and a pinch of cinnamon.

Bananas with Rum and Maple Syrup

I cook this as a Sunday breakfast treat when the gathering cloud of fruit flies tells me that the bananas need to be used up right away. It's probably better made when the bananas are less mushy, but of course at that point you don't feel any compulsion to annihilate the household supply—one of those cooking paradoxes that separates real life from the magazine version.

This is a rich dish, so figure about 1½ bananas a person. Cut the peeled bananas from top to bottom into thirds or quarters depending on their size. At this point I like to do something silly that comes from having lived with small children—skip this stage if you're more mature. Take one of the tapered, rounded banana ends and, with the sharp tip of a knife, carve out two little round eyes, a nose and a mouth, and make a few whisker slashes on either side. Voilà, a baby seal, which you can set on a white ice-floe plate for your child to admire while you get on with the work.

Take the banana chunks and slice them lengthwise in half, and then in half again. In a broad sauté pan, melt a good-sized chunk of butter (2–4 ounces depending on taste and courage), and when it starts to sizzle (but before it browns), add the bananas, pushing them around gently with a wooden spoon to make sure that they're all coated with the butter. After a minute at a low-medium heat, pour in a splash of rum and then stir in a couple of ounces of maple syrup—the dark variety is best. Cook for another minute. Some people like to add a little orange or lime juice at this point for a bit of tartness and extra flavour. I've stopped doing that because I find it makes the sauce too watery, and in my hurry to thicken it I often overcook the (already mushy) bananas. But of course you can always be more fastidious than I am and remove the bananas with a slotted spoon before thickening the sauce.

Just before serving, add a couple shakes of cinnamon, and cream if you like. I find it rich enough as is. I suppose you could also serve this dish as a dessert ice cream topping if you really wanted to go too far.

Your child, by the way, may feel separation anxieties when you try to remove the banana seal pup. This is a good opportunity to introduce the concept of anthropomorphism, if the word can be properly applied to sculpted fruit. It's probably not wise to discuss the merits of the Newfoundland seal hunt, though.

Caponata

Sicilian cooking is so provocative because it has managed to preserve ancient flavours and styles that have drifted out of fashion in more progressive and rootless food cultures. With caponata, it's the sweet-and-sour agrodolce touch that sets this stewed-vegetable antipasto dish apart.

Cut 2 pounds of eggplant into 1-inch squares. Trim the tough ends off 4 or 5 celery stalks, cut the stalks in half and lightly steam for a couple of minutes, then chop up into 1-inch-long pieces.

Heat a good amount of olive oil in a large pan, and soften the egg-plant, then add the celery, 1 large sliced onion, 1 large tablespoon of capers, 2 dozen serious olives (black or green), 1 tablespoon of sugar, 2 tablespoons of wine vinegar and ½ cup of puréed tomato. Stir, and cook for 15 minutes. Season with chopped parsley, salt and pepper, refrigerate for a day and serve at a cool room temperature. Caponata goes well with canned tuna if you want to chop some in before serving.

Raw Mushroom Salad

Raw mushrooms are ordinarily seen as bland vegetables waiting to be turned into something cooked. But this recipe shows the transforming powers of olive oil, lemon juice and garlic.

Take ½ pound of mushrooms, either the run-of-the-mill regulars or the fancier cremini or portobello. Clean them, pat them dry, slice them (trimming off any tough bits at the end of the stalks) and put them in a bowl. Dress with 4 to 6 ounces of olive oil, the juice of 1 large lemon, 1 very finely chopped clove of garlic and freshly ground pepper. Don't add salt at this point; it will just leach out juices from the mushrooms and make your dressing watery.

The mushrooms will absorb all the oil easily. Make sure that you mix them around so that all the cut surfaces can pick up the flavours of the dressing. Leave to sit at room temperature for an hour, and just before serving add plenty of finely chopped parsley and enough oil to make the mushrooms moist and juicy, as well as lemon and salt to taste. Chunks of smoked meat (especially chicken, duck, pheasant) can be added if you like.

Since the olive oil is your principal flavouring here, it's best to use an assertive extra-virgin variety—I like locally produced Greek oil when I can find it.

Summer Pudding

My memories of walking through the hedgerows of England always include (1) the welcoming sight of plump, brambly blackberries hanging from the vines and (2) a sudden jerk from behind as a baby in a backpack lurched to the side to get a free feed from the passing fruit. I've long since given up foraging for summer-pudding ingredients with a purple-mouthed child on my back and now feel like I'm recovering from the chronic effects of infant-induced whiplash. But creaky as I am, I still find great pleasure in the fresh outdoor taste of this very simple English sweet.

This dish can be made with raw fruit, which preserves the nutritive qualities of the berries, but it works better if you can bring yourself to cook the berries long enough to produce some juice. Take 1½ pounds of blackberries, raspberries and redcurrants (though raspberries by themselves will do if you pick your fruit from the less varied supermarket counter). Heat with ⅔ cup of sugar for a couple of minutes, and when the juice starts to run take off the stove and leave to cool. Cut 7 or 8 toast-sized slices from a loaf of day-old bread (white is the usual choice, but a nutty whole-wheat loaf gives extra flavour) and trim off the crusts. Neatly line a round, deep bowl with the bread on the bottom and sides, and make sure there are no holes for the fruit juice to seep through. Pour in the fruit, then cover with a layer of the sliced bread. Put a plate on top and weigh it down so that the pudding can take the shape of the bowl. Refrigerate overnight, then turn onto a serving dish. Summer pudding make a perfect ending to a warm-weather lunch, and is one of the few sweet dishes that go well with dessert wines.

Sesame

THE REALIZATION THAT the humble sesame seed had me in its grip came the moment I finished my cheese bagel.

Just to avoid confusion in these lawless times, I should make it very clear that this was a bagel filled with cheese, Roquefort if you must know. What it definitely wasn't was a bagel flavoured with melted cheese bits. Nor, for that matter, was it a bagel flaked with onion or powdered with garlic or baked with dried cranberry or made from life-affirming whole-wheat flour. This was not one of those fun-for-all franchised bagels that's desperately trying to steal market share away from tortillas, croissants and pita wraps. It was just a good old-fashioned Montreal-style bagel lightly coated with sesame seeds, which is another way of saying that it wasn't coated with poppy seeds, the only acceptable alternative.

Earlier that morning I'd spread out a layer of Saran Wrap—the product-placement fees are flowing in quite nicely, thank you—and sliced the bagel on the clear sheet before loading it down, desecrating it if you will, with cheese and lettuce. Every home-safety manual teaches that you must slice your bread on a cutting board, or risk hacking off your finger and inextricably mixing meat and dairy. But I've always walked on the wild side and sliced my packed-lunch bagel on its Saran wrapper.

The reason why becomes clear as soon as the bagel has been consumed at the office desk a few hours later. The haunting, nutty flavour of the toasted sesame seed is fading away, the oily, bittersweet taste has become a memory, it's time to get on with this mundane existence—tote that barge, lift that bale, punch those keys—and then, look, there's still something on the Saran Wrap: more seeds!

For some reason, old-fashioned, Montreal-style bagels are designed to shed their sesame seeds the moment you touch them. I like to think it's the baker's way of saying that life is so good and so rich we can afford to waste something as magnificent as sesame. We do not have to glean the leavings of our own meals. As best as I can recall from the Old Testament—unless it was from the Eddie Fisher song that finally drove Liz Taylor into the gin-soaked embrace of Richard Burton—the land of milk and honey featured heaven-sent sesame as its principal flavouring.

Ignoring the message that luxuries can be squandered, violating pretty well every law of Emily Post, dousing the ardour of any well-bred heiress who might enter the room and disqualifying myself from any future diplomatic posting at the Court of St. James's, I hoovered up the sesame. If I didn't actually lick the Saran Wrap, I came awfully close, moistening my index finger to get the right grip, then fastening onto the pesky little white ovals until none remained.

I tell you this not to shame myself, or not just to shame myself, but to acknowledge the power of one tiny little seed. The tiny sesame is an ingredient that receives little attention in the look-at-me culture of modern dining. That's fine for those of us who don't want to see one of our passions reduced to a trend, but sad for those who don't know what they're missing and have to settle for tofu mousse or tomato water.

Thinking back to those rare moments when the sesame in some form has found its way into self-conscious menus, I can only come up with the occasional Asian influence: flecks of black sesame seeds in white rice, cooked vegetable salads flavoured Japanese-style with toasted seeds, or cold noodles infused with the penetrating nutty scent of sesame oil. You can add to that, I suppose, the prominence of hummus at an earthier level of modern cooking. But it always seems to be the chickpea, the majority partner in this pita-ready paste, that gets the credit, when the distinctive flavour actually comes from ground sesame. Try a spoonful of sesame butter by itself if you don't believe me.

Hummus bi tahina, to give the dish its proper name, came to us from the Middle East, a vast region that has had almost no influence on the fashions of modern cooking. Our traditional North American view of sesame as a toasted topping on bagels and bread is obviously the result of several millennia of Jewish migrations, and fans of Sesame Snaps—those crunchy and sticky sesame-sugar wafers that are always positioned near the convenience-store cash register—will have noticed that they almost invariably come from Poland, which doesn't make much sense unless you think of them as a legacy of Jewish wandering.

Sesame is prominent in Middle Eastern cooking, especially as the basis of dips or salad dressings when ground and mixed with lemon, but also as a flavouring for baked fish or as the main ingredient of the wonderful chewy sweet called halvah. The seeds on their own don't seem to get used much except in the Middle Eastern equivalent of Sesame Snaps, a thicker bar of toasted sesame bound by honey or sugar (which can also be found, such is the way of the eastern Mediterranean, in Greek bakeries).

Farther east, in the cooking of China, Japan and Korea, the high-fat sesame seed is savoured as a flavouring oil—with an effect as powerful as that of hazelnut oil in regional French cooking—but is also turned into a crisp coating for sweet and savoury fritters, or used as a nutty element in the salads of cooked vegetables that turn up in Japanese bento boxes. But for those who are so taken with sesame that they track down every last seed shed by their bagels, the closest equivalent is to be found in Chinese bakeries: not the sesame-coated cookies or the sesame-topped pork pastries, but the gooey rice-flour dumpling stuffed with sweet bean or lotus nut paste, rolled in sesame seeds and deep-fried to a golden crust. Best of all, the seeds stay on.

Deep-Fried Rice Balls with Red-Bean Filling

This Chinese recipe requires you to have confidence in your deep-frying abilities. A simpler sesame soup follows for those who (like me) feel nervous around sputtering fat at a high temperature.

First make your filling. Cook 1⅓ pounds of dried Chinese red beans in 10 cups of water until the mixture is a thick paste. If you're feeling refined, you can strain out the skins afterward. Stir in 1 cup of lard or butter and 2 cups of sugar. (You can buy sweet bean paste in Chinese groceries if you want to cut this particular corner.)

Divide 1 cup of bean paste into 16 pieces. Mix into a smooth dough 2 cups of Chinese glutinous rice powder, 5 tablespoons of sugar and ⅔ cup of water. Lightly oil a countertop and knead 1 cup of your dough until smooth, then form into a long, even roll. Cut into 16 pieces. Flatten each piece into a 2-inch circle, then place a portion of bean paste in the middle and gather the edges of the dough to enclose the filling. Pinch to seal, then roll into a ball. Dip in water, then completely coat the exterior with white sesame seeds (you'll need about 1 cup). Deep-fry over medium heat for 5 minutes or until plump and golden. Remove, drain and serve.

Sesame Soup

Sweet, soothing soups are often served at the end of a Chinese feast or a greedy dim sum lunch.

Take 4 ounces of white or black sesame seeds and stir-fry them over a low heat without oil until they are fragrant and, in the case of the white seeds, golden-brown. Blend with 1 cup of water until smooth. Place this liquid in a pan with 5 cups of water, ¾ cup of sugar (rock sugar is the most authentic, available at Chinese groceries) and 1 tablespoon of soy sauce. Heat until the sugar has dissolved. Stir into a paste 3 tablespoons of cornstarch and 3 tablespoons of water. Use this to thicken the soup. Serve hot.

Both of these recipes come from the 1976 Taiwanese book *Chinese Snacks*, a splendid collection of authentic, out-of-the-way dishes filled with useful pictures and translated by the great exponent of Chinese cooking, Nina Simonds, back when she was just a young miss hidden away in the title page's small print.

BOOZE

NIGHT AFTER NIGHT I EAT FOOD, AND night after night, such is life, I drink wine. That this partnership has become habitual can't be denied. Do I knock back wine with every meal because (a) it helps me to forget whatever it was I was trying to forget; or (b) at this stage of existence, it passes for a cheap thrill; or (c) the marriage of wine and food stimulates conversation, engages the senses and enhances the pleasures of the table?

It becomes very tempting in the circumstances to choose (c), even if the circumstances rarely resemble the solemn bunfights of the International Wine and Food Society. "What's for dinner?" I ask the chief cook. And when she replies, "Chinese food," I open up the refrigerator and try to decide which of the three half-empty bottles will best substitute for conversation and numb our senses to the fullest.

The usual answer is all of them, and not just because it is hard to find the perfect pairing for sesame chicken and pork chow mein. On most nights of the working week, wine is a swiggable beverage first, a mood-enhancing drug second and a gastronomic partnership a fairly distant third. Quantity often takes precedence over quality for the simple reasons that there are times when it is nice to drink without concentrating too hard and the Rothschilds didn't make Château Lafite to go with takeout beef in black bean sauce.

It would have been nice if they had, maybe adding one of those friendly back labels that makes wine seem so accommodating: "This wine goes perfectly with red meat, game, poultry, pork, smoked and cured meat, vegetarian dishes, pasta, cheese and beer nuts. Oh yes, and with takeout Chinese food eaten on the floor in front of the Yankees–Blue Jays game while the children are upstairs cackling insidiously at the *Best of Beavis and Butthead* video." But unfortunately the Rothschilds, immured in their Beavis-free lifestyle, refuse to bend to the realities of modern life, and so we must make compromises in the way we pursue the pleasures of the table.

People talk about the marriage of wine and food as if the two were inextricably bound. But it seems to me that the grounds for divorce are there from the beginning. It's not that wine and food don't belong together or that each can't enhance the other. They can and do, if only on the principle — familiar from other married couples of our acquaintance — that when you begin to tire of one part of the partnership, you can always turn to the other.

But the problem in these semi-sophisticated times is that the life-improving qualities of good wine and good food can't be enjoyed simply for what they are. Like Bruce Willis and Demi Moore failing to make a go of it in a cruel and uncaring world, the ideal marriage of wine and food is too much at the mercy of human foibles. As the person in the house assigned the job of mating drinks with dinner — it keeps me out of the kitchen — I own several guidebooks that offer sage advice on the subject. That they go unread these days may have something to do with their complete impracticality — will the local booze outlet stock the five-year-old Fronsac required for lamproie à la bordelaise? Hold on, we're all out of lamprey—but a lot more to do with our just-in-time lifestyle.

When the ingredients for dinner, or indeed dinner itself, are picked up on the way home, it's hard to assume that the perfect match will be waiting in the wine cellar like a bride at the altar. Harder still when the wine cellar consists of three dusty bottles of aging port (one a rare Texas version) and a lot of power tools jammed into the empty racks that once, before the budget was diverted to Pampers and Air Jordans and Fender Stratocasters, held bottles that would grace a meal. Now when the chef finally consults with the wine steward, we check the fridge to see what's left over or dash round to the nearest liquor store. If we boldly drink red wine with fish at the end of the day, that's because it would have taken too long for a just-bought white to chill. Of such drab necessities are great partnerships born.

Living like this, if it can be called living, does not endear one to those who make fussy pronouncements on the need to flatter a '45 Latour with a saddle of lamb, roasted with a touch of garlic. There's something about wine that attracts know-it-all perfectionists, the kind of killjoys who love to make rules and inflict them on other people whatever reality says to the contrary. They insist that red wine must be served at room temperature or that white wines must never be drunk in Bordeaux glasses, and provided their orders bring obedience they don't care about the consequences.

But unhappy results come from letting wine's despots overrule common sense. Too many people, insecure about following their own judgments, give way to the bullies and wind up trying to enjoy Cabernets the temperature of tepid bathwater. Or they read the pompous bluster of some English expert on the mystical pairings of food and wine, a man whose taste buds were likely refined by years of private-school stodge, and suddenly become aware of the offence they gave last Saturday by daring to serve an Aussie Shiraz in the company of … tomatoes!

"Sauvignon Blanc is their only friend," intones Hugh Johnson with paralyzing fastidiousness in his *Pocket Encyclopedia of Wine*, an all-too-authoritative handbook for the easily swayed. Lording it over insecure imbibers with their pitifully insensitive palates, he tells them that caviar should be partnered with iced vodka ("Champagne, if you must, must be full-bodied"), that nothing grand may be served with swordfish, that quiche is "never a fine-wine dish," that the classic combination with dim sum is tea ("Oolong or BoLi") but "for fun," drink Sauvignon Blanc or Riesling with fried dumplings and Chianti or Bardolino with steamed.

Some fun. This is micromanaging of the palate, with a vengeance. Look at the pages of diktats in Johnson's *Encyclopedia*, where turbot demands Chassagne-Montrachet or mushrooms on toast match up with "your best claret," and you'll wonder how you ever managed to combine the dregs of a day-old Beaujolais Nouveau with a takeout Chinese dinner that included ginger beef, chicken with hot peppers, green beans in garlic sauce and mussels with black beans.

In the real world, there is no perfect fit. A sturdy Zinfandel may be the only table wine capable of lording it over the warring flavours on a modern plate, where five-spice powder and jalapeño peppers vie for domination of the taste buds. But who decreed that the wine must subdue the food? Once you accept that there's bound to be a little conflict between the plate and the glass, the choice becomes easier. Open whatever you like and sip it as just one more component in a complex meal.

While guests are reasonably adaptable when it comes to food —on the old "Anything I don't have to cook tastes great" principle—they can be surprisingly cranky about wine. One of the finest examples I know of comes from *Gourmet* columnist Gerald

Asher, who was about to sip a cooled Beaujolais at lunch one day when a fellow guest dipped a thermometer into her glass and shouted, "Stop! The temperature of this wine is only nine degrees centigrade. We must wait until it reaches ten."

No one, or almost no one, would treat their food quite so officiously. Granted, there was a time when a few people viewed sauces that deviated from Escoffier as a life-or-death matter. But mostly food is eaten with a generosity of spirit: if the cook has made an honest effort and the company is good and no one talks about mutual funds, we're content.

Discerning wine drinkers, on the other hand, are by nature critical and single-minded about their pleasure. These are people, after all, whose entire universe is contained in a mouthful of liquid. I know a few such experts, otherwise bearable, who consider it their duty as guests to rip apart the wine you supply—the pH is out of whack, there's too much sulphur floating around, the oak is obviously from some second-rate cooper in the Ozarks. The best way to deal with such overeducated bumpkins is to pour them a lot of champagne when they come through the door, throwing off their judgment, enlarging their gratitude, relaxing their rigidity and predisposing them to like anything that follows. But even then they may not be satisfied.

Wine buffs are such fusspots. As guests, they can be seen to tighten up when the meal turns out to be Thai—spicy dishes numb the sensitive palate—or rustic Italian—all those tomatoes. As hosts, they're inclined to make food the handmaiden of drink, cooking roast meat ad nauseam so that the wine won't be overshadowed.

Now it's true that if you have a special bottle of rare old wine, it won't show its best with ska-punk videos screaming on the tube and takeout tacos on the table. Some pleasures demand concentrated attention, and the endless nuances of the best wines that you paid a small fortune for nine years ago in anticipation of this day can't be enjoyed in absentminded gulps. But the mistake too many hosts make is to assume that all dinner parties demand high-grade wines.

At a crowded table where three people are talking at once, the flavours are leaping off the plate and the drink is flowing freely, a subtle, expensive wine in the meditative and elusive Old World style will be lost. If your company won't sit in worshipful silence as each sip is supped, it's often better to serve the cheaper, fruitier, upfront wines of the New World. Professional winemakers, I've noticed, prefer beer. They'd rather talk about anything else than the glass in front of them, and who can blame them?

There's still pleasure to be found in wine, if only it can actually be treated as a pleasure and not as the exclusive sacrament of the high priests. But the trouble is that drinking, which should be open to everyone, has become confused with connoisseurship, a pastime best left to a self-important few.

Connoisseurs (and those who hope to be mistaken for them) worry endlessly about the kind of glasses their wine is served in; the most fussy will shoot you a pitying glance if your champagne glasses are too broad (dissipating the bubbles) or your IKEA-bought Bordeaux glasses turn up with a Côte de Beaune, a Moselle Riesling and everything else going. Knowing which glass to present with which wine is difficult enough — the restaurants that have mastered this arcane art turn dinner into a frenzy of disappearing goblets. But having to calculate the temperature of what's being poured into the glass is far, far worse.

Too many people, experts included, put faith in that bit of dogma about serving red wine at room temperature. It's a meaningless phrase, but one with such power that even people who know better would hesitate to chill a wine if it meant losing status in the eyes of those who belong to the old school. Sure, it might have made some sense to nineteenth-century aristocrats marooned in drafty castles whose idea of indoor heating was a wool blanket wrapped tightly round the chilblained body. In the pockets of Britain that have rejected home insulation as an affront to the brisk island climate, you can still get an idea of just how cold room temperature can be when the room is left to its own devices. These are places where you go down to the cellar to get warm, because at least it's protected from the bite of the breezes. In such a setting, discerning people who want to taste their red wine have to warm it up, usually by letting it sit by the fireplace or steep rather miserably in a bucket of hot water. There is even a fancy French word invented to justify and validate such odd behaviour — *chambrer*, meaning to warm your wine to the temperature of a comfy Parisian chambre.

This antique and ambiguous notion of room temperature clearly doesn't fit our climate-controlled life. We prefer an indoor environment where one pair of socks will do, long johns are an optional accessory and your fingers don't always feel like they're about to fall off. Unfortunately what suits the digits isn't so good for the drinks. Sure, if it's volatile acidity and numbing tannin you want to savour at the table, if the burning sensation of alcohol at the back of the throat is your identifier for fine wine, then by all means let a high-strength Gigondas or an aggressive Barbaresco enjoy the wonders of central heating. But keep in mind as you're enjoying their sultry splendour that even a brisk 20°C/68°F — at the cool end of room temperature — may be too warm to flatter red wines. Many European winemakers, unaware of our thermostat regulations, actually suggest cooling their reds to between 12°C and 18°C. Lacking a wine thermometer, I stick a red in the freezer for fifteen or twenty minutes and hope for the best. If the wine comes out too cold — muting the nice flavours along with the more undesirable elements — you can always warm it up in the glass with your blood-temperature hands.

Of course, the legislators of oenology prohibit the freezer shortcut on the grounds that it "shocks" the delicate liquid. But wine is not so easily disturbed. If you read all the nervous literature on the subject, you'd think the best approach to storing a wine bottle was to treat it like a chronic invalid: no extremes of temperature, no sudden movements or sounds, keep the curtains drawn and make sure not to mention Uncle Fred's sex change. But that gutsy Zinfandel is made of stronger stuff.

If you happen to have a dark cellar that maintains a constant temperature of 13°C, all well and good. The fluctuations that most people experience in their basement storage rooms, however, aren't going to do much harm, contrary to the stern warnings of those who like to perpetuate wine's mystique. Think of the trip that bottle took to get here, roaring along bumpy country roads in the back of a truck, sitting on a dock for weeks in an unheated, unchilled container, being tossed around warehouses by guys who like to show off their upper-body strength. It can handle your unfinished basement for a while.

But before you think about loading up on expensive Bordeaux and Burgundy to put away for a few decades, it's important to re-examine a few more odd assumptions peculiar to the fine-wine business. This question of aging, for example. Why should anyone want to pay top dollar for a product that is regarded even by the experts who eulogize it as being undrinkable for years and years? Certainly there are wines, white as well as red, that manage to develop fascinating nuances of flavour as they grow old, if you can wait that long. Most people can't.

But there are just as many wines that start off woody and stalky and shorn of fruit and never get any better. Writers tremble in ecstasy when they taste these wines in their unpleasant youth, but why is a long-lived bottle of bitter grape tannins considered so superior to a rich, fruity blend that you can buy this morning and drink tonight? That's the way we approach our food—would you ever keep a cheese for ten years before eating it? So why should this last part of our meal be treated any differently?

Wine has not yet been democratized as food has. There is still a style of winemaking, and wine tasting, that is a throwback to more primitive times, when the best way to preserve fresh grape juice for the foreign connoisseur's cellar was to turn it into a puckery tannin cocktail. Necessity rapidly became a snobbish virtue, and the cult of the wine collector caught on. But in the modern world, as New World winemakers have proved with great success, it's possible to make fresh, quaffable wines with lots of flavour that can be drunk right off the shelf.

Of course, wine's regulatory busybodies look down on quaffing — it's something peasants do from their cheap, stemless glasses, when everyone knows that wine is a precious nectar to be savoured from crystal goblets with anxious sniffs, wrinkled brows and beady-eyed squints. And they're not too keen on what they call the New World either, caught up as they are in the wine connoisseur's prejudice that old is always superior to new. Read Johnson's highly influential handbook, which guides more people in their wine purchases than any other volume, and you're struck by the pro-European complacency that leads to such puffery as "France's best wines set the standards by which all the world's finest are judged." Because this comes from a writer who thinks the decline of that British clubman's favourite, Madeira (a sweet, fortified wine designed to make cold rooms feel warm), is part of some New World conspiracy, it can be safely ignored for what it is — a passing nostalgia for the old rules and the established ways.

But let's look at the situation from the other side for a moment. Suppose you have actually managed to procure an expensive Bordeaux and raised it in your designer cellars, taming its fiery youth and allowing the harsh tannins to mellow out into something that is finally drinkable without a palate-puckering shudder. What do you do with it now? Do you hoard it like a miser, taking quick sips while looking over your shoulder to see if anyone's lying in wait to steal your precious liquid from you? That would be mean. Do you invite round only those people who can truly appreciate the awe and majesty of a properly aged French wine? That sounds boring. And besides, if they're so used to old Bordeaux, where's the big thrill? So you take a risk, and decide to share your treasure with the unknowing world.

You are invited out to dinner and bring along your best claret to—how does that go?—stimulate conversation, engage the senses and enhance the pleasures of the table. The host takes your offering rather carelessly, and just as you're about to remark on the miraculous weather in the Médoc that year he pushes it to the back of the cupboard and pulls out his latest passion— homemade wine. While he prattles on about the great Zinfandel grapes he crushed last fall and the joy that comes from tasting the fruit of one's labours and the foolishness of those who pay top dollar for an everyday drink—"What do you think this cost me to make? Two bucks!"—you try to will the Bordeaux out of the cupboard *Bewitched*-style and send it back to your cellar. The homemade pasta flecked with the cook's own oven-dried tomatoes and handmade fennel sausages passes by unnoticed. The marriage is off.

Anyone who proposes to cook with wine in this land of milk and honey has already committed an unnatural act. While wine, the drink, has gained a kind of immigrant status at the table, it's still an alien in the kitchen. It costs, it's hard to come by, it's surrounded by rules and regulations that would confound a zoning-bylaw committee.

Anthropologists talk of the can of Spam or the box of corn flakes transported halfway round the world to become an object of reverence in the undeveloped world. It's the same with the status of wine in our society. Being a primitive people with limited experience of wine as a free-flowing liquid, we're too easily fooled into thinking it's a precious nectar that conveys sophistication if you sip it slowly enough.

But as a recipe ingredient, wine is something much more basic and much less self-conscious. Leave the lifestyle possibilities to the ad-agency copywriters. In the kitchen, with no one watching, the work is humbler: when the rouge and blanc are poured into the pot, wine sheds its pretensions and turns into a cooking medium, a complex flavouring agent, a tenderizer and even an acceptable preservative.

Traditional wine stews, the basis of all wine cooking, are among the most rustic and unassuming dishes of all. When confronted with a social-climbing recipe, it's always comforting to remember that the original farmhouse versions called for the wine closest to hand. Using a pricey Chardonnay when you had direct access to ordinaire was like cooking with gourmet-shop papayas when the apples were hanging from your backyard tree. There is a hoity-toity dish called coq au Chambertin made (in theory) with one of the world's most expensive wines. Let us assume, which is unlikely, that this dish is made with Chambertin in the village of the same name. Take the road south to Beaujolais and coq au Chambertin turns into coq au Chiroubles, made from a good local red wine that is nothing like Chambertin in style or price. Travel to Alsace, where white wines predominate, and the specialty becomes coq au Riesling. In Normandy they use cider without hesitation and in the kitchens of my Ontario childhood, water and flour—both, unfortunately, Canadian specialties.

It's obvious that wines taste different from each other and give different results in the kitchen. A typical Beaujolais Nouveau is grapey, an Aligoté is tart, a Bordeaux is tannic and woody, and an old-fashioned Zinfandel is brawny and bumptious. A dish made with these wines will take on at least some of their character and end up with a distinctive personality. The Bordeaux, for example, adds a bitterness that requires adjustment elsewhere in the recipe, and the Aligoté gives a sourness unless softened by cream or diluted by broth. But maybe a little piquant sourness is what you want from time to time—partly to capture the authenticity of a regional recipe, but also to vary flavours that too easily become uniform when we make everything conform to the sophisticate's evolved tastes.

Cooking is an art of accommodation. A strict rule is one that creative cooks discard first. Assuming that a cooking wine is drinkable (the test is easy and quick), one wine can very easily replace another. Since wines of the same name can range from awesome to awful, there is no room here for inflexibility. When you see a starstruck magazine calling for a glass of Chardonnay in a chicken recipe—never mind that the neutral-tasting Chardonnay grape is not a very rewarding varietal in the kitchen— you have to appreciate that a bulked-up Napa version and a watery bargain from Northern Italy aren't the same thing at all. You can still cook good food with the cheaper version, but it will take a little more cooking time (and an extra pinch of spicing) to concentrate the thinner flavours.

Cooking will transform a wine in any case. The difference between a sound wine and a great wine is scant after several hours of stewing in combination with meat, bacon, vegetables and spices. To create the illusion of fidelity, it may be entertaining to use a Barolo in a beef al Barolo from Piedmont. But since there are Barolos and Barolos (most of them too expensive to drink, let alone cook with), nothing is lost by switching to a Barbaresco or Spanna (same grape) or to a red wine of equally strong, beefy flavours from less renowned vineyards.

And why stop there? There are countless examples in traditional European cooking of whites being used where the legislators call for red, and vice versa. White wine figures as a base of many meat stews, and finishes creamy sauces that accompany red meat. Red wine is used in a number of fish recipes, particularly in matelotes of eel and other rich fish. An Alsatian recipe for salmon incorporates the local Pinot Noir. Lamb in the Bordeaux area is cooked with the local red wine but in Rome the sauce is made al vino bianco. Perhaps one dish may be classified as hearty and the other as subtle but the cook who is able to improvise and make adjustments can afford to be colour-blind.

Thus liberated, we're free to cook for taste and not by the book. If a recipe calls for Chablis, you're out twenty bucks even before you buy food. Why not switch to a Muscadet at half the price, or experiment, not necessarily with vintage port but with a red wine of similar freshness and acidity? If anyone needs to be reminded of the possibilities, read Richard Olney's book *Yquem*. Among the new and old uses he finds for sweet Sauternes (a cheaper bottle than the deluxe Château d'Yquem, I hope) are turbot cooked in a Sauternes court bouillon, eel braised in Sauternes, pork stuffed with apricots macerated in Sauternes, tongue braised in a Sauternes stock and warm rabbit in a Sauternes vinaigrette.

According to the ancient rules of wining and dining, a glass of Sauternes is obligatory with the preceding—what goes in the pot goes in the glass. Sometimes, of course, this makes sense. If you use the first third of a bottle to cook with, the next step is to drain it. But there's no sin in discriminating between cooking and drinking wines. After all, certain qualities disdained by wine connoisseurs (high acidity and fruitiness being obvious examples) are an advantage to the cook. Fussy experts have no place in a creative kitchen.

The first comparison that comes to mind is a final exam. Now maybe I'm exaggerating the fear that seizes both mind and body when a wine list is presented at the table, but the air of tension is undeniable. No matter what experience you bring to ordering wine in restaurants, the document you are asked to read and respond to is an unknown, filled with the tricks and traps examiners adore.

Sure, you have the kind of working knowledge of wine that comes from a cram course at the more affordable racks of the liquor store. But the sadists who put together the wine list you now hold in your hands are wise to your ways. They don't want you looking at their 300-per-cent markups and making an unflattering comparison with the more bearable prices on the retail shelf. So they go out and order wine privately, stocking their list with warehouse obscurities whose original price will never be known — at least not by the diner who's paying full freight.

Fear of the unknown is just the beginning: restaurant wine lists find ways to intimidate in so many other ways. While the modern menu gives a chatterbox description of the dishes you can choose from — every herb, spice and cooking technique invitingly itemized — wine lists are deliberately enigmatic. I think it goes back to the days when the test of a gentleman was whether he could recite the 1855 Bordeaux classification; that whiff of elitism still lingers. Barbaresco Serraboella Cigliuti, it may say in cold, hard type, and all most people will really know is that it's Italian, red and unpronounceable. Can't diners be told that the *Wine Spectator* gave it an 87 rating, or that the risk with a Barbaresco is that its puckery tannins will cloak the intense taste of the Nebbiolo grape for years to come?

No. Too many restaurants are just lazy, knowing that the less they say about their wines, the more they can impress and intimidate. Fear of making a faux pas is what drives people to the simpler alternative of wine by the glass, or the dreaded house wine. But these can be even riskier choices. Many restaurateurs use the wines-by-the-glass category as the dumping ground for bottles that don't sell. Wines don't sell for a number of reasons, and it's possible you'll hit upon some nice old-vine Auxerrois from Alsace that lacks the star power to market itself by the bottle. But often you'll end up with a Chardonnay that's getting a little long in the tooth, or a run-of-the-mill backwoods Burgundy from a shipper who made his name with finer stuff from the Côte d'Or. And when the wines are sold by the glass, especially when a huge range is on offer, there's no telling how long the bottle they come from has been open. Good restaurants put a date sticker on the bottle as it's opened, but even good restaurants get busy and forget about the little things—and then, voilà, your Oregon Pinot Gris tastes flat and oxidized.

But something identifiable by the glass is far preferable to anything from that vague and deceptive category referred to as house wine. House wines are euphemistically known in the business as a profit centre. The markups are outrageous, but it's a price restaurateurs know timid diners will pay to avoid having to fiddle with the tongue-twisting names of Chianti estates or select from the array of higher-priced (but better-value) Aussie Cabs. In the greediest restaurants, the anonymous house wine has been made in u-Brew style from barrels of grape concentrate freshly imported from the wine factories of Chile—figure a 1000-percent profit there. In others, the deception is a little more ingenuous. "Where's your house wine from?" you ask the waiter in an attempt to gain his respect by making an informed choice. "It's Burgundy," he answers without hesitation, "Moreau Rouge. Very nice."

Moreau does have offices in the Burgundy region, but the wine in the bottle, like so many others shipped from a Burgundy address, is in no way a Burgundy. The flag of convenience notwithstanding, this is just another not-very-interesting commercial blend from who knows where. Maybe the waiter doesn't have a clue himself. Or maybe he's learned to tell inexperienced diners what they like to hear (the way that white house wines, though often a little sweet, are invariably described as dry). Or maybe he's engaged in a kind of fraud that's still depressingly common in ordinary restaurants, the same restaurants that pass off carbonated bubbly as the house champagne.

So what do you do apart from staying home, where every wine is ultimately a house wine? Well, I could take the final-exam analogy one step further and suggest that you should actually study harder. Get a restaurant's wine list in advance and analyze it with a wine guide close to hand. For those not in the habit of cribbing for their night on the town, a few tips might relieve some of the exam-night anxieties. First of all, keep in mind that strongly flavoured food — fusion cuisine or cooking that uses concentrated reductions — goes best with the full-flavoured wines made from outgoing grapes such as Zinfandel, Sangiovese, Viognier, Pinot Gris and Gewürztraminer.

If it's a dry wine you're after, watch out for semi-sweet and off-dry bottles lurking on even well-made lists. In the oddball French of Champagne, the word "sec" does not mean dry, but medium-sweet; for truly dry champagne (which is surprisingly rare), look for phrases such as brut nature, brut ultra or brut zero. Many U.S. Rieslings, Gewürztraminers and Chenin Blancs are perceptibly sweet and taste sickly beyond the apéritif stage. Most of the high-end Vendange Tardive (late-harvest) bottles from Alsace are noticeably syrupy, and even some of the so-called dry wines from the region now carry residual sugar as if it were a virtue.

On a list organized geographically, certain areas stand out for good value and consistency: Alsace, the berryish red Chinons, Saumurs and Bourgueils of the Loire Valley, older whites from Austria, almost anything out of Australia (but especially the Shiraz reds). Where a wine list is badly overpriced—at a conservative Michelin-starred restaurant in France, for example—it's possible to save face as well as money by ordering the local wine. Even the snootiest sommeliers in France have to pay lip service to the wines of their region, which are likely to be cheaper and livelier than many of the classics.

But anyone who insists on spending big on big reds should beware. Deluxe lists in self-important restaurants are top-heavy with name-brand Bordeaux that won't soften up for a decade or more. The appearance on the wine list of a tannic and unpalatable wine such as the latest vintage of Mouton (which will only be at its best when many of us are dead) serves an unfortunate dual purpose: it attracts big spenders who are impressed only by the name on the label and the inflated price, and it makes the other overpriced wines on the list look cheap by comparison.

Finally, don't hesitate to ask for advice when the list is formidably long. If they insist that you should have something pricey, order draft beer all round.

So what's wrong with beer then? The snobs in the restaurants disdain it and the cooks in the kitchen have never heard of it. Ever since I was a lad sneaking glances at *The Playboy Gourmet* and pining for my own extra-long flambé matches, wines and spirits have ruled. From coq au vin and baba au rhum to salmon in champagne sauce and Glenfiddich chocolate cake, the vintner and the distiller have been elevated in the culinary pantheon while the brewer has drooped lower and lower.

As a beverage alone, beer deserves more attention from people who care about their food. In a society that feigns concern about health, it has the advantage of being relatively low in alcohol and high in water. And for those who long to free their diet from our era's more self-conscious complications, beer is the appropriate drink. It doesn't come loaded down with pretensions, for a start (though they're available on request). But more important, beer's prickly bubbles and hoppy malt cleanse and refresh the overworked palate. It can be drunk like a drink, not sipped like a sacrament.

But here I go down the slippery slope. It's the problem that faces all dedicated beer drinkers. They concentrate so much on praising the drink for its quaffability that they forget about its place in the serious kitchen. They become so casual, so stress-free, that they end up flipping burgers or ordering pizza instead of attempting something challenging.

Now the tendency at this point for the obsessed fan is to elevate beer into a miracle ingredient that is supposed to supplant all previous sauces and flavourings. But it would be a mistake to make too much of beer. Because it's over 90 per cent water, it has to be used with care, or whatever you're cooking may taste diluted and bland. As for the flavouring elements in the remaining few per cent, they have their own particular beery character —bitter, malty, herbal—that won't necessarily improve every recipe.

The safest way to experiment with beer in the kitchen is to work with time-tested recipes from traditional brewing regions. This approach has its limitations—beer is historically a northern drink, and the cuisine of the north is more often about brute survival than hedonistic bliss—but a recipe's grounding in real-world cooking is no bad thing. At a time when cabbage and parsnips creep onto fashionable menus, there's no reason why barley-wine shouldn't piggyback on their success.

And fortunately for those who need Gallic validation, there's a part of the French-speaking world where beer is used in the kitchen. I speak of the much-unvisited area around the French-Belgian border, where mussels are cooked with the fine local beer instead of vin blanc. The writer Michael Jackson—an unfortunate choice of name, perhaps, but he had it first—gives a recipe from a Belgian café in his stimulating *Beer Companion* where ten ounces of beer replace the usual glass of white wine. A large plate of french fries is the traditional accompaniment with this dish, which just goes to show that people who cook with beer don't fret too much over making an impression (though the same Belgians don't hesitate to combine beer with crème fraîche, egg yolk and saffron in a sauce for mussels and scallops).

Jackson's recipes, emanating from Belgium, naturally call for Belgian beer, in particular a tart, yeasty style of brew called gueuze. I wouldn't want to think you'd be discouraged from trying this dish because the local beer emporium hasn't heard of it —by all means try another brew and see what you think. But keep in mind that Coors Light was not what the original framers of moules à la gueuze had in mind.

If you search out recipes from the corners of the world where they care as much about their food as their beer, you will come across such classics as coq à la bière (much like coq au vin, but with a generous dash of gin and juniper), carbonnade flamande (beef stewed with brown ale), Welsh rabbit (melted cheese cooked with beer) and steak and kidney pie made with English ale (I've also seen recipes using Guinness). These are recipes of a certain type, perhaps, the sort that beer tends to attract: hearty, simple and warming dishes for cold-weather months. But even a conservative drink such as beer has attracted a few experimenters: Jackson gives beer-inflected recipes for goat's cheese and pear salad, lamb with beer and artichoke hearts, pheasant in Scotch ale, a sweet beer tarte, cherry-beer ice cream and even beer foam. That would be the northern peoples' answer to zabaglione.

⊶⊨ White Wine Soup

Not the sort of thing you want to be eating before a job interview, perhaps, but this uncompromising soup from Fred Macnicol's inspired book *Hungarian Cookery* is a good way to get warm on a cold winter night.

Beat 1 egg lightly in a soup pot, sprinkle it with a pinch of flour and gradually add 10 ounces of water (or chicken stock for a more refined taste). Heat separately 20 ounces of an aromatic white wine such as a spicy Hungarian Harslevelu, flavouring it with a clove and the grated rind of 1 small lemon. Add this slowly to the egg mixture, and stir in a little sugar if needed. Put on the gentlest heat and whisk and beat until it begins to thicken. Strain the soup into mugs and serve very hot with croutons.

⊶⊨ Chicken with Riesling

The endless variations on coq au vin that you find all over France (including coq à la bière in the north—worth trying) all start with the assumption that you're cooking with an older, tougher free-ranging male bird and not the tender young things of the supermarket meat counter. Such birds aren't designed for the long stewing required for the usual coq au vin rouge, and usually end up falling off the bone in the time it takes to subdue the fieriness of the red wine. This more delicate—relatively speaking—cream-and-white-wine version from Alsace is better suited to the standard quick-cooking chicken of today.

Dice a 4-ounce piece of bacon and soften in 2 ounces of butter. Add 2 peeled and chopped onions, or 12 peeled and chopped shallots, and soften for a minute or two. Then add 6 to 8 chicken legs and breasts, and let them brown before adding 12 ounces of

Riesling in the Alsatian style, which means very dry and slightly sharp. A sweet German-style Riesling won't do. Bring to a boil, then simmer for about 30 minutes, moving the chicken around once or twice to make sure that each piece is in contact with the cooking liquid. After 20 minutes, stir in ½ pound of sliced mushrooms. When the chicken is cooked, transfer it to a warm serving dish, thicken the cooking juices at a higher heat if necessary, slowly stir in 8 ounces of 35% cream and season to taste with salt and pepper. When the sauce is ready, pour it over the chicken, sprinkle with lots of chopped parsley and serve on a bed of noodles.

Pears in Red Wine

This cold-weather dessert is a good way to warm a drafty house in winter, and the glistening purple fruit that emerges from the oven is a beautiful sight in a drab season. You can use ordinary table pears, but the long, slow baking is best suited to large, firm cooking pears that can't be softened in any other way — just make sure they're not too green and underripe. The kind of red wine you use will determine how much sugar you need to add and also affect the final flavour. I've had the best luck using a rich Portuguese or Australian ruby port; a thinner, stalkier Cabernet Franc will give more of a wine quality, even after all that cooking. I've also made this dish with dried purple pears that I found in a basket at a farmers' market. The result was fascinating, like a combination of figs and pears, but almost too intense.

You'll need a tall baking dish, a little higher than an upright pear. You may also want to do a couple of batches together, to make better use of the long cooking time. Peel 6 to 8 pears, but leave them whole, with the stalks still on. Stand them in the pot — they should support themselves, but you can always trim the bottoms of the fruit to make a level base. Pour in wine to the halfway point of the pear, then add water to the top of the stalk. If you're using port, add 1 tablespoon of sugar for each pear. Otherwise add 2 tablespoons. Bake in a 250°F oven for about 6 hours. As the cooking liquid reduces, spoon the juices on the tops of the pears every hour. This dish can be served hot or (better) cold. If you find the taste of the wine syrup too concentrated, pour on a little cream, which also gives a pretty colour contrast to the deep purple of the fruit.

MUSSELS

THE SEA REACHES deeper into the imagination than it does into the kitchen. Sitting in the grid-locked wastes of downtown Toronto, engaged in the typical Toronto task of fingering a keyboard in a climate-controlled office, I can still call to mind the smell of salt water and the sound of storm-whipped waves collapsing on the resisting rocks. But let me try to take my idle thoughts to the next level—tonight's dinner—and the dreamy images begin to break apart.

Who knows how long our fish have been out of the water or by what roundabout route they found their way here from the briny depths? That corpse of a mackerel on the fishmonger's slab —it sure looks far from home. Why are its eyes so sunken and where's the silvery sheen on its skin? What's an imagination heated up by sea fever to make of flesh that's lost its bounce and a tail that's starting to curl?

Painted with olive oil and thrown on the grill, poached in tart white wine and served up as an appetizer, stewed with onions, green peppers and tomatoes, used as the basis of a dense, garlicky soup, the aging fish may distract taste buds dulled by skinless chicken and vegetable pasta. But to the dreamer staring out the window at the slushy sidewalks and pining for the sea, it will never taste remotely like the saltwater ideal. And then I think of mussels, and all is well.

Well, not entirely well, since the slush is still oozing on the sidewalk and the tangy sea air is still a few thousand kilometres the far side of the driveway. But wellish, because there is no better way of bringing the maritime spirit to town, and the town to its senses, than by cooking up a pot of mussels.

It shouldn't be surprising that most ocean fish don't travel well: they're dead, after all, and started decomposing long before coming to rest on a bed of ice in a not-always-trustworthy fish store. The more remarkable thing is that the taste of mussels is so convincing this far from the source. Having feasted on them ad lib (and, eventually, ad naus.) in the bivalve heartland of Stanley Bridge, Prince Edward Island—just a few kilometres past the Anne of Green Gables Laundromat—I can't go so far as to say mussels are actually better inland; but they are not appreciably worse, and the wine used to steam them is much cheaper.

Of course, mussels are bound to fare better than fish since they can be kept alive on their cross-country trip. I make no comment on the quality of that life—though it can't be much less stimulating than clinging eternally to a rock—but for whatever reason (probably not excessive pampering, since they remain remarkably cheap), expatriate mussels are true to type. In landlocked regions far from the ocean, you're more likely to come across cultivated varieties, which have led a more stress-free existence. But this doesn't seem to have taken away from their flavour (in the way that farmed fish are blander than wild)—cultivated mussels are plumper and cleaner, advantages which are hard to scorn.

It's worth adding for the easily intimidated that mussels are quick and easy to cook. Not that this is entirely true. But when you actually dump the mussels into the sink to rinse them and strip away the beard—the fibrous material sticking out of the shell that is basically their connection with the outside world— the work will be so engrossing and so much like what real chefs do that you won't notice it's laborious. (With some mussels, the beard and any clinging limpets have already been mechanically removed; cooking really has become too easy.)

Once cleaned, what next? You could eat them raw, I suppose, just to prove it can be done, but my preference in the great divide is for cooked. And if cooked it is to be, then the best approach is à la marinière, in the sailor's style.

You have to hand it to those French sailors. While not terribly skilled at winning sea battles that saved civilization, they created recipes that made civilization worth saving. I've always been impressed, in any case, by sailors who travelled with shallots and a nice Muscadet in their rucksacks, so unlike the usual seagoing necessities of hardtack and rum.

But at the risk of coarsening the refined maritime sensibility of the French, let me say that you don't need shallots: onions will do. As for variations and refinements, cream and tomato turn up in a lot of magazine recipes—they are to be avoided, since they only make things different, not better. I also keep garlic out of my quick-cooked stews on the grounds that it turns something intrinsically northern and cold-water into something southern and warm. By the same principle, beer or dry cider can be substituted for the wine.

The strong taste of mussels makes them a good candidate for smoking (much cheaper than the oyster equivalent) and an excellent match with Chinese black bean sauce—they have the advantage of being easier to get at than the periwinkles (a.k.a. "snails") that often appear on Hong Kong–style seafood menus. Green-shelled New Zealand mussels have lately caught the attention of those whose preference runs to exotica, but our humble, common black-shelled guys have a finer flavour. I find them easier to chew as well, but maybe New Zealand molars reared on mutton chops are made of tougher stuff.

Leftover mussels, like other kinds of shellfish, don't reheat very well. They're better off being added to salads (good with potato or celery-root in mayonnaise), seafood soups or cooked rice. But I doubt that you'll have all that many. By some strange culinary rule, the amount of mussels that can fit into a pot is exactly the number sea-starved diners are capable of eating.

Mussels Steamed in Wine

You already have many recipes for mussels, I'm sure, but I include this exceptionally simple dish as a caution against trying to be too elaborate. Though this is the easiest method of preparing mussels short of boiling them in water, it is by far the best way to cook them. Anyone who suggests adding tomato or cream or egg yolks or saffron should be dispatched back to Cordon Bleu or fitted for a guillotine.

Use a deep pot for this dish.

Clean 4 pounds of mussels (good for about 4 people as a lunch or first course), and strip away the beard, the fibrous mess that attaches the shell to its rocky home. Finely chop 1 medium-sized onion (don't worry about recipes that insist on shallots) and melt in an ounce of butter.

Don't be tempted to add garlic, because its southern aromas tend to overwhelm this very northern dish (and surely we're getting too much garlic in our diet these days anyway). Add 1 glass of dry white wine (Muscadet, Pinot Blanc, a tart Riesling), or dry apple cider or 8 ounces of good lager. Heat until it bubbles and steams, then add the mussels and cook covered until the shells open, turning them once or twice so that they cook evenly. Sample as you go to avoid overcooking (at which point the nice plump bivalves start shrivelling up). When ready, throw on some finely chopped parsley and transfer them with their broth to a deep bowl, from which people can help themselves. Crusty bread (for mopping up the broth), a bottle or two of the same wine you cooked with and fistfuls of napkins are all you'll need. Any un-opened mussels can be saved to poison your enemies.

SIMPLICITIES

I T'S HARD, ONCE YOU'VE DISCOVERED WHAT money can buy, not to feel you're missing out by being short of cash. No matter how many times you reassure yourself that wealth brings its own problems — the costly security systems, the upkeep on the Tuscan villa, those tiresome charity galas — the sense of falling short never quite goes away.

One of the perks that come from being in a high-income bracket, for example, is that you instantly turn into a better golfer. Pay enough money for a titanium-head driver and you can knock the ball farther and truer. The rich may have a hard time entering the kingdom of heaven — Matthew 19:24, and even back then the poor were looking for consolation — but they have a much easier time reaching the green in two.

Such discrepancies can be found in almost every part of our lives, since the entire economy of the West seems to be based on creating personal advantages — ABS brakes, wider seats in business class, graphite racquets with their generous sweet spot, gold-card benefits that move you to the front of any line — for an additional charge. Where the nineteenth-century idea of wealth was based on possessing baubles that no one had any practical need for — diamonds, paintings, titles — the more democratic version in this cutthroat era is designed to make you actively better than your neighbour on a daily basis.

I'd always thought that food was immune from this class warfare. Many poor people eat badly, it's true, but so do many rich people. Anyone who has had to dine in an expensive boarding school, a private club or a luxury health spa soon realizes that taste can't be bought. Knowing how to cook or shop is a far more important factor in producing a good meal than knowing how to make money.

Brave words. Still, I was brought up short when someone told me, more in sadness than in anger, that she couldn't afford the artisan French cheeses I'd been praising as one of life's essentials. It's true that at $40 or $50 a kilo these misshapen lumps of curd can be considered luxury goods. But it's also the unhappy truth that they're the standard by which all other cheeses should be measured, which makes them, for anyone who cares about food, a necessity.

Not an everyday kind of necessity. That would be boring, and ennui in the face of luxury is the preserve of the rich. But a wild and savage raw-milk brie needs to be sampled, if only once, to keep the taste buds honest. Knowing the range of flavours a humble French farmer can conjure up out of his full-fat milk, it becomes a lot harder to put up with our tasteless mass-market cheeses that have the single virtue of being affordable.

Some economists believe that the desire for luxuries is what drives the economy and spurs people forward to work harder and better their lives. I'm not so sure, and I can't argue very hard with someone who would rather put money into clothing her children than assembling a state-of-the-art cheese tray. But since we're all going to spend money on food anyway, a tight budget shouldn't prevent anyone from eating well. Quality is often an insignificant factor in the price of expensive food. You're also paying for scarcity value, labour-intensive production, the cost of air freight, the intermediaries' rake-offs, the gouging rents in swish neighbourhoods, the interior designer's bills or the wages paid to the good help that is so hard to find these days.

In short, you're paying for other people's time and expertise and often for other people's tastes as well. As good as a truffle may be, it's not five hundred times better than a raw carrot, whatever the price tag says. Once you go to the trouble of making carrot soup, anyone with an open mind—not always easy to find in food circles—could easily prefer your creamy broth, with its lingering taste and vivid colour, to the fungus being grated with fawning respect on a plutocrat's pasta. And that's without taking into account the pleasure involved in cooking a soup: reading over old recipes, chopping cold carrots to the rhythm of Glenn Gould playing (and occasionally humming) Bach, reducing the chicken stock till it's a concentrated essence, adjusting the flavour with a little chopped chervil or grated ginger at the end and presenting it to grateful companions who know you made it yourself. We won't try to put a dollar value on this experience, except to say that people who pay other people a lot of money to do the cooking and the fawning miss out on it completely.

I'm not trying to make a case for the nobility of poverty— leave that one to the Gospels—but I know that some of the best meals can be put together with cheap ingredients and hard, unpaid work. When there's a glut of peppers and eggplants, you make ratatouille that doesn't need Air France luxury and a villa in the Côtes de Provence to be nonpareil. When the winds turn cold, instead of having to curse the valet parking at an overpriced restaurant that can't tell summer from winter, you turn your mind to braising Chinese greens, experimenting with borscht, roasting and peeling chestnuts for a warming soup, cooking down the baskets of Spys and Anjous into a sweet purée you'll never find in high-priced kitchens, baking the oatmeal cookies to go with the apple-pear sauce, or simmering the tough hunks of beef for hours until they fall apart and produce the kind of rich stew despised by the finest menus.

And best of all: buying an expensive stove won't make you a better cook.

Becoming a better cook is something of a delusion anyway. It's not about money, as much as we hanker for the six-burner Garland and the slate-tile floors. And it's not about serving ready-to-photograph masterpieces that can only be concocted with a step-by-step manual at your right hand and a team of faithful assistants at your left. When making an impression is a priority, we may mimic hotshot chefs, but the insecurities of party-giving should never be confused with good food.

The next time you find yourself in the company of people who like to eat, and who don't feel their gastronomic reputation rides on their answers, ask them what foods give them pleasure. At a point in world history when style triumphs over substance in every restaurant where cash counts, the comebacks will be simple and direct: toasted almonds, someone volunteers. Cherry tomatoes, smoked salmon, Portuguese barbecued chicken with hot pepper sauce, corn on the cob, pad thai noodles, steak charred on the outside and bloody inside, crusty sourdough bread, a hamburger, runny Camembert, vanilla fudge, cinnamon ice cream, strong espresso, a ripe and juicy peach.

What people don't volunteer, unless this display of studied simplicity makes them turn ornery, are the clichés of fashionable chefs. No one summons their taste memory, punches the retrieve button and comes up with carpaccio of tuna framed by daikon radish spaghettini and a medley of shiitake, enoki and portobello mushrooms, or grilled breast of duck on a bed of braised green lentils with wilted radicchio leaves and thyme-flecked aioli, or—

don't you want a ripe peach just about now?—a tarte of black walnuts set in a maple custard accompanied by elderberry coulis and a sorbet of marc de Bourgogne.

High-minded, long-winded restaurant food has its place— the big celebration, the gastronomic adventure, the fleeting escape from homemade drudgery, the act of self-delusion that makes us think we inhabit a world other people only read about in glossy magazines. But if we end up treating good food as something elusive and rare, something expensive and privileged, we do ourselves wrong. Overspending on someone else's thyme-flecked handiwork is a minor consideration, usually resolved when American Express no longer returns calls. What's more worrisome is the relegation of everyday food to the world of the ordinary.

Say your idea of the perfect food is cheddar cheese. Unfortunately, the recent meanderings of Western civilization, so kind to baseball salaries and cable television, have not done well by this basic product. You can't just walk into the local supermarket and expect to find the aged wheels of nutty cheddar that made it a byword for good eating a generation ago. You can turn up something named cheddar, it's true, even something shackled in plastic wrap and dyed deep orange called Olde Cheddar that pretends to be heir to a great tradition. Grilled on toast or tucked into a ham sandwich—transformed or hidden—it's perfectly edible, but no more.

What went wrong with cheddar? Well many things, to be honest—don't get me going on milk-management boards—but the one that concerns us here is the lost respect for good simple things. In a chef-centred culture, where people gain status by turning dinner into a performance art, a slice or two of old-time cheese just can't compete. Put a well-made piece of properly aged cheddar on a plate at the end of a meal—always assuming you can find some; the cloth-wrapped English farmhouse versions are

best, though some Quebec cheesemakers have kept the faith—
and people used to finishing with the mango and star anise mille-
feuille in a macadamia-grappa glaze will barely suppress their
sneers.

They're the ones we should be sneering at. If honest foods
such as cheddar were more honoured in the mansions of gastronomy, the entire web of pretension might suddenly dissolve and
simple pleasures would get their due. It's not all that hard to
imagine either, not to anyone who's spent time in Italy and discovered that the most acceptable way to end a good meal is with
a slice of nutty parmigiano. But for a back-to-basics movement to
succeed, you'd still have to win over the food producers who've
forgotten what flavour is all about. The succulent juiciness I like
to imagine in my peach, the perfect balance of sweet and ever so
slightly sharp, the lingering flavour that stays in the mind and
comes to represent an ideal of taste—all this is more and more
confined to the realm of fantasy. The fruit growers who supply us
worry about yield and size and uniformity of shape and resistance
to rot and transportability long before they have to think about
flavour.

If cheddar is made to be grated into a tortilla, or a tomato is
going to be hacked into an overdressed salad or the peach is simply the starting point for a wunderkind's fevered work of genius,
then you can hide a fair number of faults. But when you ask a food
to stand on its own, there's nothing to disguise the imperfections.
And this is where grandiose restaurants have a role to play. Instead of taking dull, ordinary peaches and gussying them up into
extravaganzas with granitas and crèmes and parfaits, they should
seek out perfect fruit, pay a premium for excellence and set it
before us au naturel. It would take some daring—$4 for a peach?
—but that is the role of avant-garde restaurants. It may be the
only way to make those simple pleasures precious to us again.

Of course the chef who dares to strip away the ornamentation from our rococo cookery, who carries Escoffier's keep-it-simple commandment to its logical conclusion, puts her reputation squarely on the line. Just as a peach, perched alone on a plate, looks unimpressive to diners used to a pâtissier's three-ring circus, so the purist meals served by back-to-basics chefs like the pioneering Californian Alice Waters bewilder more self-indulgent types.

"That's not cooking, that's shopping," scoffed a New York rival on seeing Waters' low-key dishes. At her Chez Panisse restaurant —considered the place to dine before you lead a protest at Berkeley—you must book weeks in advance for an uncomplicated meal of fresh shellfish, mixed greens, grilled chicken, poached fruits and cheese. The $100 or so you're asked to pay for such simple pleasures will come as a shock to those who want their dinner-time investments to exude luxury. But Waters' cooking style— *le style sans style* as Escoffier might have observed—is less about those well-travelled Cal-Ital trends popularized by LA's slaves to fashion (whatever happened to duck sausage pizza?) and more about treating the best raw materials with respect and restraint.

It's an earnest and even obsessive form of hedonism that has its roots in the hippie Enlightenment, with an anti-materialist approach to self-gratification that values organic produce over a glittery guest list. Waters' outlook on food, as detailed in her earthy *Chez Panisse Vegetables*, is very much what you would expect out of Berkeley, an iconoclastic place where even mealtime is seen as part of the political struggle. While other kitchen icons spend their spare time developing mass-market product lines, Waters busies herself with the Edible Schoolyard, a "food curriculum" that "uses active participation in a school garden and kitchen— planting, harvesting, cooking and eating—to teach children respect for the planet and each other."

But what redeems Waters from holistic piety is that her back-to-the-land ideals have taken their inspiration more from her invigorating experience of Mediterranean cooking than from holier-than-thou hippie communes. Her 1982 *Chez Panisse Menu Cookbook*, which almost singlehandedly propelled garlic, goat's cheese and tapénade into fashion, was full of infectious enthusiasm for the cooking of Provence, which neatly approximates the California climate. Instead of acting out some dour brown-rice form of Whole Earth rebellion, Waters' book celebrated the uninhibited flavours of backwoods France, the same simplicities that captivated the great English food writer Elizabeth David when she defined good cooking as "the avoidance of all unnecessary complication and elaboration."

But because Waters works in North America, where market forces have made it increasingly hard to see simplicity as a virtue — do we dare put that pulpy peach on a plate by itself? — she has ended up going in a different direction from David. Travelling through Provençal villages not yet affected by the Peter Mayle–inspired real-estate boom, David could take it for granted that the local ingredients were able to stand on their own. Not so for Waters. With perfect produce so rare in this part of the world, gardening has ended up becoming the foundation of her cuisine, and the grow-your-own mentality of the hippie dropouts has resurfaced in the austerely beautiful *Chez Panisse Vegetables*.

It's a back-to-the-basics approach to be sure — "That's not cooking, that's composting," you can hear her critics saying. But for anyone who wants to escape the fanciful delusions of the star chefs, the produce basket can bring cuisine back down to earth. There's always the danger of falling a little too ardently in love with the perfect carrot — some elaboration may be necessary. And yet as dedicated cooks know, the most inventive and least self-conscious recipes start with a glut from the garden. When tomatoes are in season, you don't try to think what tricks you can play or what exotic names you can drop to turn a simple vegetable into a work of genius. You stop looking over your shoulder to see what other people think and instead, like Waters, get down to the business of turning raw materials into a succession of never-the-same lunches and dinners: Greek salad; tomato salad in a balsamic vinaigrette with basil, bocconcini and garlic croutons; the salade niçoise sandwich called pan bagna; bruschetta; tomato-and-garlic spaghetti; roasted tomato sauce; a tarte of tomato and Cantal cheese; tomato, onion and potato au gratin; tomato-and-bread soup; chilled tomato soup; pasta with tomato comfit; baked tomatoes with the usual Mediterranean flavourings and—back to California—fresh tomato juice.

Maybe we could take Mars as our metaphor. For years, the wizards of Hollywood have tried to persuade us that weird and exotic creatures populated a planet with a momentous landscape that put the extra in extraterrestrial. But when we finally land a camera there, our intragalactic neighbour looks like nothing more than an abandoned rock garden in one of the less popular Arizona deserts.

And so it is with food. For years, ambitious chefs indifferent to Alice Waters' vision of a tomato's simple beauty have laboured to fill our plates with shapes like nothing ever seen on this planet. Giant strips of dried plantain rise up out of seared grilled tuna bathed in murky tomato water. Spears of chive dart skyward from garlic mashed potatoes in a poblano chili reduction. Thrusting antennae prod and poke their surroundings as they ascend out of the nutmeg-flecked foam of a lobster cappuccino.

It's all too strange. Good food, we will finally discover when space modules land on Earth in search of our reality, is nothing out of the ordinary. If far-off Mars can turn out to be a down-to-earth kind of place with a remarkably restrained sense of colour and style, then maybe our dinner plates can be rescued from those who turn them into alien monstrosities. The signs are good. Just as scientists with a practised eye can study the Martian barrens and barely contain their excitement, so I look at the drab photos in *The River Café Cookbook* and see visions of a brighter future. The River Café is a very expensive London restaurant that specializes in Italian farmhouse cooking—*la cucina rustica*—and while there are obviously elements of Prince Charles playing shepherd at Highgrove, the style of the book's photographs is still inspiring.

Never mind that a true cucina rustica book wouldn't have any photographs at all. There comes a time when we have to be confronted with heightened visions of ordinariness just to comprehend how far exoticism has taken over. After years of ornate and artificial photo-studio set-ups, going back at least to the fastidiously plated filigrees of nouvelle cuisine, it's a relief to see a flat overhead shot of a white soup bowl filled to the brim with beans, vegetables and broth-soaked bread in various shades of monochrome. Or the charred skin of two whole sea bass, topped only with slices of lemon, fennel and purple onion. Or a gratin pan of oven-roasted potatoes with pancetta or an unadorned slice of yellow-brown polenta, almond and lemon cake situated on a plain little plate surrounded, not by nasturtiums, vintage bottles of Château d'Yquem and a distant view of Long Island Sound, but by grains of ground corn.

Photographs of food are not just decoration. In a society where most people are uncertain about their culinary heritage or their mealtime longings, these images represent an ideal to strive for, a way of thinking about food that can have ramifications well beyond the page. The earthy pictures in *The River Café Cookbook* suggest that food can recover its integrity once we scrub away the professional's cosmetics, that it is possible and desirable to eat traditional dishes the traditional way: with humility, not amazement.

It's a studied kind of simplicity, to be sure, and the price you're asked to pay for a working man's meal of pork and beans at the River Café is as amazing as it is humbling. But if we're in-secure enough to let the upscale restaurants set the standard for the rest of us, then we may need them to remind us how artless-ness in the kitchen can be the greatest art: the purple-tentacled Martians will leave our planet alone at last and there will be no more stage sets erected on our plates.

It's not easy for the ordinary to take on the extraordinary. While homespun cuisine is much the same to look at wherever you go, exotic food, like extraterrestrials, can assume many forms. The new and unusual will always be more spectacular than the old and familiar, and as long as cooking is considered a form of enter-tainment, chefs will take the blockbuster approach to their cre-ations. But just as *Mars Attacks!* doesn't tell you anything about the real Mars — while being exceptionally eloquent about the limita-tions of our earthbound culture — so the special-effects silliness of the kitchen superstars ends up being a distraction from real food.

A good meal doesn't need art direction. It can be simple, plain and even a little negligent without losing anything in the taste. Is there any food more drab than an unadorned french fry? But does anyone think that a serving of frites would ascend to the next level by being immersed in a papaya-lobster jus, surrounded by perky baby-eggplant dumplings, dusted with finely chopped Thai basil and — there's no stopping us now — made camera-ready with a sprinkling of freshly picked tea-rose petals? The only adornments a fry needs, if it needs any at all, are a dash of salt crystals, a bowl of homemade mayo on the side, a splash of vinegar if you're an unrepentant traditionalist and maybe some steak juices just to vary the routine. None of these accessories photographs well, but if you're planning on having a long-term re-lationship with your food, take personality over looks every time.

And even with personality, you don't always want it to be too assertive or edgy. Reputation-making food critics extol food that (to borrow a few of their favoured clichés) jumps off the plate

and explodes in the mouth. You would too if you had to eat out
and discover genius night after night. But those of us who aren't
obliged to put our taste buds on public display shouldn't feel we
have to overwhelm our palate with every bite we take. Just because strong flavours and harsh textures are used to waylay a
jaded palate in a noisy restaurant, there's no reason to assume that
the same techniques work best in the comfort of the home. The
opposite, if anything.

No serious restaurant, not even one tempted by the modish
simplicity of la cucina rustica, would ever dream of trying to tan-
talize critics with cornmeal mush. And yet as the yellow porridgy
mass is ladled onto my plate, I feel a deep sense of contentment.
This is what I will have to eat when I am old and toothless and
pining for Lawrence Welk—food that can be gummed. And I
don't mind it in the least.

Now it helps that the way we cook cornmeal chez nous is to
treat it like risotto and inflict all kinds of flavourings on something that, stark naked, would taste like liquid wool. Add some
olive oil, pour over a light stock, chop in some chilies, push a few
shrimps into the heaving mass of maize near the end, cook until
gummable and finish with grated Parmesan. But at the heart of
the dish, no matter how many fripperies and folderols we clever
chefs impose, it is still a seething mess of goo.

Goo is good, and if I seem to say that with an air of belligerence it's because conventional wisdom has long pointed in the opposite direction. Soft, gentle textures—the conventionally wise
would not use such nice words—are the sort of sensations you're
supposed to have abandoned with your baby food, or can look
forward to if you survive long enough to be forced into the old
folks' home. They are not meant to be a part of a sophisticated
adult life.

Sure, stylish chefs tolerate the occasional purée of parsnip
and Jerusalem artichoke or a plate of garlic mashed potatoes as an

ironic throwback to a toothless era when more people ate mush. This is called comfort food, but it is meant to be comforting not in the sense that you or I would think of it—"That soft stuff feels nice in my mouth"—but in a more remote and artificial way— "That muck is supposed to be like the stuff my mother used to make, but Mom couldn't cook. Still, it's nice to be reminded of how much happier I was then than I am now."

The same chefs will serve you something called barley risotto, and if you start thinking back to those pillowy pearls of grain in the soups and stews of long-ago days you'll be sorely disappointed. Barley has gone from being a soft, puffy plaything full of meaty broth—lamb, preferably—to being a meagre spoonful of firm, tiny dots sitting lonely on a plate.

Goo is good, as I said, but many cooks, especially those who work from books rather than their own sense of taste, think otherwise. They will serve you a risotto with rice that is still raw and starchy at the centre, because some tyrant told them that this was the only way—never mind that it isn't edible and hasn't absorbed the flavours of the enveloping broth. Or they will try to persuade you al dente means spaghetti that chips your teeth when you try to take a bite. It should have some resistance, granted, but not so much that eating feels like work. If you can hear yourself chew, or find yourself mesmerized by the way your jaw is slowly grinding up and down, up and down, then the pasta needs more cooking. Blame the chef, not yourself.

Food becomes a chore when a chef forgets the simple truths and starts deferring to the whims of fashion. I know I sound like someone who has a dentist appointment coming up and is trying to see the bright side of decomposing molars, but bear with me. There is a fear of overcooking vegetables that has gripped the land and caused people to serve food that is unpleasantly underdone. It does no harm from a health point of view (though digestion may be a problem if you can't be bothered chewing up your rock-hard broccoli completely); but a vegetable that snaps is a vegetable that can never be described as succulent or luscious.

So you never thought of describing vegetables that way? Then you should start experimenting with cooking time just to appreciate the difference. Asparagus and cabbage, for example, strike me as greens that can do with more cooking than they normally get, particularly when they're served with the sauce or the broth they were cooked in. Even Chinese chefs, who are presumed to have blessed the world with crunchy vegetables, accept that there is room for variation. The onion and green pepper with your sautéed beef must be crunchy and sweet, but the leafy Chinese cabbage in your lion's head casserole is so sodden with the juices from the pork meatballs that it practically melts in the mouth. That, by the way, is a good thing.

Just as there are some vegetables that should never be under-cooked (potatoes for a start, except the most delicate new potatoes), there are a few vegetables I would never want to taste well-cooked, such as peas (except in a soup) or carrots (except in a purée). But the other refugees from the seed catalogue can do all kinds of interesting things when given the chance to hang around the stove a little longer: long-cooked eggplant served cold the next day, sliced tomatoes slow-baked on a pizza until they're almost a paste, even peppers melted down in the Hungarian style until they're a pepper concentrate.

Bring on the dentures. I'm ready.

For years, the round, blue tin with the Russian letters and the picture of a shiny, slinky fish sat untouched on a ledge in my refrigerator. I just couldn't bring myself to open it, partly because the Communist-era design was so striking but mainly because I was afraid of what I'd find inside.

The price was too low for caviar. At $45 for a couple of ounces of the world's most expensive eggs, it undercut by far the tariff demanded by high-rent gourmet shops back in the metropolis. When I bought the tin, I was pleased with myself for finding a bargain. Almost immediately I began having doubts.

My problem, or at least my weak spot, is that I've got a taste for luxury. While acting as a public defender for simple pleasures, I still believe there are some foods that shouldn't be condemned just because they move in high society. You may think that something the size of a small cat-food tin, with the nutritive value of a cheese sandwich, should never be priced in the mid-to-high double figures. But all I can say is that I have tasted real caviar—savoured it slowly egg by egg—and decided it has a place at any table where food is loved for its own sake.

But my deluxe tastes are compromised by an intense discomfort with the high-margin lifestyle. Do you really require a château thronged with servants to produce Bordeaux wine? Can Verdi only be sung in gilded theatres to a front row full of fur coats? Must caviar be packaged in gift-wrapped boxes and priced to provoke class warfare? These are only fish eggs, after all, and if they came from the herring or mackerel instead of the sturgeon, no one would get too excited. I used to be suspicious of all luxury, the way arch-xenophobe Don Cherry, another lover of simplicity, was suspicious of all Russian hockey players. I figured that caviar and foie gras and truffles and chocolate-covered ants were what the overly rich ate to distinguish their tastes from ours. Remember when Henry Kissinger was described as one of the sexiest men around, and short, balding, guttural-voiced professors everywhere wondered what he had that they didn't? The undemocratic answer was "power." Well, in the same way that power is the greatest aphrodisiac, when it comes to food the highest price creates the greatest desire.

This is unfair, of course. But it doesn't follow that we should laugh off caviar as one of the more feeble props of the rich and famous. And, I keep asking myself, is $40 (the minimum investment if you want more than a spoonful) really too much to spend on a food that is the essence of pleasure? For the price of an un-ambitious speeding ticket or the worst seats at a bad hockey game, you and yours can play czar and czarina for as long as your paltry few grams can be made to last.

I agree — czars may not be the greatest role models. And if you're looking to democratize the price of caviar, I've already figured out a shortcut: all we need is a caviar factory outlet (with maybe a few spare shelves devoted to foie gras) where all the costly trappings that usually attend the sale of processed fish eggs fall away, and only the food itself remains.

That's what I thought I'd found when I spotted my tin of caviar on sale in a small town in Northern Ontario, where I'd gone to visit a soon-to-be-closed uranium mine. I snapped it up before anyone else could beat me to it, paid what I figured was at least half the going rate in the cruel city — and only then asked myself the crucial question: What was Russian-speaking caviar doing so far from Gorbachev's dacha?

You remember those Russian hockey teams that celebrated glasnost by skating their way around the free world, buying VCRs and blue jeans every chance they got? In exchange, they sold caviar. Who knows how good or how fresh it was, or how care-lessly it had been stored? If they looked after these precious eggs the way hockey players look after the rest of their equipment bag — kind of like a teenager's room on a road trip — there was every chance I'd wasted my cut-rate investment. And who knows where you go to complain when the stuff turns out to be spoiled: the Red Army ice rink? Such are the torments of one who chases luxury on a tight budget.

There are people who will tell you quite confidently that fish eggs are overrated, but chances are they have been done in by the cheapest of imitations, the dyed lumpfish roe that squats in too many fridge doors. This is the stuff that tastes like brine and leaks its imitation blackness all over the Fettuccine Natasha with the slightest application of heat. It is to caviar as Al Jolson is to Paul Robeson. Avoid.

Real caviar comes from the salt waters of the increasingly polluted Caspian Sea, which is shared (with uncharacteristic generosity on both their parts) by Iran and Russia. Although Russian caviar is better known to those weaned on Petrossian's best beluga, Iranian caviar according to my all-too-inexperienced palate is the better buy—on the understanding that if you obtain your caviar from the bargain bin at the corner store, all bets are off.

Iranian and Russian caviar come in three varieties: beluga, asetra—or osetra—and sevruga. Much is made by connoisseurs of the differences among them, but they are more like each other than any of their imitators are like them. Asetra and the smaller sevruga have more flavour. Beluga is the most expensive for reasons that have more to do with the luxury lifestyle than with taste: the eggs are bigger and harder to come by. If you're going to drop a name around a Las Vegas buffet table, this is it. (Malossol, another favorite of name-droppers, is simply Russian for lightly salted; the Russian product tends to be saltier than the Iranian.)

The high price that attracts the jet set does have a good side: you do not chew good caviar between the molars absentmindedly while watching the ball game and knocking back a brewski. Instead, you savour it by rolling a few eggs onto the tip of the tongue, pressing them against the roof of the mouth and catching the juice that sprinkles down. I hope I'm not making that sound too mechanical—it should be deliberately and shamelessly self-indulgent. In a tin of good caviar—one that hasn't travelled the North American hockey circuit—the eggs are a pale grey colour (not black at all). Rather than being mushed together in a primordial ooze like your fridge-door lumpfish, the plump sturgeon eggs are all separate and whole. Their characteristic saltiness is submerged in a nutty sweetness, almost a fruitiness, that lingers in the mouth and only hints at the bitterness found in lesser varieties.

Because caviar is perceived as a luxury, it has become the victim of ritualistic one-upmanship. True caviar lovers, already born with silver spoons in their mouths, are supposed to step it up a notch and take their eggs in a spoon of gold from a serving receptacle that could pass as a reliquary for splinters of The True Cross. Quite frankly, the eggs taste just as good if eaten like the simple, uncomplicated pleasure they are: scooped with your pinky finger directly from one of the elegant tins, or licked from the navel of a loved one if you're into erotic snacking.

Either way, avoid garnishes (sieved egg, chopped raw onion, sour cream, capers). Laid out as it is in classy hotels, all this fussiness looks like a devious rite of passage for admission to the Oddfellows. It just gets in the way, like the shaved ice in your fast-food Coke or the Hamburger Helper in your ground round. If you're going to pay too much money for salted fish eggs, you don't want to get distracted by the extras. Those of us who need to ration our pleasures have a keener sense of their value.

Mushrooms on Toast

Realism in recipe names isn't something to be encouraged. Doesn't "Mushrooms on Toast" sound dull and predictable? Successful chefs have the knack of naming their concoctions with such exaggerated finesse that even dull dishes sound spectacular, and many's the plate I've laboured to enjoy simply because the menu's salesmanship was so persuasive. Thinking about this luscious breakfast recipe, which I first made from huge field mushrooms picked in an English meadow, I wish I could come up with a title that did it justice. But some austere Lutheran impulse holds me back, some feeling that the high priests of the kitchen use their flowery language to intimidate as much as to impress. Anyone can make a dish called Mushrooms on Toast, and the best part about the straightforward name is that it ends up being an understatement: this is food that's much better than it sounds.

Take ½ pound white mushrooms, slice them thinly (trimming any tough bits from the stem), sauté in butter for 2 minutes, add about 4 ounces thick cream and a dash of nutmeg, and reduce the sauce at a moderate heat for about 5 to 7 minutes. Don't overcook the mushrooms. If the sauce seems too thin, remove the mushrooms to a heated plate and simmer the sauce on its own for a minute or two more. Serve on toast. The one danger with a breakfast like this is that the rest of the day's meals will be a disappointment.

Tapénade

Spreading olive paste on toasted bread is one of the best ways I can think of to start a meal, and after my first taste of tapénade, the Provençal version of this piquant purée, I was tempted to put out a pot every time people stopped round. If there was any left over—which was almost never—I'd use it as a sandwich filling. For some perverse reason, I especially enjoyed taking a tapénade sandwich to the ball game, to pull out during a late-inning pitching change when everyone around me had to settle for the last of the red hots. And if you're going to get caught eating a smarty-pants sandwich at the ball park, better pizzeria-approved olives and anchovies than some Silver Palate picnic concoction of nasturtium blossoms and brie.

Tapénade is more versatile than we give it credit for. The strong, sharp flavours are good with almost any cold dish that needs a pick-me-up, especially hard-boiled eggs and slices of left-over roast lamb or chicken. If you make your own pizzas, try smearing on a thin layer instead of the usual tomato sauce, or add a few small dollops as a salty topping instead of pepperoni or sun-dried tomatoes. For a change from the usual vinaigrette, try spreading a little of the paste on your sliced fresh tomatoes, or use it as a substitute for the peanut-butter filling in your ribs of celery. Bittersweet Belgian endive leaves also make a good companion for the taste of puréed olive.

The word tapénade, lest we forget, comes from the Provençal word for caper, which makes capers an obligatory part of the recipe however freely we want to play around with the other ingredients. Rules are rules. Of course, I've tasted lively tapénade made quickly with fat, bland, canned California olives, so I don't want to be too dogmatic. But to have a better sense of what this spread can be, start with tart capers and interesting olives bought loose from the tubs in Mediterranean food stores. Black olives are the usual, but green make a striking variation. There is obviously a huge range in the taste of olives, from wizened and oily to moist and vinegary, and part of the pleasure in making this dish is the different flavours you can end up with.

Take ½ pound pitted olives, and then blend into a coarse paste with 6 to 8 anchovy fillets, 2 tablespoons capers, 2 ounces canned tuna (optional), a squirt of fresh lemon juice, a few sprigs of parsley, 2 tablespoons good olive oil and a dash of black pepper. Some recipes call for a few drops of cognac or rum. Spoon into earthenware pots or bowls and serve at room temperature.

Toasted Cheese

On those nights when we get to dinner late, or just feel lazy, toasted cheese is a great salvation. There are all kinds of variations on the theme, but here are two of my favourites. The first is almost too simple to qualify as a recipe. Grate old cheddar or

Gruyère or a mixture of the two, and spread over tortilla circles. Add finely chopped onion to taste, top each tortilla with another one, press down to bind. Melt some butter in a broad pan and cook at a low-medium heat until the underside browns and the cheese starts to melt. Flip over, brown the other surface and serve cut into quarters.

The second, from Elizabeth David's book *Summer Cooking*, is a little more ambitious if you extend yourself to making the tomato sauce. Preheat the oven to 450°F. Cut 6 to 8 slices of crusty white bread (or 20 to 24 baguette slices) about ¼-inch thick. Cover each piece of bread with a slightly thinner slice of cheese (cheddar, Gruyère or Emmenthal) and arrange in a baking tin, leaving a little room between each. In 8 to 10 minutes, the dish will be ready, the cheese melting and the bread just getting crisp. Sprinkle with freshly ground pepper or top with tomato sauce.

To make the sauce while the cheese is cooking, coarsely chop 2 large, ripe tomatoes and sauté in an ounce of butter, then add a little finely chopped garlic and parsley, salt and pepper. Cook for about 3 minutes only.

Pour over the cheese toasts as soon as they come out of the oven.

Strawberries in Vinegar

When, overcome by their scent at the market, you buy an entire flat of strawberries, you'll need many recipes to dispose of the glut come the cold light of day. If you find yourself eating all those dishes that only a marketing board could dream up—scrambled eggs with strawberries, strawberry-Camembert melt, pork with strawberry salsa—you have only yourself to blame. In a pinch, chicken salad with chopped strawberries replacing the usual pineapple is bearable—though fresh pineapple is tarter and less mushy

—and cold strawberry and yogurt soup is at least superior to the tepid watermelon and orange juice combination that had me swearing off fruit soups long ago.

Strawberries show best in simplest surroundings, which is why I appreciate an easy variation on strawberries and cream dreamed up by cooking-school teacher Lydie Marshall: In a cold mixing bowl, blend together to the consistency of whipped cream ½ pound fresh cream cheese, 1 ½ cups heavy cream, ¼ cup super-fine sugar and a little orange juice, eau-de-vie or fruit liqueur. Dollop lavishly on the hulled, sliced berries.

A simpler treatment of strawberries, and one that makes them seem a more contemplative, less frivolous kind of fruit is this meal-ending dish from balsamic vinegar country. Hull and rinse your strawberries, then gently pat dry. If small, keep whole, but if large cut into sections. Pour 2 to 3 tablespoons of good quality balsamic vinegar over the berries, mix well and let sit for 15 minutes. Add sugar to taste, and serve. If the idea of vinegar seems odd to you, then I won't mention an equally meditative French variation that partners strawberries with freshly ground pepper.

CHOCOLATE

ONCE A MONTH on average, if my teeth and waistline allow it, I splurge on Lebanese baklava. You'd
understand my hesitation if you tasted one of these
pastries, because they're very sweet and very rich.
Not as sweet as their syrup-soaked Greek cousins, perhaps, but
sweet enough to make the teeth tingle. And rich enough, with
their buttery layers of phyllo pastry wrapped around a honeyed
filling of finely chopped almonds, pine nuts, pistachios or walnuts, to make me realize how beautiful life must have been in
pre-war Beirut.

It's one of the many small pleasures of living in a peaceful
refuge like Toronto that I can find these pastries in my local convenience store, just beyond the hockey cards and the licorice
sticks. Every food ultimately tells a story, I suppose, of explo-
ration or escape or ingenuity. But just as I was speculating on the
history of my baklava assortment, and getting ready to mispro-
nounce their names to the Lebanese sales clerk, I noticed that the
story had changed.

"What's that?" I asked, pointing to a tray of pastries that was
markedly different from the rest. While the others all had the dull
yellowish tint of flaky cooked pastry, this one was covered with
squiggly dark-brown lines.

"That is chocolate," said the clerk proudly.

Chocolate-topped baklava. The spirit of innovation was hard at work. It was like revisiting a quaint Mediterranean fishing village and discovering that the old Venetian castle had been turned into a Club Med.

Chocolate is the most imperialistic of foods. It moves in and takes over wherever it can. I love chocolate, as everyone does, but there are times when I hate it, and this was one of those times. My Lebanese pâtissier, thinking he was on to something good, had decided that the best way to expand his market was through the universal ingredient: chocolate.

Over the past few years, chocolate has dominated desserts the way Monica Lewinsky took over U.S. politics. Order a pecan pie in an innovative restaurant, and the chances are good that it will arrive with a chocolate topping. Ask about cheesecake, and the one that comes with the warmest recommendation will be chocolate. Fruit is dipped in chocolate, pretzels and potato chips have been coated in it and birthdays are celebrated with chocolate truffles wrapped in gilt and ribboned curlicues.

Everywhere there are cakes described as decadent or sinful and they're all made with chocolate, chocolate and — why stop there — more chocolate. Triple chocolate cake is a favourite for over-the-top celebrations and children are now raised to see chocolate chocolate-chip ice cream as just a starting point. Jewish bakeries sell chocolate Danishes. French pastry shops do a brisk trade in pain au chocolat (chocolate bread: think about it). When you're feeling ascetic, you don't dispense with the chocolate, which might make sense. Instead you get rid of the flour and make a flourless chocolate cake. My preferred source of shortbread cookies turns out shortbreads filled with massive hunks of bittersweet chocolate, and the bittersweet truth is, I like them.

Or at least I can't leave them alone. Chocolate is addictive. The space between just enough and too much is very short, and often crossed. For the first bite or two, the taste of good chocolate is subtle and lingering. After that it's simply overpowering, and nothing can stand in its way, certainly not the elusive taste of phyllo pastry or chopped pine nuts.

I won't say chocolate ruins everything, only that there are places where it doesn't belong. Chocolate has a domineering effect on almost every cookie it goes into, and levels out the individuality of oatmeal cookies, granola bars or (it pains me to say) shortbreads. It has no place in the company of fruit (apart from orange peel, which is scarcely a fruit and adds a layer of subtlety to dark chocolate ice cream). As for cheesecakes, I can't imagine how chocolate got into them in the first place, since the pleasant sourness of the cheese is utterly neutralized by the bitter sweetness of chocolate. All I can guess is that most people don't really like the taste of cheesecake. There can be no other explanation.

The need to protect the integrity of baklava is self-evident — why isn't the UN working on this one? — and I pray that the chocolate version was just some cultural misunderstanding, a bit of anthropological trivia along the lines of the custard sauce that you risk getting on a baklava served in England. But remain vigilant, just in case. And beware of the chocolate falafel.

A house is not itself after Christmas. Even the habitually neat let their habitat go to ruin during the seasonal celebrations, as if to signify that it can't be a holiday if you're always tidying up. Stacks of presents take up space once devoted to decaying cats or frayed backpacks full of unwashed gym shorts. Eventually the Calista Flockhart autobiography will rise up off the broadloom and find its way to the bookshelf, squeezing out the mint-condition Kelsey Grammers and Stephen Hawkings of years gone by. The *Pavarotti Sings Motown* CD, for the past few festive days just a painful sensation underfoot, will soon assume its natural position at the bottom of a landfill site. Even the ostrich-hide cellphone holster and the oversized boxer shorts decorated with the manic face of Tom

Green, things nobody can bear to put in a room and call their own, will finally get picked up and moved elsewhere, reopening the essential living room–kitchen lifeline.

But the chocolates, ah, the chocolates. Disposing of this perennial reward for the hard-to-please has never been a problem. While stacks of other Christmas presents abide and grow weary, chocolates disappear. Since I eat them before I go to bed at night, having heard on the street that they're a good narcotic, and eat them again when I wake up, having persuaded myself overnight that they're a good pick-me-up, I'm not surprised they don't linger. Even in the Christmas lassitude, the chocolate madness is so strong that I'm convinced midnight prowlers are sneaking the incomparable soft caramel creams from the assortment I've stashed by the German dictionary on the top shelf of the bookcase.

Yes, I'm an addict, and I have the addict's horrible, schizoid need to say bad things (see above) about the thing I crave. *Odi et amo* is my Latin motto. I hate and I love.

That I go too far with my love during the chocolate season of late December is beside the point. Everyone feels unwell that time of year, and better a chocolate overdose than being poisoned by turkey stuffing or crushed by Boxing Day. But what I find interesting, as a result of eating chocolates in place of breakfast, lunch and dinner, is how much their tastes can differ. When you cook too relentlessly with chocolate, you reduce every dessert to a numbing likeness of the one that came before. But when you eat chocolates one by one from their precious Christmas boxes, every taste is distinct.

If you don't like chocolate, if merely hearing the word chocoholic makes you fear for the future of the race, then you are easily persuaded that it's all much the same: sickly sweet, gooey and sticky for the indomitable young, boozy and creamy for the toothless old.

But after years of giving and receiving chocolates, I know that the levels of partiality are as highly developed as for Chardonnays or hockey sticks. I—this information is included only as an example and not as a hint—can't stand milk chocolate, which always seems insipid and sugary. The bitterness of dark chocolate makes it easier to eat more, which is clearly an advantage, but it also makes a more stimulating contrast with the invariably sweet fillings.

Now fillings are another point of contention. I happen to think chocolate and nuts were made to go together, and while hazelnut is clearly the best because of its slightly burnt taste walnuts, almonds and chestnuts give a good chocolate the kind of heft and seriousness it deserves. Others—those in the more weight-conscious sector of the human continuum—prefer the lightest and frothiest of creams, as if insubstantiality in the mouth persisted in the body.

Maraschino cherry fillings we will ignore as beneath discussion, toffee crunch because it's so juvenile and mint because there's not much to say about mint beyond the fact that it's so breathtaking you almost forget you're eating chocolate. And so we come to alcoholic fillings, the Scotch and rum and cognac and Grand Marnier extravaganzas. These are the best, because finally with high-strength spirits we have found flavours and sensations that can compete with the domineering power of chocolate. Children can't stand them, which is a good thing, since they will last longer around the house (the chocolates, I mean, though probably the children too). Friends mature enough to enjoy the gentle burn of chocolate-coated spirits are worth cultivating, because they are happy and sophisticated and likely to give you a good supply next Christmas. Every addict in denial needs a support group.

Chocolate and Almond Cake

This satisfying cake is a longtime favourite for our birthday cele-brations. It's so dense that only a little bit disappears during the birthday meal itself, and you can live off it for days on end. The almonds make it taste less sweet and frothy, but the power of the chocolate isn't diminished in the slightest. The boozy raisins aren't too restrained either.

Soak ½ cup of raisins in a glass for a couple of hours with enough rum to cover. In a small bowl, beat the yolks of 4 eggs (re-serve the whites) with 1 cup of white sugar (vanilla sugar is best). In a saucepan, melt ½ pound good semi-sweet chocolate, and then add 4 ounces of unsalted butter (which has been chopped up to melt faster). Remove from the heat and add the egg-sugar mixture to the chocolate, then stir in 8 ounces of freshly ground almonds (much better than the packaged version), 4 tablespoons of flour, a generous pinch of salt and the plumped-up raisins to-gether with whatever rum is left.

Whip the reserved egg whites until stiff, then blend in with the rest of the cake ingredients. Pour into an 8- or 9-inch spring-form pan, the bottom of which you have lined with a circle of waxed paper, and bake in a 350°F oven for 25 to 30 minutes (it should be moist but not runny in the centre). Let it cool before icing.

To make the icing, melt 4 ounces of semi-sweet chocolate, and then add 2 tablespoons of icing sugar, stirring well to incor-porate all the sugar, followed by 4 tablespoons of butter. Spread the mixture over the cake and put in the fridge until the icing hardens. You could, if you wish, add chocolate chunks or truffles after the icing has set, but it's probably better at this point to heed that Greek rule of nothing in excess.

WORD OF MOUTH

THERE ARE FEW SUBJECTS IN THE CRASH course of life that require as long a reading list as cooking. To get up to speed on something as basic as child-rearing, you might buy two or three books. Personal health will require another couple of volumes if you're a woman, none if you're a man. Home repair, auto mechanics, physical fitness, the French language — two or three handbooks is enough and any more seems like wasteful self-indulgence.

Most departments of life are self-taught, if they are taught at all — you don't need much in the way of reference materials. My children are bloody-minded nonconformists, my asthmatic wife is married to a hypochondriac, the drain forever needs unclogging, the car could seize up at any moment, the flabby abs await their ten-minutes-a-day miracle exercise program, the irregular verbs remain elusively irregular — and to make good all these deficiencies we have only a handful of manuals.

But should we need to find a recipe for poulets fumés rôtis aux raves caramelisés, why it's right up there on the overcrowded bookshelf in Madeleine Kamman's book *Savoie*, between *The Original Boston Cooking School Cookbook* (1896) and *Chez Panisse Pasta*,

Pizza & Calzone. And so are the recipes for every other turnip dish that's ever been cooked or contemplated in the stirring history of root vegetables.

Like most people who take undue pleasure in food, I can't imagine the edible part of existence without an ever-expanding collection of cookbooks taking over an ever-shrinking house. There must be several hundred scattered round the place, each with its own peculiar reason for existence (though the three aphrodisiac cookbooks seem increasingly redundant). The next time I kill a baby seal—it doesn't happen a lot, but best to be prepared—I can pull down Marielle Cormier-Boudreau and Melvin Gallant's *A Taste of Acadie* from the bookshelf and turn out a batch of homemade Acadian seal-fat cookies. When I catch myself pining for the dreaming spires of Oxford—or alternatively, when I find myself with a spare pig's head to dispose of—Elizabeth David's *Spices, Salt and Aromatics in the English Kitchen* supplies the recipe for head cheese with Oxford brawn sauce (Dijon mustard, brown sugar, olive oil, vinegar, and actually both heady and dreamy).

Put me in a cookbook store when it opens, go off to deal with existence as it transpires at ground level, and I'll still be there at closing time, looking to fill the gaps in our family holdings. A cookbook store is an escapist's paradise—all fantasy, no mess—and the shelves are full of possibilities that the compromises of real life can never quite subdue. Good books about food open up the world and expand the ways that mealtime can be turned from drudgery into one of life's most accessible pleasures. They are more than just user manuals: a well-made cookbook is that rare place where sensuality and intelligence meet. Set against the earthy and visceral images of saffron releasing its flowery scent into a risotto milanese or grainy mustard thickening a sauce for a tender cut of well-aged Angus beef is a rich story of human inventiveness throughout history and across ethnicity.

We fill our shelves with books that promise to transform our lives, making the hard parts easy and the ordinary things extraordinary. If it's a delusion, it's a happy one, at least as long as I'm filling the shopping cart at the cookbook store. But if you asked me, once I get home, how many of these books I actually draw recipes from, I'd have to admit that this culinary resource centre of mine is pretty impractical. As much as I once liked to gaze at the fried taro cakes in Huang Su-Huei's *Chinese Snacks* or be startled by the recipe for date omelette in Penelope Casas' *Foods and Wines of Spain*, I don't remember ever cooking these dishes.

It's the peculiar nature of cookbooks that the more you have, the less you're inclined to use them. This rule of inverse proportion doesn't apply to mystery novels or travel books or video-game magazines, but when I cast a guilty eye at the bulging cookbook section of my library I know that I cooked more when there were fewer. While I can make all kinds of excuses for why this is so — more money for buying books being exactly paralleled by less time to use them — I have to admit that bibliomania has gone too far. The sad truth is that in our modern urban culture, there are too many choices for what to eat and how to make it.

Some of the best meals I ever ate were cooked very quickly on a two-burner hot plate along the backwaters of Brittany, where the dinner menu was determined by what the fisherman had caught that day. I don't find that multiplying the ingredients available to me by a factor of a thousand has improved my meals in the same proportion. If anything, the greater freedom of choice (and though I'm not saying this to bring about a restoration of conservative values, it makes you think) has become paralyzing. "What should we have for dinner tonight?" someone asks, and instead of fumbling for an answer I cringe in what seems like fear.

It's like those horrible questions that philosophy professors use to separate the true geniuses from the rank and file. "What if?" is all it said at the top of the exam paper, and you had three hours to answer. Only the question was so vague and so wide open that you'd spend most of the allotted time trying to figure out where to start. Or slowly going mad in the attempt.

Dinner has become a "What if?" question, and few of us are going to pass the test in the limited time available. Sure, it's an open-book exam, but that only makes it harder: the tomes we keep around the house to guide us admit far too many possibilities.

That should be more than enough to drive us round the bend, but no, the cookbook industry is still not satisfied. Though a good volume of food wisdom should never wear out, the makers and publishers of cookbooks have convinced us that our collection is in need of constant turnover. Bought a microwave? Time to throw out your old books and start over just as you did when you converted from vinyl to CD. Finally admitted to being a chocoholic? How could you have got through life to date without ten books devoted solely to your addiction? Hooked on *Oprah*? Then you (and ten million others) will have to buy a copy of *In the Kitchen with Rosie*, the low-fat diet book from Ms. Winfrey's chef that may not have made the talk-show host skinny but at least discouraged her from getting much bigger. And think of how much more compassionate you'll be if you indulge in her skinless chicken recipes —all the ills of the world that aren't solved by sitting around a TV set and talking can be cured, according to contemporary cookbook writers, by taking the skin off your chicken.

Like a daytime talk-show host, they promise to help us, these books that now take up so much space in the cookbook store. They look at society's besetting worries—the shortage of free time in a ruthlessly busy world, the dissatisfaction with the ordinariness of the daily routine, the encroaching mortality of an aging population—and propose an instant remedy: recipes.

Playing on our insecurities, the up-to-date recipe targets the universal nervousness about health, and promises a stronger heart, a cancer-free body, perhaps a longer life, certainly a smaller waistline. A generation ago, when good eating was about the amount of cream and cognac in your steak sauce, people who were treated for heart attacks used to leave the hospital with a handful of photocopied recipes prepared for their eternal torment by the staff dietician. Health-oriented cookbooks in those days were bland and resolutely unfashionable handbooks full of drab charts and doctors' sermons, intended solely for victims and sufferers. But the number of actual diseased people who want to fill their bookshelves with new cookbooks is necessarily limited. And so the hip new volumes of edible cures take the preventive approach instead, crafting trendy recipes for a broader, younger market. The medical problems of a few have been appropriated and made mainstream.

The problem with propagandistic books like these is not so much what is there — although the medical presence is dismal — as what is excluded. Perhaps someone under a cardiologist's care should avoid dairy fat and strip the skin off every last boneless chicken breast. But the rest of us are missing something important — and pleasurable — when we limit our intake to what has been approved in the grim confines of the hospital labs and the boardrooms of the opportunistic charities and businesses that link themselves to these projects. "If these scareheads succeed in taking over," Julia Child once said between sips of her trustworthy gin and tonic, "they're going to kill gastronomy."

My own personal death watch started when I was warned away from a dish of chicken with ginger in black bean sauce at a posh Cantonese restaurant. "That's only for Chinese people," the well-coached waiter told me. "You won't like it." And why did he assume I wouldn't like it? Because in the best, and most flavourful, Chinese way, the pieces of chicken that the chef expertly hacked up with his cleaver came with both skin and bones. After many complaints from health-conscious scaredy-cats who were distressed at even the sight of fatty chicken, the restaurant decided that spineless Westerners prefer their chicken denatured and denuded.

The redoubtable Julia, whose slow-cooked ratatouille and saffron-flavoured tomato and rice soup were staples of my formative years, who credits her own longevity to healthy doses of beef and booze, believes that the "nutrition police" are conducting a reign of terror in the kitchen. Terror? The people I know who rely on the fashionable miracle-cure handbooks cook with the kind of zeal you see only in fundamentalist religions. They believe. But aren't all forms of fundamentalism ultimately based as much on fear as faith? Start thinking for yourself, start disobeying the rule-makers' commands, and you will no longer submit to their lucrative diet plans. And if you recoil at the sight of full-fat Roquefort or a melting slice of foie gras, if you require full nutritional analysis and an MD's reassurance before you'll even look at a recipe, then you have ceased to enjoy all that food has to offer. Imagination sets the cook free. Dogma, by definition, has its limits.

One thing at least can be said in favour of low-fat, no-dairy, beef-and-gin-are-bad, I'm-going-to-live-forever (and you're not) cookbooks: by excluding so much, they simplify the dinner menu. Nervousness about health makes it easier to deal with the unsettling array of choices open to the modern cook, if only by ignoring them. "What if?" is not a question you ask when you already have The Answer.

But soothing the fears it has itself created doesn't satisfy the voracious cookbook industry, not when there are so many other insecurities to prey on and profit from. Every time we feel like social failures — I'm afraid to entertain, I have no time, I live a humdrum life, my best recipes must be years out of date, I can't even pronounce jicama, let alone tell you what it is — there's a one-stop, ready-made solution. Sustained by books full of never-fail recipes, up-to-the-minute garnishing tips and unrelenting optimism, you too can organize clambakes in the Hamptons, cook an au courant Thanksgiving dinner for forty, hold your own among the supercilious connoisseurs of Latino gourds and — why not? — update the time-honoured techniques of Chinese cuisine to fit your needs rather than the other way around.

That doesn't sound so bad? So why does my heart not leap when I read the blurb for *China Express* by the very wise and very worldly Nina Simonds? This is a writer who lived and trained in Taiwan, translating cookbooks to make ends meet and developing as fine an understanding of Chinese cooking as you'll find in the world today. And this is the fainthearted way her publisher describes her creation: "At last, a cookbook for those without the time, energy or resources to cook the classic way."

These books sell; such is the awareness of the role food plays in the good life and the slow death. But for those who see mealtime as one of life's basic pleasures, the volumes of self-improvement are all too often exercises in self-denial. The fantasies they hold out can never be realized as perfectly as the pictures show, except in a parallel universe where disease strikes only the deserving, speed is a virtue, no one is tired of jicama — yet — and well-behaved children put aside their anthologies of French poetry to help with the Thanksgiving floral display.

Cookbook readers divide into two camps. In one are those who value a book for its author, for the stories she tells, the people she encounters, the pretensions she deflates and the recipes she unearths from the hidden past and the unglamorous present.

In the other are those who prefer something they can look at. They may be fraught with fears about their social inadequacies, they may be consumed by worries about a colon that has kept company with far too many saturated fats, but whatever their abiding concerns, a pretty picture will put it right. These people do not like to exercise their imaginations if they can force-feed them. What they require of a cookbook above all is that it looks smart, that it ornaments a lifestyle in a constant state of wish fulfillment. The most help a cookbook author can give these people, having laid out a stunning mise en scène for their discreet salivation, is to identify the Japanese obi cloth resting under the candied clementine tart so they can rush out and buy it for themselves.

It's a battle of words against image. And while good prose elevates the creation of food, good photography too often demeans it. Photographers and food stylists and food-magazine editors have a very narrow concept of cooking: they insist that it looks beautiful and enticing, that it elevates the hopes and soothes the fears of the flawed people who seek perfection in an image. In this, they are much like the people who cast movies in Hollywood and insist that the part of the unglamorous single mom is exactly right for Helen Hunt.

And just as you wouldn't go to see a movie about an ordinary working-class woman if it actually starred an ordinary working-class woman, so you shouldn't expect to find regular food in a lavishly illustrated cookbook. No matter what a recipe's source or history, no matter what jokes are told as the meal was prepared or how many hunks of meat fall on the dirty kitchen floor, cooking through the lens becomes homogenized into an art director's dream: distant yet desirable, perfect yet attainable.

Now I'm not suggesting that you throw out *The Taste of Italy* and Lee Bailey's *Long Weekends*, *Martha Stewart's Pies & Tarts* and all the other books that are based on creating an illusion of absolute good taste. They do set a standard for what you could accomplish if you had faithful retainers, devoted assistants, a passion for crafting chocolate ivy leaves to garnish chocolate pecan lattice tarts and the best collection of Fiestaware in Westport, Connecticut. After the first prick of despair that you have wasted your life by comparison with the indefatigable Martha, you too can rouse yourself to make perfect golden raspberry tartlets (remembering first to plant the raspberry bushes and shop for some amber-pink Depression-glass serving dishes).

But life is short and cooking that is so singlemindedly devoted to making an impression, allowing so many opportunities for soul-destroying imperfection, can prolong our agonies beyond what even a formal dinner party deserves. The best reason to cook from a book without pictures is that there is no lofty standard against which you must measure yourself. Antique-shop flatware and perfectly aligned asparagus spears of the deepest green, or off-brown soups spilling over the edge of mismatched bowls and cats leaping up on the table just as the main course is served—the choice is up to you.

Some amateur cooks will find this terrifying, having to make their way in the dark toward an unrecognized destination. I'd say it's liberating, for the very same reason. When you have only the words to work with, the recipe rapidly becomes yours and the focus is on the cooking, not whether the tarte will match the cut glass and the chintz. The credit, when it is given out at the end of the meal, need not be shared with a professional home-entertainment consultant.

Cookbooks in mindless Ektachrome aren't about to disappear from the bookstores any time soon, since they captivate comparison shoppers in a way that no mere writer can hope to do. And many people prefer the ordered simplicity of being dictated to. But there have been encouraging signs that pictures are being used with a little more respect for real time and place. Look at Patricia Wells' *Food Lover's Guide to Paris* from the days before she too went glam, where the black-and-white photographs of Parisians actually enjoying their food restored a healthy dollop of normality to cookbook illustration. Spontaneous scenes of real people tucking into their meals with un-Michelinlike enthusiasm, with no digressions on the provenance of their place settings, reminded cooks that in Paris, France, just as in Paris, Texas, and Paris, Ontario, eating could be a simple and basic pleasure.

A cookbook with a strong sense of place supplies its own integrity. Yes, the more opportunistic books play into the landlocked cook's sense of make-believe or turn the stews of poor shepherds into the expense-account diner's peasant-chic plaything. And yes again, after *A Year in Provence* and *Under the Tuscan Sun*, elsewhere became *the* place to be in the food world. Part of the desire to know where our food ultimately comes from is based on those pleasant feelings of instant escapism that food can so easily provide — the mess on your plate tastes a lot more interesting if it can be larded with stories about setting suns over the Cyclades or hard walks through the olive groves around Lucca. While wine bottles have fanciful labels to perform this role — associating aristocratic names and paradisiacal settings with the liquid coursing down the throat — a recipe needs its background sketched in at the table.

But a more important reason to prefer regional cuisine is that it gives food a firm grounding in reality. A trip to France may be a highly attractive means of escape viewed from the North American vantage point, but when you arrive it becomes real awfully quickly. A good cookbook writer — which brings me back to Elizabeth David, the best cookbook writer of all — immerses herself in the way of life that gives birth to the recipe and provides its pedigree. A dish of eels in red wine that might seem suitably outlandish if dreamed up by a Manhattan artiste makes perfect sense in the Touraine region of France where the richness of the river fish is sharpened by the tart local red wine.

Cookbooks more concerned with improving your health or your lifestyle always seem to find their recipes in a no-name place where the fats are forever unsaturated and the vegetables are crisp and colourful. Cookbooks tied to the land and steeped in its history provide their own appellation contrôllée, a guarantee that generations of people who like food have preceded you in their passion for a dish. If you find the Italian beef in vinegar too sour or the Indian carrot dessert too sweet, the baby eel offensive or the chicken skin disgusting, maybe that says more about the self-imposed limitations of our own time and place.

Not all regional books do the job, I admit. In some of them (Paula Wolfert's *Cooking of South-West France* comes to mind), the scholarly commitment gets too laborious and the peasant's family recipe turns into a cooking-school exam. High seriousness is the abiding sin of the regional-cooking devotee. It takes Wolfert more than five pages to describe how to make duck confit. In her *French Country Cooking*, David dispatches duck stew in twenty-four lines. The point is not so much which one would taste better, but which you're more likely to cook. The most authentic dish is one that ends up being eaten, not one sampled lovingly during a quiet moment in the cookbook store while you pride yourself on your low cholesterol level and your mastery of napkin folding.

There is an art to writing a recipe that manages to be nourishing, timely, tasty and undemanding. But it is harder to develop a love of food and an understanding of cooking from know-it-all books that impose rules and regulations. Some of the best writers about food are hopelessly imprecise in their attitude toward measurement, knowing that you cannot evoke the way people actually make good food in Provence or Liguria or Cyprus by measuring out ground pepper by the grain. There are stories to tell, and the fixation on cooking times and lipid levels and publishing tie-ins gets in the way of the telling.

There is no muse of food writing. It is one of the lowlier of the arts, and most of the time it is not an art at all. Just as a western must culminate in a shootout, all of food writing predictably leads to the recipe, and to the meal that disappears into happy oblivion soon after the recipe is put to use. A collection of good meals is at least as creative as an anthology of minor poetry, but there is no artistry in a recipe. That you have to make for yourself.

And this is where cooking becomes a collaborative art between the writer and the reader. The best food writers catch the attention of the distracted cook, hand out sound advice and cranky opinion, speak from experience both charming and harrowing, and fasten on to your imagination even as you go shopping or peel the garlic or dream of places far away. Elizabeth David was that kind of writer.

Many of those who now tell us what we should eat seem to operate in a vacuum. They know a lot about microwaves, perhaps, or animal fats, or the emotional needs of well-heeled New Yorkers. But they don't know a lot about the world. Elizabeth David was extremely worldly. When she described the typical diet in the hill villages of Provence, you had the feeling she knew what she was talking about from her own sleuthing, not from a press junket to the Riviera or a chit-chat in Soho with an expatriate restaurateur. Without being overly dogmatic about it, she shied away from star chefs and discovered her recipes in honest bistros off the dreary autoroutes or long-lost cookbooks from the France of Napoleon III. She knew her back roads and her back pages equally well.

Her cookbooks are disordered, by modern standards, and very wordy, except when it came to writing up a recipe. She quoted at length from exuberant French writers, gave a lengthy and hilarious account of the Fascist recipes devised by Italian Futurist artists (mortadella with nougat, marinated eel in iced minestrone) and took great pleasure in serving up mutually incompatible recipes for the same dish, because she knew the one important fact that eludes most cookbook writers and almost all cookbook readers: there are as many different recipes for a dish as there are cooks and kitchens. She respects her readers too much to lecture them like an all-knowing teacher. She never caught on to the idea that many otherwise intelligent people are helpless in front of the stove, and could do with more orders, and less disorder. Nowadays you cannot publish a recipe without calculating every ingredient down to the last grain of pepper. Elizabeth David gave the imagination and resourcefulness of her readers more credit, and wrote books instead of user manuals or nutritional tracts. As a result, you feel less like a student or a slave and more like a friend when you succeed with one of her recipes.

Her influence has been sadly marginal on this side of the Atlantic, where a bossy style and a naive allegiance to technique have always been preferred. "In personal ways," noted Christopher Driver in *The British at Table 1940–1980,* "Mrs. David's background could hardly have been more English: descended directly from a Victorian Home Secretary (Viscount Ridley) and a Conservative MP for Eastbourne, educated at an ill-fed English girls' school, married for a while to a British diplomat. She tried both painting and acting before turning in her late thirties to cooking and writing. She had behind her two formative experiences: several months living in Paris with an exceptionally greedy famille bourgeoise; and a spell on a Greek island followed by war years in Cairo, running the Embassy library and exchanging ideas in the kitchen with her Sudanese cook."

Something in this wayward combination of experiences — Mr. David disappeared early on — produced a food revolutionary, though one always inclined to look back in order to move forward. Her closest equivalents in the American food world were perhaps James Beard and Julia Child, but they had a keener sense of how to sell themselves, which is what much of North American food writing is about after all. Elizabeth David was reclusive and aloof, and not inclined to turn the subject of food into prime-time entertainment or lifestyle hucksterism.

Proof for this could be found in her first book, *Mediterranean Food*. The war was over and she didn't have much to show for it except the recipes she'd collected in her travels and a few clippings from her food articles in *Harper's Bazaar*. But that was enough. In 1946, she took herself to a small hotel in Ross-on-Wye near the Welsh border and set to work. In cold, gloomy, impoverished England, where even the dullest and most basic foods were rationed, she made it her goal to "bring a flavour of those blessed lands of sun and sea and olive trees" into the kitchen.

Her books were written to affirm the value of pleasure, and they were all the more vivid for being written in a country where eating was a form of penance. She took special delight in other writers who brought joy and energy into the kitchen while barring the door to guilt and smugness. Through Elizabeth David, I discovered Sir Harry Luke, an official in the British Colonial Service who as Chief Commissioner in Georgia, Armenia and Azerbaijan dines off salmon trout surrounded by its roe and accompanied by a sauce of water buffalo cream, fresh walnuts and horseradish. Then there was the Italian poet Filippo Tommaso Marinetti, who declared pasta to be obsolete and proposed a bold new cuisine where roasted pheasant was warmed in baths of milk and sweet Sicilian muscat, then stuffed with candied fruit and preserved pears and cherries flavoured with mustard oil. Mussolini, for some reason, took a liking to his forward-looking recipes. But my favourite discovery of all was David's friend Norman Douglas, another British diplomat, who left the service in disgrace to settle down in Capri and write libertine novels when he wasn't eyeing the young boys. From him came the aphrodisiac recipes collected in a book called *Venus in the Kitchen*, for which Graham Greene wrote a very respectful introduction. Squid-ink risotto, pie of bulls' testicles (based on an ancient papal recipe), leopard's marrow cooked in goat's milk, carnation marmalade—

the strangeness of it all is an antidote to the urgings of drab and earnest cooks.

The world seemed like a bigger and more interesting place with Elizabeth David. But unlike many of her successors who have adopted the Mediterranean as their second home, she was not a writer who habitually resorted to tourist-board cliché. Her Mediterranean could be hard-edged and challenging, and not just a place for overpriced bouillabaisse. In the introduction to *Mediterranean Food*, when rationing was still in effect, she lures in her well-bred, timid, narrow-minded readers with the words, "Anyone who has lived for long in Greece will be familiar with the sound of air gruesomely whistling through sheep's lungs frying in oil." The image, like the woman, is unforgettable.

But even the no-nonsense Elizabeth David, like so many of us from cold and sober places, could feel the lure of Provence and its food. "It's civilized without being overcivilized," she wrote in *French Provincial Cooking*. "That is to say, it has a natural taste, smell, texture and much character. Often it looks beautiful, too. What it amounts to is that it is the rational, right and proper food for human beings to eat." The golden tiles on the roofs, the glint of the Mediterranean as you top the last mountain, the scent of the wild thyme crushed underfoot, all these things suddenly seemed more real—or at any rate, more like what reality should be.

This idealized Provence of the cook's dreams may well exist, but I'm not sure I want to find it. My maps show a region of the same name in the south of France that fits in neatly between the Rhône and Italy along the coast of the wine-dark Mediterranean. But I can't bring myself to believe that any place on earth is as appetizingly perfect as so many food writers make Provence out to be. Waverley Root, one of those old-time foreign correspondents who believed that politics and dinner were subjects of equal interest, once declared in his *Food of France* that "the most magical of all the provinces of France is Provence." Now suppose that

with a quick abracadabra you could relocate to the summer forever underway in the sunny south. If, instead of fragrant lemon
groves and gnarled olive trees, terra-cotta hill towns and white-
washed fishing villages—the Provence of legend—you found
hardened starlets on the make, vistas disfigured by deluxe resorts,
ersatz bouillabaisse priced beyond the reach of the dollar, and the
cold mistral winds cutting through the hillside's scrub: could you
still believe in magic?

Let's put the rabbit back in the hat (or into the stew pot with
a few anchovies à la provençale). Better to treat Provence as the
armchair cook's faraway ideal—the eternal sunshine on relentlessly rainy days, a perennial holiday refreshed by sea-blown
breezes and earthenware jugs of pink wine, the picture-perfect
land where food is created by honest artisans for ever-hungry,
never-fussy connoisseurs. Yes, all those ingredients that seemed
weird or alarming or (worst of all!) unknown to my Methodist
grandparents—garlic, eggplants, fresh figs, salt cod, black olives,
anchovies, ugly fish with ugly names like rascasse—flourish there,
and the Provençal cook does nothing to disguise their intense
flavours.

Naturally, if you found your way to one of those villas outside
Nice or Nîmes that deflect the monied classes from the grind-
stone, the dream would be compromised. You'd expect, as a matter of course, to eat a goat's cheese omelette for breakfast in
the shade of an orange tree, and you would be very disappointed
if the pure mountain breezes didn't waft the scent from those
oranges while shavings of peel simmered with the daube de boeuf
on the wood stove. Provence has a lot to live up to.

No, the best way to savour the enticements of this wonderful
place is from afar. When summer seems slow to show its face,
scan the bookshelf for *The Cuisine of the Sun* by Mireille Johnston;
the very title lifts the spirits. Or slip into the world that Leslie
Forbes has recreated in *A Taste of Provence*. Having unearthed

tantalizing recipes from grandmothers, vine-growers and truffle-hunters, Forbes has placed them in the vivid setting of a vacation sketchbook. Her drawings steer clear of the grosser excesses of Provence that can turn it into a tourist's *cage aux folles*. Instead there are the pictures that daydreams are made of: a plate of grilled eggplant and red pepper framed by tickets to the Arles bullfight, a milestone en route to Montélimar, nougat capital of France, and a watercolour of two gurgling fountains in the elegant town of Aix-en-Provence. There, after an inspection of the Cours Mirabeau, known as "the most beautiful main street in the world," we lunch on a terrine of artichokes in a red pepper purée, followed by ratatouille and noisettes of lamb in a creamy garlic sauce. And somehow we find room for the local biscuits of ground almond and candied melon, known as Calissons d'Aix. Or just stare longingly at the drawings, which are more enduring than a biscuit could ever hope to be.

A postscript on recipes: they don't all come from Provençal hill towns or New York's hippest neighbourhoods. The ones that cling most stubbornly to the subconscious often originate in much more unassuming surroundings. An example: sneaking a square of semi-sweet cooking chocolate—not quite Belgian chocolate, but useful in a pinch—I noticed a huge amount of typography inside the box. Investigating further, I found a credible-looking recipe for chocolate pecan bars that in the time-honoured manner called for—surprise—an entire box of Baker's semi-sweet chocolate. (The most ambitious of these package recipes, of course, manage to include mayonnaise, cheese slices, peanut butter and whatever else the corporate conglomerate has ownership of; hence the indigestible cuisine of the fifties). And so somewhere a child engaged in a senseless act of random destruction will rip open the chocolate box, discover the recipe cleverly printed inside and start a family taste for chocolate pecan bars that will last for generations.

These commercial promos lack the diverting stories or the pretty pictures that we expect of our recipes. But there is no denying their reach across age groups, income levels and religious divisions. Many of the chocolate chip recipes on this continent started not with a chef's secret recipe or a course at the Cordon Bleu or a clipping in *Gourmet* but—where else?—with the small print on the back of a package, the work of some underpaid corporate recipe creator who shaped (at waist-level at least) the course of a nation.

I went searching for the source of a broiled coconut-and-brown-sugar cake topping that caught my attention every time I tasted it at country bakeries and family funerals. I assumed I'd eventually end up in the kind of place people like me always think recipes start, in the kitchens of some poor-but-honest peasantry. I already knew that the Germanic peoples of Southern Ontario liked to top their cakes with coconut, and when I found a recipe in a classic book about Mennonite cooking I felt my theory was vindicated.

But recipes are strange things. A search of my late grand-mother's recipe collection—she who used to win prizes for her peach pies at agricultural fairs—turned up a surprisingly large number of variations on the coconut-and-brown-sugar theme, which apparently took North America by storm in the days be-fore Sara Lee. But contrary to my preconceptions about honest peasants crafting the truest, most timeless food, what I also found throughout this handwritten family recipe collection was an over-whelming corporate presence. The Jell-O salads go without say-ing, but there were also Eagle brand condensed-milk cookies, Graham-cracker pie crusts, Fleischmann's dried-yeast coffee cakes, Kellogg's Corn Flakes casserole toppings and so on through the capitalist hierarchy. And that got me to thinking: How could co-conut ever have been a basic ingredient in the Old World Germanic kitchen? Is it possible that the ancient, nostalgic recipes I was so taken with were just the creation of a company flak with a product to promote and a deadline to meet?

I look on seal-fat cookies with new respect—at least they haven't been co-opted by the corporate culture.

Galettes au Petit-Lard de Loup Marin

A delicacy from a Provençal hill town? Not quite. It's just that the French name for this Acadian recipe sounds so much more appetizing than seal-fat cookies. Unless you spend time in the seal-hunting regions of Eastern Canada, I don't expect you'll have a chance to make this treat from the fascinating book *A Taste of Acadie*. But I like to look at it from time to time just to remind myself that not all recipes have to come from twenty-four-year-old chefs living in the moment, that the beginnings of creative cooking are necessity and opportunity.

The Acadian phrase petit-lard refers to the milder-tasting fat of younger seals, the ones that are slaughtered for their pelts to the great distress of cute-animal lovers everywhere. I don't know how this ancestral recipe was modified by the Acadians who made their way to Louisiana and turned into the Cajuns. Baby alligator-fat cookies just aren't the same.

Take a 1-pound chunk of seal fat, cut into small pieces and boil for an hour. Drain, and mash the fat with a fork. Mix in 1½ cups flour, then stir in 1 egg, 1 cup whole-fat milk, 2 teaspoons baking soda, a good dash of salt and 2 tablespoons vinegar. Pat the dough on a floured surface and knead, adding more flour until it has the consistency of biscuit dough. Roll it out until it's ½-inch thick, cut into rounds, then bake at 400°F for 20 to 30 minutes.

Coconut Frosting

Having had enough of the highway to Hell, we eased our way off the exit ramp at a small town named Ingersoll, once home (as the memorial plaque stated proudly) to The World's Largest Cheddar Cheese. If you're going to build the world's largest something, a wheel of cheddar may not be the best choice. It lacks both the longevity of the pyramids and the CN Tower's panoramic views, and there's nowhere to put a revolving restaurant. The cheese was long gone, a victim to the changing tastes of mass tourism, sold off for a song (or so I told my children) to a local mouse-catcher with dreams of going global.

So instead we shopped nostalgically from the cookie display at Zurbrigg's Bakery, and commandeered a dozen peanut-butter, a dozen coconut and raisin, a dozen thickly iced Easter cookies shaped like chickens and rabbits (for great-grandma in the nursing home) and — turning to the impulse-purchase display by the cash register — a Styrofoam tray of something brown and squiggly.

It was the last one that tempted me when we sat down to sample the goodies in celebration of another car trip survived. Compared with the riotously excessive creations that urban bakeries turn out as entries in the World's Largest Dessert competition, this cake was a model of small-town restraint, the sort of thing that gets passed around in the church basement after a funeral. Even to call it a cake was a bit pretentious since it actually fell into that old and nearly abandoned category of dessert squares. The base was a dense chocolate brownie, but what really caught my attention was the baked frosting, an irresistible mixture of toasted coconut, brown sugar and walnut.

As soon as I put the first square into my mouth — or if not the first, certainly by the sixth — I knew I had tasted that combination before, somewhere long ago after a similar diversion when my father was behind the wheel and the World's Largest Cheddar cheese may still have been with us. It was certainly not a taste you come across these days in smart restaurants or fashionable cookbooks. But it was so striking that it had kept a place in my memory long after I'd willingly forgotten triple-chocolate layer cakes with their cappuccino sauces and almond-ginger whole-wheat tartlets with out-of-season fig coulis.

Well, maybe not entirely forgotten. But there was also room for this humble square with its powerful frosting, a place denied it by world-class diners forgetful of our sweet-toothed past. Here's the simple recipe, culled from Edna Staebler's classic book about traditional eating, *Food That Really Schmecks*.

Mix together ⅓ cup brown sugar, 2 tablespoons of melted butter, 2 tablespoons cream, ¾ cup shredded dried coconut and ½ cup chopped walnuts or pecans. After letting your cake (almost any cake will do) cool for five minutes, spread the mixture over the top and broil until it bubbles and browns.

Raie au Beurre Noir

It's impossible to pick out a single Elizabeth David recipe that reveals all the pleasures that come from reading and cooking with this great writer. So many of her best thoughts on eating well are mentioned along the way, in the introductions to the wonderfully detailed chapters of her masterpiece *French Provincial Cooking* or in her terse, recipe-free observations on how to put together a good meal. Her random notes on assembling a plate of crudités, for example, are far more inspiring and encouraging than the lengthy descriptions of more involved hors d'oeuvres in most French cookbooks: "Radishes, washed, trimmed of excess greenery but left otherwise as God made them rather than disguised as water lilies." Yet from those no-nonsense orders, she can shift with sudden elegance to a vivid description of an unusual charcuterie in provincial France. "It was designed twenty-five years ago by M. Montagne's grandfather; the lapis-coloured tiles were really to discourage flies, for it is well-known that blue repels them but, using the blue as his starting point, old M. Reymond achieved a most original and oddly beautiful combination, a kind of mosaic which turns the charcuterie into a cool and orderly grotto, if such a thing can be imagined, with the rows of hanging sausages and hams for stalactites."

Many of her recipes are so simple and straightforward, from the whites of leeks poached in red wine to her many renditions of the southern beef stews called daubes, that the range of her genius only emerges when you realize you've been cooking from her books for months without encountering a bad or boring dish. This recipe for skate is wordier than the Elizabeth David norm, but perfectly shows how she brings knowledge and passion together.

"Skate, that spectacular fish that looks like some fantastic kite, has, when cooked in ideal conditions, a very fine flavour. It is one of the rare fish which is better kept for an interval of two to three days after it has been caught rather than eaten fresh from the sea but, since the circumstances of having too fresh a skate is scarcely likely to arise in most people's lives, it is more important to know that the creature should reach the kitchen as soon as possible after the requisite wait of two to three days, for stale skate can be disastrous, and because of the powerful ammoniac smell which it gives out some fishmongers do not care to buy it. In England, a good deal is sold to the fried-fish shops, but poached and served with brown foaming butter according to the well-known French recipe, it can be a real treat.

"The common skate, *raie batis*, and the thornback, *raie bouclée*, are the two varieties of skate most often to be found in French markets and here, and these fish are extraordinarily voracious. M. Donies, author of a manual called *Les Poissons de mer*, asserts that in the stomach of one monster specimen of the common skate were found two large plaice, a lobster, two mackerel, a thornback nearly half a metre long, and a salmon. A well-nourished fish, in short.

"Supposing that you have a piece of wing of skate, weighing 1¼ to 1½ pounds, the other ingredients are an onion, a few sprigs of parsley, vinegar, and butter. You also need a pan sufficiently wide for the piece of skate to lie flat while cooking. Into this pan you put the skate, cover it completely with cold water, add a sliced onion, a couple of sprigs of parsley, a little salt, and 2 tablespoons of vinegar. Bring gently to the boil, with the pan uncovered. Thereafter let it barely simmer for 15 to 20 minutes. Lift it out and put in on a dish or board so that you can remove the skin and the large cartilaginous pieces of bone and divide the fish into 2 or 3 portions. This has to be done with some care, or the appearance of the fish will be spoiled. Transfer it to a fireproof serving dish, sprinkle it with chopped parsley, and keep it hot over a low flame while the black butter is prepared.

"For this, you put 2 ounces of fresh butter into a small fryingpan and heat it over a fast flame until it foams and begins to turn brown. At this precise moment, not sooner or later, take the pan from the fire, for in a split second the butter will take on the deep hazelnut colour which is beurre noir. (It should be only a little darker than beurre noisette, which is light hazelnut colour.) Pour it instantly over the fish. Into the pan in which the butter has cooked, and which you have replaced on the fire, pour 2 tablespoons of wine vinegar, which will almost instantly boil and bubble. Pour this, too, over the fish, and bring at once to the table; for, like all dishes in which beurre noir figures, the ideal is only attained when the dish is set before those who are to eat it with the sauce absolutely sizzling.

"In one of those noisy, busy, cheerful Lyon bistros renowned for very simple, rather rough but well-cooked food, in copious quantities, I had skate with black butter beautifully served. We were sitting within a yard of the kitchen but even so the patron almost ran from the stove to our table with the little covered dish containing the skate and its hissing, bubbling sauce, to which a few capers, cooked with the vinegar, had been added."

Risotto Nero

I first encountered Norman Douglas as a novelist, and not one I could read with total devotion. *South Wind*, his classic work about unrepressed people on the island of Capri, was undoubtedly stylish, but the liberating effect it once had on the young Graham Greene seemed to have diminished over the years as modern literature became a little too liberated.

Then I came across references to his defiantly eccentric 1952 cookbook, *Venus in the Kitchen*. When I tracked it down I found a collection of allegedly aphrodisiac recipes that made most modern cookbooks look exceedingly dull and narrowminded. Douglas, writing under the name of Pilaff Bey, loved to undermine the recipe he'd just solemnly dictated: "Rather banal," he'd say of puréed celery, or "not so bad as it sounds," of elderflower fritters. He took great delight in going beyond home economists' ideas of good taste, supplying recipes for odd concoctions and then rating their lust-provoking effect (frogs' legs in a white-wine sauce is summarized as "a noble aphrodisiac"; a recipe for andouille sausages, which begins with the command, "Take some pigs' guts" concludes with the judgment, "This one works in the opposite direction with me").

But when he wasn't challenging the accepted customs of cookbook writing, Douglas could put together a good, uncomplicated recipe that drew on the tastes of an elderly Englishman in Italian exile.

"Clean well half a pound of cuttlefish, keeping apart the little bag containing the ink. Cut the fish into small pieces and leave them in fresh water for half an hour.

"Chop fine a big onion, two cloves of garlic, half a red pimento [sweet red pepper]; add pepper and salt. Put these in a saucepan with three spoonfuls of fine olive oil. Fry. When the onion is getting brown, throw in the fish and let it cook till it gets yellow. Then add half a pound of chopped spinach and let it cook for 30 minutes. Add then a pound of rice and the little bags from the fish which contain the ink, mix well with a wooden spoon in order to break the bags and pour in little by little some hot water with diluted tomato sauce in it. When the rice is cooked, add a piece of butter and some Parmesan cheese. The rice must absorb all the liquid and be nearly dry if you want good risotto nero."

One pound of rice sounds like too much, but on Capri as in the rest of Italy, they like their risotto in quantity. You could cut back to half a pound, especially if you're serving this as a first course. Arborio is the variety of choice.

You could also substitute smaller squid for the cuttlefish if you liked. In either case, this is still something of a shocking recipe in the liberated turn of the century. Imagine how daring it must have seemed when *Venus in the Kitchen* was first published.

RISOTTO

SHALL WE START with pronunciation? For a word that seems to be on everyone's lips, risotto is all too easily mangled. Those of us unfortunates who have learned our Italian from menus and cookbooks will never get it exactly right, of course, any more than U.S. auto-racing fans could ever wrap their tongues round the name of Jacques Villeneuve. But we are a lot more likely to cook a dish authentically if we start by making an attempt to say it right.

The trickiest part is that vowel right in the middle. People who've just discovered the great rice dish of Northern Italy tend to pronounce it long, which is generally a good approach to Italian vowels. But not in this case. Instead of rhyming with "owe toe," risotto should sound something like Ow-toe. Advanced students can move on from here to work on the first syllable (pronounced like the Welsh name Rhys, not like a rhyme for wheeze) and the troublesome double t's (which should be articulated distinctly and crisply, an almost impossible task for non-Italians, especially when their mouths are full).

Having stumbled over the basics of culinary Italian, we will now be less likely to make risotto with chicken-stock cubes and parboiled long-grain rice on the one hand or, on the other, to mess it up with artichokes, goat's cheese and duck confit. A sense of nervous respect isn't a bad way to approach foreign cuisines, not if it forces you to follow the traditional methods closely and avoid both store-bought shortcuts and the flights into Californian self-absorption that make so many modern dishes taste exactly the same.

Debased ingredients used to be the besetting sin of the not-quite-Italian risotto, the salty stock cubes and squirts of tomato paste and dusty imitations of Parmesan. Now the danger is over-elaboration. It isn't that a risotto can't be made with truffles—it can be, very successfully, if your truffle pig's done its work—but that it shouldn't be made with truffles and lobster claws and crab legs and six other things. The essence of a good risotto is the rice. Perhaps you can use the rice as a setting to showcase one favourite ingredient, but whatever else is added must blend in quietly.

Risotto is a long-cooked, meditative dish that encourages patient, thoughtful eating. If that sounds dull, blame me, blame the accelerated culture that has replaced introspection with talk radio and Roseanne's annual facelifts, but don't blame risotto. It's restrained, granted, but only in the most obvious way. A bowl cooked with saffron in the Milanese style can be a meal in itself—except that it is so often partnered with osso buco—and is capable of standing up to self-important wines in a way that few other rice or pasta dishes could ever hope to do.

The difference is in the rice. Good risotto uses the best strains of Arborio (and its upscale cousins Carnaroli and Vialoni), the longest and fattest of the short-grain rices. You can make a decent risotto with the smaller, cheaper types that are simply labelled Italian, but Arborio gives off its starch in a way that produces a creamier risotto. At the same time, the individual Arborio grains hold onto their own autonomy just a little longer and don't collapse into sticky porridge the way cheaper varieties do if you let them cook too long.

My only complaint with Arborio, Carnaroli and Vialoni is with the little white kernel of starch at their core. It's generally accepted in cooking risotto that some of this starchiness should remain—the risotto equivalent of al dente—but as far as Marcella Hazan and I are concerned, the less the better. Macho cooks —the sort who like to cook beef bleu and chili red-hot—will serve risotto to you so undercooked that it tastes like chalk. Here's the test: if it feels like work, it's not good risotto.

The quality of rice is important if you want to achieve the essential creaminess. But to get to that stage, you must also make a good stock from chicken or veal—vegetarians are on their own here, though a fish broth would suit a seafood version. The stock needn't be overly concentrated—the idea is not to take over the dish—but it can't be too watery or fatty or taste of long-cooked chicken bones. Once you've made your stock (and don't think you're making risotto if you buy ready-made broth) the rest is easy: melt butter, add finely chopped onion, cook till golden, pour in a glass of wine, add rice and stir to help it imbibe the flavours. You must add real grated Parmesan at the end (except in the seafood version), and be sure to stir in some crushed saffron if you're making the classic accompaniment to osso buco. My favourite risotto is made with mushrooms—plumped-up dried shiitakes are appropriately earthy, though the fresh ones do the job almost as well. I make a primavera version with fresh vegetables in the Canadian spring (that would be somewhere around mid-July) but in the dark depths of winter it comes across as meek and mild. For the starker, more austere months of the year, I always think back to a dish that broke the rules, an Umbrian version that used two glasses of red wine to make the darkest of all risottos. Or should that be risotti?

Some cookbooks equivocate on the need for wine in a risotto. So let's be dogmatic: you must add a glass, if only because there are few smells nicer than that of wine bubbling in butter and onions. Since you're about to spend the next twenty minutes adding stock—you are keeping it warm on the stove, aren't you?

—and since you're going to be stirring the resisting rice on a low heat till your rotator cuff injury flares up, you might as well have something good to smell.

Note, in passing, how singleminded and attentive the risotto chef must be. That's why it's so hard to get perfect risotto in a busy restaurant. For once, the cook at home has the advantage.

Dark Risotto

There are few more satisfying cold-weather dishes than this one. Risottos are often served as a first course, but for the amount of work involved at home they're better served as a main course with a good wine and a salad and not much else—risottos are disarmingly rich and filling, especially when your guests have seconds as they should. Leftover risotto immediately becomes porridge and should not be served to anyone you're trying to impress, though it does make a very forceful alternative to corn flakes the next morning.

Much fuss is now being made over pricier varieties of risotto rice such as Carnaroli and Vialoni. I've always been satisfied by plain old Arborio, which is easier to find and faster to cook.

Make a stock out of cheaper chicken parts or a whole stewing chicken, an onion, a celery stick and a good dash of salt. Go easy on the carrots—they tend to make the stock too sweet. If you don't want to be bothered making a stock, skip this recipe. The stock needn't be overly concentrated, but it shouldn't be watery or fatty (make a day in advance and chill so the fat rises to the top and can be easily removed).

Before cooking, trim a dozen or so medium-sized dried shiitake mushrooms of their stalks and soak in tepid water until they soften. Heat the stock in a pan. In a deep, heavy pot, melt 2 ounces of butter, add 1 finely chopped onion, cook until golden and add 2 cups of rice. Stir so the rice is coated with the butter and onions, then add a glass of wine, white if you're feeling delicate, red if you're feeling hearty (in which case you might as well make it two glasses). Stir and let the pleasant fumes evaporate into the air — this is the real joy of cooking. Add the shiitake caps. As the rice starts to dry up, add a ladle or two of warmed stock, and keep stirring gently. Repeat, cooking until the rice softens and loses its starchy taste, which takes about 30 minutes. About 15 minutes in, add ½ pound of fresh mushrooms, preferably a mixture of oyster and portobello. When the rice is ready to serve (it should be a little chewy but also tender and creamy), mix in grated Parmesan (real parmigiano reggiano) to taste. One cup is about right. Serve with a little chopped parsley on top, and pass round a bowl of grated cheese.

HEAD CHEESE
AND THE HUMAN
CONDITION

THERE ARE MANY THINGS YOU CAN SAY about Hungarian cuisine — that it is heart-warming, unpretentious, respectful of tradition, underrated — but there is one thing that only I can say: Hungarian cooking cost me a job.

While living in England, I'd written the exams for the Canadian diplomatic service and, much to my surprise, been summoned to attend a day of interviews in London. To steel myself for the interrogation, I came down the night before, checked in at an overpriced hotel and went out into the December damp in search of dinner.

I walked through the lively restaurant district of Soho, reading menus, calculating prices, and ended up outside a Hungarian place with the improbable title of The Gay Hussar. The name gave me pause — flamboyant soldiering not being any guarantee of good food—but the hour was late, the night cold and the press clippings intriguing. The Gay Hussar seemed to be the local hangout for Labour politicians who wanted to eat well—foie gras led the menu—but couldn't afford to be seen at the expensive French restaurants preferred by their Conservative rivals. So they salved their consciences and soothed their appetites with the best cuisine the Eastern Bloc could offer.

This gave a useful political dimension to my meal, one that I could reflect on as I ate and perhaps use to advantage the next morning to impress sophisticated diplomats. Entering, I discovered a much plusher setting than I was used to from the student hangouts that made up Toronto's Hungarian cafés. The sommelier asked if I wanted wine—I was used to raspberry soda with my stuffed peppers—and trying to think what a suave Canadian *fonctionnaire* would do in these circumstances, I asked for a carafe of Bull's Blood. The menu was long and impressive and hard to disentangle. With a less than gay Hussar tapping his boots beside me, I quickly ordered the specials: wine soup, roast goose and an apricot pancake. When the sommelier brought my carafe, it turned out to be a litre.

The food was delicious, but all too Hungarian in the way it stuck to the ribs and expanded them endlessly outward, making sleep almost impossible when I finally got around to collapsing into bed. The potent wine seemed pleasant enough, though by the seventh glass I was drinking it more out of duty than thirst. It was only the next day that its effects really took hold. Whatever hopes my written exam had raised in diplomatic circles were dashed by my semi-comatose performance in the flesh. I confused the French president with the French prime minister right off the top, failed to extricate a Russian defector in a role-playing exercise, nearly had a breakdown on the spot when I couldn't decide if it was right to bribe a Mexican drug agent who'd discovered my girlfriend with a joint, and made up various character flaws in the psychological assessment just to break up the embarrassed silences.

But my big mistake came at the end of the day-long session when I hesitantly presented the bill for my feast at the Gay Hussar. The diplomat in charge of expenses looked at the name of the restaurant, looked at what I'd had to eat, looked at what I'd had to drink, looked up at me accusingly, looked down at the total cost after tax and said in an angry voice that should never have been allowed to speak for Canada, "How could anyone have spent so much on Hungarian food?"

We never did get to talk about the effects of Soviet hegemony on the agricultural production of the Warsaw Pact or whether the foie gras of Hungary was superior to that of France. Canadian diplomacy, all too sensibly, seemed to involve a dedication to things Canadian. Terrine of goose liver, the sort of thing that was the mainstay of nineteenth-century *ententes cordiales*, that kept Henry Kissinger going during the Paris peace talks, did not figure large in my country's list of priorities.

Neither did I. The don't-call-us letter arrived a few months later, but by that time I'd persuaded myself I could never have gone to work for people who felt such disdain for Hungarian food. This was a cuisine that sustained me and my university classmates, with its gulyàs soup, creamed lentils, chicken paprikás, pork schnitzel and tart cucumber salad, to say nothing of poppyseed strudel and the sweet curd-cheese crêpes that made it so easy to linger in the boisterous cafés with their whirring espresso machines and steamed-up windows when we should have been studying Canadian diplomatic policy during the post-war period.

I'd always imagined that everyone, at least after 1956, counted Hungarian food as a basic part of their coming of age. I only discovered when I went out into the wider world that the coupling of academe and Transylvanian wooden platters piled high with mountains of meat was a historical accident unique to Toronto.

So perhaps the nostalgic argument for Hungarian cooking is not the strongest. In that case, I should point to its basic integrity, an earthy cuisine that has enough confidence in its dumplings, paprika and sour cream to resist the flavours of the month. And though these humble dishes may not be quite as important to Canada-Hungary relations as the sale of a nuclear reactor, they're much easier to digest.

Good food has always found a way to keep my worldly ambitions in check. When I first went to university in the early '70s, I could have dined in the college dining hall like everyone else and bought myself more time to work in the library or pad my résumé. But the food was so unbearably bad that I set up house in a co-op off-campus and devoted almost all my waking moments to making meals out of my counter-culture handbook, Adelle Davis's *Let's Cook It Right*, and then cleaning up the whole-grain, additive-free messes that resulted.

After a year of enlightened drudgery, I decided I'd better back off a bit if I was ever going to accumulate the kind of degrees expected of future ambassadors and Supreme Court justices. I deliberately took an attic apartment without a kitchen so that I wouldn't keep experimenting with new uses for potato peelings, and instead decided to live off Toronto's fine collection of cheap student restaurants.

It was a good idea in theory. The mistake I made was in thinking I could just dash in for a quick dish of chicken paprikás night after night and go back to *Oedipus Rex* half an hour later as if nothing had ever happened. But something did happen. Building on the basic knowledge of cooking techniques I'd acquired through Adelle Davis, I started to see my dinner not just as something that tasted good but as an extramural course full of endless fascination and education. If I started going over the list of mealtime options during dull moments in seminars, if I diverted some of my research skills to the study of the local newspapers' underground-gourmet columns, if I lingered a little longer at my nighttime hangouts to try a regional dessert, it could only enhance my educational qualifications. Who wouldn't prefer a Supreme Court justice with a firm grounding in menu Spanish?

And thus I reached the turning point in my relationship with deep-fried food—if the word relationship has any meaning in the wake of Dennis Rodman and Carmen Electra. A café with the promising name of El Cid had opened near the University of Toronto. Always looking for an excuse to bone up on European history, I set out to learn more about the legendary Spanish hero, or at least his cooking.

Determined to earn my sophistication the quick and easy way—what else are the university years for?—I ordered two dishes with exotic-sounding Spanish names. *Sopa de ajo* was easy to recognize as it arrived from the kitchen, the advance smell of garlic quickly identifying the anonymous-looking milky broth. The main course was more puzzling. *Calamares fritos* it said on the menu, and I guessed from the word fritos that whatever it was, it would at least be pleasantly greasy in the usual way of fried food. But what I saw on the plate set before me was a set of perfectly symmetrical golden rings, looking like oversized Cheerios.

One tentative bite told me they weren't at all greasy. A second told me that the slightly rubbery, mildly sweet circles of meat inside the crisp batter tasted not too bad. But by the third bite, I still wasn't any closer to knowing what I was eating and turned to look for the man who'd taken my order. He wasn't hard to spot since he was looking right back at me with what I would now guess was amused anticipation but at that point looked much more intimidating.

Please keep in mind that this was 1971, when words such as *calamares* and *calamari* were not yet part of every Canadian schoolboy's vocabulary and deep-fried rubbery rings had not yet supplanted cocktail weenies as the boozer's nibble of choice. "Squid," he said to my surprise, if not horror. "Fried squid."

Well, perhaps there was a brief spasm of horror as the subconscious brain called up terrifying, tentacled images from *20,000 Leagues Under the Sea.* Maybe I even hoped for a second that this was one of those fabricated, just-kidding names like Welsh rabbit or Bombay duck. But the waiter, like some solemn knight in a medieval epic, looked gravely serious and it soon became clear that (a) I was going to lose face pretty fast if I couldn't rise to the challenge of deep-fried squid and (b) whatever version of jumbo squid Captain Nemo had wrongly ordered, it was nowhere near as good as the stack of benevolent morsels I had in front of me.

In the interests of higher education, I've since eaten squid-like creatures cooked every possible way, and some impossible ones as well (a soup of dried cuttlefish with sea cucumber comes to mind). But none has ever caught my attention as quickly as those first simple battered rings.

Deep-fried food is much scorned now, at least if you move in culinary circles where health is the prime concern. It's hard not to move in such circles when even the slumbering salty-snack market has awakened to the benefits of low-fat tortilla chips and baked potato chips. At the haute end of cuisine, it's only the most daring and perverse chef who will put a fried-in-batter item on a menu dominated by grilled and baked and roasted. Even then, when I see a carte that lists, say, Vidalia onion rings in lambic beer batter with a rouille dipping sauce, I tend to think the chef is pulling our legs, showing off his regular-guy side while charging double figures for a greasy-spoon staple.

Deep-fried food deserves better. I know the fast-food industry has used the deep-fryer to dire effect, and I also know from personal experience that there are few sights more disgusting than the dripping paper bag holding day-old pakoras and their now-dispersed cooking oil. But if we judged all cooking techniques by their worst examples, we'd have to do without roasted red peppers because of Grandma's leathery Sunday joint and baked risotto al pomodoro because of your college roommate's cornflake-crusted tuna casserole.

So instead consider (and imitate, if you've got a deep pan, a deep-fry thermometer, a serene temperament and guests who let you cook to order) the glories of deep-fried food. Tempura comes first to mind, and not just for the ease with which it provides an entree into Japanese cooking. What other cooking technique, more to the point, focuses and concentrates a vegetable's natural flavours to such a degree?

I have an inexplicable liking for deep-fried cheese (even in this age of tasteless mozzarella sticks) which I won't force on anyone else, but instead will go on to praise deep-fried oysters (especially with mayonnaise as part of a po' boy sandwich), falafel on its own or in pita with purple pickled turnip, Chinese shrimp (provided the batter is fully cooked and thinner than the shrimp), zucchini flowers in season, the Italian fritto misto (best of all with creamy brains) and the okra in batter you find in the more unpretentious Southern restaurants. When I spotted deep-fried milk on a Chinese restaurant menu, I decided that anything could and should be fried in batter. But my heart, or what's left of it, still belongs to squid—though with the courage and wisdom that come from too much experience, I now have learned enough to take the tentacles over the rings.

Having found the key to the pleasures of intellectual life, I stuck around universities for a while, eventually making my way to England on a scholarship that miraculously rewarded my breadth of knowledge while not being too concerned about its murkier depths. Libraries, my benefactors had kindly decided, were not the only place, or even the best place, for feeding hungry minds.

I took them at their word. I spent time in dusty study halls, to be sure, poring over learned articles about ancient military alliances while equally ancient radiators wheezed ineffectually and students from all over the globe coughed in unison. But there was also an astonishing liquid called real ale undergoing a renaissance in the pubs, boisterous markets where you could choose between eel or hare, and an annual publication called *The Good Food Guide* that depended for its all-knowing coverage of the country's restaurant scene on unpaid reports from enthusiastic omnivores like me. I was in England, and to my surprise I was in my element.

So I knocked back pints of beer with names like Winter Warmer and Ramrod, got up before the sun to fill my backpack with the market's specimens, hurried home to skin the hare for a stew or bone the eel for a marinade, studied the nuances of English cheeses to the point of actually bicycling through the pastures of Wensleydale, plotted my London visits to include field trips in Soho's Chinatown — *The Good Food Guide* wanted my thoughts on dim sum — and generally confused my priorities so completely that when my time was up I'd become a food writer.

I refused to acknowledge it, of course, food then as now ranking low on the official list of things that really matter. I looked for jobs in the Canadian diplomatic corps, was approached about career opportunities in the British secret service (and scared off the spooks, I believe, by my habit of holding staring contests with barbecued pigs' heads in Soho windows), seriously considered teaching in Somerset schools where lunch consisted of boiled gristle (to be near the village of Cheddar, I now like to think), briefly entertained thoughts of spending a stop-gap year playing hockey in the south of France (to perfect my bouillabaisse recipes, perhaps?) and finally decided that it was time to get serious, go home, and study law.

So I went home, started law school, and discovered that I preferred tortes to torts. Somewhere along the way, quite clearly, I'd lost the ability to be serious. And the more time I spent trying to read the lifeless words of bloodless judges, the more my thoughts drifted to the dinner I would sneak in before I had to get back to my life's work. It was during this last gasp of my student existence, when I still thought I could stand being a lawyer for the rest of my days, that I discovered the great consolation of the Chinese soupe du jour.

In the simplest Chinese restaurants, where the steam rises up in clouds above the simmering noodles and the lacquered ducks hang throttled in the window, hungry students seeking a quick escape and other wise people of limited means like to order rice plates. These are the cheapest items on the menu, and for good reason. They tend to be the fastest, least elaborate dishes the kitchen can produce—beef with green pepper in black bean sauce, say, or crackling roast pork with bean curd in a sludgy gravy—and they're cooked up as half-sized portions of the regular menu items before being spooned onto a king-sized bed of steamed rice.

Unlike the usual Chinese fare, which comes in banquet-sized servings and must be shared round the table just to keep the doggy bag down to something portable, these plates are a meal meant for one. They're designed for people who like undemanding food that is filling and cheap, but haven't succumbed to the cult of the Happy Meal.

Rice plates take next to no time to cook, which is not the least of their virtues. But for the solitary diner, or the young people who haven't learned to make an evening out of a meal, next to no time is still a little too long. So for the terminally impatient, there's an added bonus. While the peppers are sizzling in the wok, thoughtful restaurants set down a time-filling bowl of soup in front of those who can't wait.

I'd asked the waitress to bring me an order of the barbecued duck with Chinese greens that adorned a heap of rice at the next table. Then I settled in for a good five minutes of worrying about whether a tavern was liable for damages when a customer got so sozzled on draft one night that he wandered onto the highway and tried to face down a transport trailer. I don't think I'd even got to the fifteen-second stage of this meditation—the point where I wondered why I was thinking about this stuff at all—when the waitress reappeared unasked with a bowl of soup.

In the past I'd eaten what I thought were typical Chinese soups—won-ton dumplings floating above coiled noodles, hot and sour soup studded with wood-ear fungus, porridge-like rice congee that was flavoured with preserved egg—but I'd never encountered anything quite like this before. The ceramic bowl in front of me consisted of a clear and fragrant broth in which were floating nuggets of potato, translucent slices of white cabbage and scarlet chunks of tomato. I'd defy anyone to spot it as a Chinese soup—Poland and Ukraine might get some votes—but when I set the broad soup spoon in motion, I realized I'd hit on something that transcended nationality: this was the universal soup of the day.

I don't know about you, as Bertie Wooster always says when embarking upon a discussion of the world's failings, but I have spent much of my life—too much, the legalist's mythical reasonable man would say—searching for the perfect restaurant. This would not be, to my way of thinking, some gilded palace of gastronomy where the stairways are decorated with thank-you notes from the Belgian royal family, the truffle soufflé is the cheapest item on the menu, and the super-rich leave the table merely rich. My ideal restaurant is a place you can go to every day, where the food is recognizably of this world, where they know your face and don't care about your name. And where the soupe du jour is laid in front of you as a matter of course.

Memoirs of Paris in the twenties are full of restaurants like this, and the details of the cheap, warming soups that fortified hungry expatriates — cream of cauliflower, thick tripe soup, even soupe à l'oignon gratinée — survive more vividly than the novels that were never finished and the paintings that were never sold.

But try finding a modest French restaurant you can call your own in these times, at least anywhere outside the less-visited towns of provincial France. The last time someone bought me lunch in a place that passed itself off as a downtown restaurant du quartier, the soup of the day — a cream of roasted eggplant that has so far gone unmentioned in *The New Yorker*'s "Letter From Paris" — cost $6.50. I think they were taking credit for the day as well as the soup. The potage in question was certainly more ambitious in concept than my Chinatown standby and came with a name more likely to woo fashionable diners than whatever the Cantonese is for potato, cabbage and tomato. But it failed to do the job of a soupe du jour, which is excite the appetite, warm the body, adapt to the season's ingredients, work with the kitchen's limitations and cost very little.

Chinese daily soups come cheap because the hard-working kitchens are geared toward producing broth from the bones and trimmings that are part of the daily routine. Cooks at home are at a disadvantage: they have to go out and find the leeks, chicken necks, shin bones and stewing beef that make a good stock, and then return home to perform industrial work on a domestic scale. The effort is worth it.

De minimis non curat lex, my law books used to say so pompously — the law is not concerned with trifles. Which explains in large part what I found missing in the law. The trifles that make up life outside the courts are so much more important than the high-priced legal minds who stick to weightier matters will ever know. Which is why, balancing Chinese soups against the scales of justice, I went with the soups. The little things make all the difference.

When, through the unfair laws of primogeniture I was first allowed to choose what the family had for dinner (at the advanced age of eight), hamburgers were my one and only choice. Hamburgers for birthdays, hamburgers when friends came by, drive-in hamburgers on the open road, restaurant hamburgers before the Maple Leaf game, holiday hamburgers at the family Christmas dinner as the guarantee of good behaviour, breakfast hamburgers at the local greasy spoon as the price of silence while my parents slept off the night before.

Back in the days when beef was not a naughty word and the McDonald's chain was but one of many, I talked up hamburgers whenever and wherever I could. Why were hamburgers so good? Because you could cram so many different flavours into your mouth. Because you didn't have to be polite around them. Because they were so juicy. Because you eat them without ever getting full (my record was eight). Because girls didn't like them. Because you could chew on them with one hand, read *Batman* with the other and still watch *The Three Stooges* on TV.

Years before I caught myself daydreaming about dinner in the law school library, I was already living in the realm of food fantasies. While other people mixed up their paste and went to work designing the next great construction-paper steam shovel, I was composing mental lists about the hamburger. With all due respect to the mothers who used to ply the peewee hockey team with patties before Friday-night practice—Mrs. Starkman put hers on challah, to our surprise—restaurant burgers were always better than those at home (why? we asked each other). The top three, in my professional opinion, were the double-patty specials at Fran's restaurants in Toronto (king-size hamburger with french fries, chocolate milk shake and a hot fudge sundae, please), Laube's Old Spain in Buffalo (it came with a knife and fork, of all things, but the Zorro decor made amends) and the Rocking Chair Buttery in Detroit, where I ate Abe Lincoln burgers for breakfast, swivelled on the counter stool in the interests of speedy digestion and dripped ketchup on the murder section of the *Free Press*.

It was an obsession, I suppose, and had I been born thirty years later I would have been sent to a therapist until I finally lost interest. But if it wasn't hamburgers, it was going to be something else. Some minds are just bent that way—I was apparently mangled by the obstetrician's forceps, which compressed the part of the brain that stops thinking of food between meals so that it can go off and do something useful.

Even as a barely conscious baby, living in an England that was still in the grip of rationing many years after the Second World War, I had an unhealthy fixation on food. Unhealthy for other people, anyway: I used to commandeer the family's meagre egg and fish ration entirely for myself, and would scream without end if my parents tried to deprive me.

One of my first food memories was of trying to figure out how to make the obligatory Sunday scrambled eggs more bearable. I noticed that my sisters liked to cover up the taste with ketchup. But to my fussy mouth, the sweet-vinegary flavour of tomato paste was far too strong and overpowering. I asked my father to mix the ketchup with the eggs as they started cooking, and the results were a pretty impressive balance of flavours, provided you like your eggs a rosy pink.

So it wasn't just hamburgers. When I went to the movies, a wave of disappointment came over me if the snack counter was missing a particular brand of candy-coated peanuts. Every pee-wee hockey game had to be followed by a post-game Willard's coconut chocolate bar and an Orange Crush. When we went out for Chinese food at the Lichee Garden, the crunch on the bean sprouts in the egg rolls had to be just so, or I'd look over at my father with sadness. He'd make inquiries, and the manager would confess that the number-one egg-roll chef was off that day. I now think he was playing along with my father, but at the time it was important for me to know why we'd fallen short of perfection.

Most people grow out of this emotional identification with food, and learn to subordinate it to the serious things that really should awaken strong feelings, like education or the deficit. I could never do that. At heart, when I start getting excited on Sunday mornings about slipping out for shrimp dumplings and radish cakes with chili oil at the dim sum restaurant, I'm still the boy who longed to start the day with hamburgers.

My father's best friend from medical school ran a clinic in Port Colborne, a town along the Welland Canal that connects Lake Ontario with Lake Erie. He lived in a spacious apartment above the clinic — a bachelor pad, I liked to think of it — and when my parents went to stay with him one weekend, they invited me along. I slipped off to bed early that Friday night, after watching my uncle, as I called him, lay out the vegetables he'd found at the farmers' market that day and start cooking a few recipes from *The Playboy Gourmet*. While the adults caroused, I stretched out snug in bed, listening to the mournful foghorns and happily making plans for my hamburger breakfast.

I woke up around six, the standard time for any nine-year-old Canadian boy who's used to starting his Saturday with a pre-dawn hockey game. I dressed, knocked on my parents' bedroom door, got no answer, walked in and proposed that we go out for breakfast. My mother moaned a little. I decided that it would be wrong to wake them up, took some change from my mother's purse and hit the town.

Port Colborne didn't have a lot to offer at 6:15 a.m. I found my way to Woolworths, assuming that it at least would be open, and was disturbed to find that I couldn't get my hamburger until eight. So I walked the streets, studying the drunks passed out near the taverns, peering at the flotsam that bobbed in the canal, staring off into the distance to see if I could spy a freighter that would start the bells ringing and force the huge movable bridges to rise up above the water.

A policeman stopped his car and rolled down the window. I said I was waiting for Woolworths to open. That seemed good enough for him. For the last fifteen minutes before the clock got round to eight, I stood at the five-and-dime's door and tried to will the employees into opening it. Finally someone took pity on me. I walked—ran, more like it—to the lunch counter, didn't even bother with the menu set before me and called for a hamburger, fries and a milkshake.

They weren't sure they could do it. Nobody had hamburgers for breakfast. The patties were still frozen. I started to cry. They quickly threw a burger on the skillet, and every sputter of fat held promise of the pleasures to come. It was awful. The bun was cold and too soft, the mustard was runny, they'd put tomatoes on without asking me, and the overcooked, overprocessed meat had no flavour. I tried to make allowances—this wasn't a sophisticated spot like Buffalo or Detroit—but in my heart I knew I'd made a mistake. Desire had got the better of judgment, and we all know where that leads, with food as with so many more important things.

Three decades later, I got it right. Our end-of-summer ramblings had brought us back to Port Colborne, and to the outdoor market that supplied my uncle with better food than I was ever going to find at Woolworths. As endless freighters made their slow way to the Atlantic past the Main Street hair salons and discount stores, we came to a stop in front of tables loaded with peaches.

My daughter and I were on a mission. We had risen at six— an hour I hadn't seen much in recent years—and raced down to the Niagara Peninsula half blinded by the early-morning sunshine. The old obsessiveness never dies, it merely adjusts—we were on a mission to find the best example of the main ingredient for a peach crisp.

True, we had also scheduled stops at a panzerotto place in Niagara Falls half remembered from a rainy March break and a shop in Niagara-on-the-Lake that makes buttery vanilla fudge. It's hard to justify all those hours of suppressed frenzy on the highway, after all, without at least three edible destinations. More to the point, I knew it would be a lot easier to drag my daughter peachward if I could also promise her a greasy lunch and a box of fudge—four boxes of fudge, as it turned out, but who's counting? —by the end of the day.

That she had an Original Crystal Beach Sugar Waffle in her hand before the day had barely got going was simply good luck on my part and a practised eye on hers. We'd left the car a few blocks away from the market square and walked slowly along the crowded sidewalks, sizing up the shopping baskets of the early-risers who were leaving as we were arriving. By the time we got to the market—to call it the parking lot behind the firehall would be to strip away its simple dignity—I was thinking well beyond peach crisp, to roasted red peppers and grilled tomatoes, to three-melon fruit salad and plum tarte.

Lacking her father's powers of concentration, my more practical daughter pointed out the end-of-summer hornets that were just as abundant, in that symbiotic way of theirs, as the produce. I suppose this is what the more pessimistic French philosophers have in mind when they moan about *la condition humaine*, that state of ambivalence that always combines moments of true happiness with a menacing buzz.

But fortunately our condition humaine included sugar waffles, which hove into view just as the cloud of hornets picked up the scent of some blueberry muffins and cleared off. The peaches could wait. Maybe, I reasoned, with that crude let's-make-a-deal mentality that passes for parenting these days, I could win her round to the joys of farmers' markets via the sugar-coated waffle.

I needn't have worried. The peaches, in their own subtle way, were just as alluring as the sweet and greasy pride of Crystal Beach. Taking advantage of her enhanced comparison-shopping gene, my heir went back and forth between the more flamboyant Redhavens and the muted Lorings, made comments about blemishes here—hornet marks, I guessed—and undersized fruit there —what they can't sell to supermarkets, I quietly suggested— and cast her vote for the plump, golden Lorings.

Their scent filled the car as we drove back to the city by way of the turbulent Niagara River and the even more frightening, if slightly less majestic, Queen Elizabeth Way. We arrived home with the puffed-up pride of people who have successfully plundered a farmers' market and provided for their family. We put the peaches on display where they could accumulate the maximum amount of cat hair, and then tried to figure out what to do next.

Blessed with the gift of enjoying new foods only when they are tried outside the home, my daughter had recently developed a fondness for fruit crisp at a restaurant in the lovely town of Kingston, Ontario. We set to work looking for a similar recipe and scanned index after index with no luck. The history of cooking, to judge from our concentrated research, was a series of missteps that came close to peach crisp but never quite grasped the central idea. There were plenty of crumbles, cobblers, crunches, brown bettys and charlottes and no end of strange New England dishes with pre-trendy names like grunt and slump and buckle. But a little too taken by a sense of delicacy, they all based their toppings on white flour or bread crumbs. None of them managed to figure out the importance of good coarse rolled oats.

Stumbling upon this situation—literally, with Evan Jones' monumental *American Food* now blocking the path to the living room—my wife quickly produced a collection of recipes she'd assembled for her sister's wedding, featuring proper peach crisps that were rolling in oats.

My daughter made the heirloom peach crisp, and doubled the topping just to be on the safe side. It was a great success, not least with the cook. You could hardly taste the peaches, which were a little too ripe for cooking and should have been eaten very quickly on their own. It didn't matter at all. Our needs were met.

At 12:48, six hours after we'd finished breakfast in Forrest City, Arkansas, and hit the open road, any kind of food would have done. Picky and patient a few exits back, I now ordered an all-out search for the dreaded golden arches and even contemplated a stand-up lunch at the next Interstate rest area—maybe corn chips and Mountain Dew from vending machines encased in a security mesh, followed by a dessert of spearmint gum.

It's summer vacation. We're on the annual odyssey, driving through thousands of miles of blurred landscape to leave our children with lasting memories that they have already forgotten. Standards have been relaxed if not actually dropped. Instead of the hill towns of Provence, the Texas flats. Instead of Texaco's Metropolitan Opera on the radio, Rush Limbaugh in a rage. Instead of a charming bed and breakfast in the Finger Lakes, a motel hard by the off-ramp with twin beds, HBO and enough air-conditioning to drown out the eighteen-wheelers.

And instead of fine food, fast food. Eating up the asphalt at 75 mph, praying that you won't be stopped by a state trooper, talked into visiting Graceland or sideswiped by a wacked-out reb scanning the dial for Rush, you don't fuss about cuisine. In the headlong flight from Forrest City, Arkansas, to Richardson, Texas, a leisurely three-hour lunch of regional specialties or a charming market with no end of local produce are nothing more than roadblocks.

Still, when I saw the billboard promoting The Bodacious B-B-Q eight miles down Interstate 30, I began to wonder. While clearly no Tour d'Argent—the spelling of barbecue was the give-away—The Bodacious had possibilities. First of all, it existed, which is recommendation enough on an empty patch of highway six hours after breakfast. Many culinary reputations along the lonely Trans-Canada Highway are based on nothing more. Second, and nearly as important, it was a barbecue restaurant.

Barbecue, as you may know if you've journeyed south of Ohio or dipped into the *Collected Works of Calvin Trillin*, is almost a religion in the God-fearing South. Entirely unrelated to the north-country weekend rite of the same name, it scoffs at grilled chicken breasts and veggie kebabs. Barbecue in these parts is a hand-me-down from the red-meat days of old and is treated much like the spoken word: slowly, deliberately and with due rever-ence. Whether the meat is pork, mutton or beef, ribs, shoulder or brisket, it is slow-cooked over burning logs for days on end to the point where it develops a smoky crust, then is slathered in sweet, pungent barbecue sauce before being served with bread, beans and slaw.

How this method of cooking evolved in a hot climate is be-yond me. Fighting fire with fire, I suppose. And if it's unsuited to the weather—101°F and counting—it's even less appropriate to hit-and-run eating. Most franchised fast food is hand-held pap that can be gummed with minimal effort in a matter of minutes. This has its value. Except for a slight pain in the gut as you wheel out of the parking lot, and a lingering taste of Secret Sauce on the palate, you'd never know you'd left the road. Barbecue, even long-cooked barbecue that breaks away into strands of sinew at the first bite, demands some effort and attention, if only because it's all meat and the standard serving feeds six. After a meal of barbecue, you don't think about lashing on the old seat belt and risking death on the highway. You think about cushioned rocking chairs on breezy porches and George Brett's chance of hitting .400 this year—never mind that he's long since retired—and whether getting a haircut will take more energy than you can muster.

Along with chicken-fried steak, turnip greens and coconut cream pie, barbecue answers a hunger for lost innocence well beyond the point of satiety. When Jane and Michael Stern, the omnivorous authors of *Roadfood*, get down to Arkansas and Texas, they can talk of little else. Praising McClard's Bar-B-Q in Bill Clinton's boyhood home of Hot Springs, they write, "The beef is sirloin, slow-sizzled over smoldering hickory until it begins to disintegrate, crusty and rugged outside but soft and yielding within, heavy with natural juices, shot through with the kick of smoke and glazed with dizzying sauce that achieves balance among pepper's heat, sugar's sweetness, lemon's zest, the plushness of tomatoes, and the pungency of vinegar." Whenever I see Clinton get that vacant, slack-jawed look of his, while others may think he's dreaming of health-care reform, I know that he's pining for uncomplicated, non-critical barbecue.

The eight miles sped by in seven minutes and The Bodacious loomed on the far side of the highway, alongside a whole series of franchise outlets. We turned off at the ramp, but so did everyone else. It took five minutes just to get through the stoplight and cross over to the far service road. Time was wasting. We needed to get to Dallas before rush hour. The Bodacious looked pretty run down: bits of neon were hanging loose and the word "Restaurant" on the sign was ominously missing the middle six letters. The back-seat lobby expressed its doubts. We joined the throng to McDonald's instead—can't go wrong with hamburgers. Maybe next time, when we're not in such a hurry.

Unlike the U.S. Interstates, the long-distance footpaths of Europe offer few temptations to eat badly. I once managed to pass out on a tour of a French château after a forty-kilometre stroll where I'd lunched fitfully on pears stolen from passing trees. But my horizontal view of the roofline at Azay-le-Rideau—What is the French for "I have just walked 40K and eaten an unbalanced meal"?—owed more to stupidity than any shortage of creature comforts. I could have eaten a plat du jour every hour as I tramped through the many well-fed villages of rural France. But instead I preferred to forage, learning only too late that he who lives off the land ends up lying upon it.

The people at the château were very nice—grateful I wasn't dead, anyway—and we ended up talking about the local industry that specialized in making Camembert boxes. But I resolved in the future to eat well even as I lived rough. When an English friend talked me into going on a walk through the Niagara Peninsula along the Bruce Trail, I looked forward to some good meals made more appetizing by all that open air. If backwoods France was full of delicious pâté de campagne and blanquette de veau, then this prosperous, well-populated part of Canada should be a vagabond's paradise.

Two hours in, we'd finished the last of our water. Trudging up and down and over the stony ledges of the Niagara Escarpment was hard work. Our New World walk, we rapidly came to realize, was different from the paths of Europe. While they linked village to village like some ancient pedestrian highway, this trail was going out of its way to avoid the many and varied contributions of the human race. We saw birds and trees and dubious berries and possibly polluted streams and all the other things North Americans expect to behold when they confront Nature. But we couldn't see our next meal.

The walk became harder as we grew thirstier and hungrier. I knew we wouldn't starve—not in the Golden Horseshoe, home to Canada's largest concentration of frozen french fries—but I began to wonder if fatigue would make us slip up. One missed step on a wet rock above a narrow crevice and the only food we could look forward to would be hospital Jell-O.

It was then, as we crested a rise and looked round for the blazes that would tell us where to go next, that relief appeared: the dark forest floor was suddenly full of chalk-white puffballs. My English friend, an innocent when it came to the more outlandish forms of fungi, decided that hypoglycemia had made him hallucinate. Huge round excrescences rising out of the land like the dead at the Last Judgment were not what he expected from his daily ramble. Whenever he goes for a walk, the only thing that appears out of the mist is a good pub.

I was better prepared. Several years before, I'd encountered baskets of the things—a word that accurately describes their appearance—at the farmers' market, the kind of strange treat you can find if you get up good and early and aren't easily frightened. I bought a couple of the creatures, sliced them into mushroom steaks and watched them absorb half a pound of butter in the frying pan. With a little parsley and chopped garlic, they tasted like parsley and chopped garlic. What more could you ask of a lunch?

Unfortunately, we didn't have any parsley or chopped garlic, or butter or frying pans for that matter. This was meant to be a civilized walking tour in the European manner where the local chefs did the work, not a back-to-the-land expedition. The taste of pure puffball on its own was enough to make us pick up the pace.

Within an hour, the trail absentmindedly broke away from the wilds for a moment to touch down in the garden of a pub selling egg-salad sandwiches. My naive English friend who had never seen a puffball had likewise never seen a pub selling egg-salad sandwiches, and in our perilous state they tasted as good as, oh, I don't know, prosciutto and Mission fig panini.

Thus restored—though the second pint of Niagara Gritstone ale might have been a mistake—we went back to working up an appetite for our next meal. To judge from the map, we had four hours of high-stepping ahead of us, followed by a nice shower at a winery B & B and a quick cab ride to a local restaurant.

The map had the distance right but it misjudged our speed. As night was falling, we pulled in at the deserted winery feeling much as we had when we encountered the puffballs but with another 20K on the odometer. Collapsing in our self-contained cottage, we knew that we were too tired to dine out. It was time to improvise. I raided the refrigerator that held our breakfast fixings and the survival mechanism kicked in. The bacon went on the grill, the butter for the eggs sizzled on the frying pan, the orange juice became the basis for a fruit salad made from the Welcome Tired Travellers fruit basket and the All-Bran cereal almost turned into the first course before I came to my senses.

With a bottle of dry Riesling thoughtfully left for us in the fridge, it became the perfect meal for diners who were in the most uncritical state possible—tired and hungry. I only wish I'd thought of bringing along a puffball to fry with the eggs.

Good cooks are the first to acknowledge their own limitations. Those complicated, five-page recipes that have you rolling out the puff pastry on one page and trussing up the goose on another— good cooks leave them to novices who don't realize such dishes are to be perused, not made. Good cooks prefer to cook what they cook best: trusted recipes that will uphold their reputations, dependable dishes that will go with the wine and satisfy the appetite with a minimum amount of fuss. They have long since mastered the skills that produce a pizza from scratch or a beurre blanc from memory. Secure in their abilities to put good food on the table in a matter of minutes, indifferent to culinary gamesmanship, they leave the make-believe fantasies of Michelin supertoques to the once-a-month chefs.

The considerable qualities of the good cook are easy to appreciate. I know for a fact that they are wonderful people to live with (even if they do shake the confidence of those of us who take six hours and a bottle of Tylenol to make a simple risotto). But every now and then, at the risk of going hungry or getting sick, I long for something more outrageous. By outrageous, I don't mean the Parliament buildings sculpted in salt cod or goat's testicles stewed in Eau Sauvage. Cooking is not like couture in having to call attention to itself by courting the bizarre. What I long for is the more ambitious and elaborate idiocies I used to cook way back when I didn't know any better.

Such as head cheese. Good cooks, especially in these subdued times, never cook head cheese. Unless you are practised in the charcuterie arts — and who beyond a Method actor trying to mug up the part of a French butcher would ever get the practice? — turning a pig's head into head cheese takes the better part of a day. To spend eight hours remaking an animal's face into something most people won't eat once they hear its name, when you could be nurturing the young or cultivating ground cover, is nowadays considered nothing short of obscene.

So why make head cheese? Back then, I saw it as a rite of passage, a way of making the instant leap from a novice who could poach eggs and grill fish to master chef. As a university student with little knowledge of the famous kitchens, I had no idea what a master chef did but I assumed it had something to do with cooking dishes that no one else could or would make. Head cheese definitely fell into that category.

Operating on the assumptions that the greatest food would be French and abstruse and highly manipulated — anyone can grill a fish, after all — I had prepared myself for my culinary ascendancy by buying a book called *Charcuterie and French Pork Cooking*. Night after night, while normal people were finding the Carter presidency a refreshing change and marvelling at the promise of a young Sylvester Stallone, I feverishly scanned my pig manual's earnest pages with their line drawings of bains-marie and rolled spleens. Was I was ready to stuff my own sausages (being still incapable of making a béchamel)? Would the real-guy side of Paul Bocuse be impressed by the *queues de porc aux lentilles* on my résumé?

Looking back, I see a series of missed opportunities and roads not taken, the chance to become the next Martha Stewart evaporating as I plunged more and more deeply into the principles of pig-slaughtering instead of mastering the recipes of Julia Child, Martha-style. But back then it seemed the best chance to leapfrog past all the good cooks blocking my way and really achieve something memorable.

And when I saw the giant pig's head smiling at me in the spare-parts section of the butcher shop—there were still such things in those days—I knew I had found my calling. Having allowed the butcher the honour of chopping it up into portable pieces—salvaging the brain for a light supper dish of cervelles au beurre noir—I picked up an extra couple of pig's trotters to jellify the fromage de tête and bicycled home. Ignoring in my enthusiasm the cookbook's instructions to salt the head for a day or two, I got down to work. The head and trotters went into the largest pot I could find. To these were added four onions, four carrots, four leeks, four cloves of garlic, bay leaves, parsley, thyme, pepper, vinegar and water to cover. For eight hours I simmered the beast, and when the meat was falling from the bones, I took it and the tongue and some of the ear for a bit of crunch and ...

Yes, I had gone too far. This was an unreality that had little to do with the world I lived in, where people pined for poached salmon with tarragon sauce or a beef stew in red wine flavoured lightly with orange peel or—stop trying so hard—a nice juicy hamburger. While I had dreams of boning chickens for my galantine and skinning hares for terrine de lièvre, wiser apprentices than I were mastering vegetarian pastas, twelve basic sauces and short-crust pastry. Slowly but steadily, they became good cooks whose only regret is that they married men who once made head cheese.

Po' Boys

I didn't expect my food sensors to go on the alert in Meridian, Mississippi, which just seemed to be a Best Western stage on the drive home from Texas to Toronto. But Meridian, in no hurry to bend to the ways of the modern world, turned out to be the home of a venerable restaurant called Weidmann's. Venerable is not the most desirable quality in a restaurant, but the sociology of local eating was worth the visit in itself. Beneath faded portraits of Meridian's leading cheerleaders and football stars, we ate the fried oyster sandwiches known as po' boys with the gusto of people who've spent the day on the Interstate expecting the worst. And as we did, we watched a massive man overhanging the counter stool attack his dessert.

Slowly, methodically, he chewed on his billowing slice of coconut cream pie, sparing a few words of dispassionate observation for the waitress as she ambled by. And when the pie was done, he paused contentedly, and then ordered a complete fried-chicken dinner just as we were paying our bill. When we drove by the restaurant later that night in search of the town's vintage carousel, we saw him sitting on a bench parked thoughtfully just outside the door, not doing much of anything, just working up an appetite for whatever came next.

The po' boys were more than enough for me. Oysters are filling on their own, particularly the fat Gulf oysters of the American South. Bread them, fry them, slip them inside a bun or a baguette lathered with mayonnaise, and you have the very model of a hand-held meal. Though they're a specialty of New Orleans, where bar-hoppers would cart them home at the end of a long evening's drinking, the best one I ever had was at Rodney's Oyster House in Cavendish, Prince Edward Island. The oysters were local, which always helps, the mayonnaise was real, which is uncommon even in New Orleans, the Muscadet was Muscadet, not 7-Up, and there was an order of fries on the side, which gave me something to do with my other hand.

To make a po' boy, always assuming there isn't a handy stall just outside your local pub, shuck a dozen oysters, heat your oil in a frying pan to a medium-high heat, dip the oysters a few at a time into a mixture of 1 beaten egg and 1 cup of whole milk, then coat with fresh bread crumbs. Fry for about a minute on each side, and serve on a submarine loaf or a scooped-out baguette with home-made mayonnaise and sliced raw onions. Some people like to add pickles.

Peach Crisp

Peaches move far too quickly from rock-hard to overripe, but this child-friendly recipe (and let them help make it if they're going to eat it) can quickly solve the problem. Double the ingredients for the topping if you like a thick crisp.

Peel, pit and neatly slice a dozen peaches, and sprinkle with 1 tablespoon of lemon juice, ¼ cup of sugar, ½ teaspoon of cinnamon, ¼ teaspoon of nutmeg and a dash of rum. Mix well and turn into a glass baking dish. Combine ½ cup of flour, 1 cup of uncooked rolled oats, ½ cup of firmly packed brown sugar, ½ teaspoon of salt and ⅓ cup of melted butter. Spread evenly over the peaches and bake for 30 minutes at 375°F. Turn the dish around halfway through if your oven, like mine, heats unevenly.

Head Cheese with Oxford Brawn Sauce

I have made this dish exactly once. It was delicious and well worth the considerable effort involved in turning a pig's head into a couple of loaf tins full of real charcuterie. In fact, it was probably more delicious because of all the effort. "To cook it at home is a scarifying performance," the redoubtable Elizabeth David once wrote of a mere calf's head, and who wouldn't want to rise to that challenge? I still remember the great feeling, after eight hours slaving in the kitchen early one Saturday, of grabbing two bricks from the backyard garden to weigh down the meat-filled tins, and then disappearing for the rest of a long weekend with the thought that my head cheese would be there to greet me on my return.

Why have I only made it once? That head. I have enough trouble buying one and lugging it home, but try finding dinner companions who will knowingly eat meat that used to adorn a pig's cheeks and jowls. So make this a very large and troublesome dish for one.

Take one pig's head (I've always wanted to say that). Actually half a head is probably enough if it's a big pig. In the old days, and in the old country, you would have asked for a set of brains as well. These may be harder to come by now, but if you get them they're best turned into fritto-misto fritters in the Italian style or sautéed with a beurre noir of drizzled butter and a little wine vinegar added to the pan juices.

Have your friendly butcher chop the head into a few pieces, so that you can actually fit the thing into your stewing pot. Also acquire a couple of chopped-up pig's feet to ensure that the cheese will jellify. Fill the pot with the pig parts, 3 coarsely chopped onions, 4 chopped carrots, a large chopped and cleaned leek if you've got one, a celery stick or two, a couple of garlic cloves, 2 bay leaves, fresh herbs to taste (a clump of parsley, a few sprigs of thyme), a dozen whole peppercorns and a tablespoon or so of salt. Cover with water, bring to a boil, put the lid on and simmer very slowly, until the meat is tender and falls away from the bone. This should take between 4 and 6 hours.

The next stage is crucial, but simple if you're patient and methodical. Make sure you have a spacious, clean area of the kitchen to work in uninterrupted. Take out the pieces of pork and set them aside to cool while you separate the cooking liquid from the cooked vegetables. Put 2 cups of this liquid into a broad pan, add the same amount of dry white wine, and reduce by half. While that's cooking, start separating the meat on the head from the bone and gristle, and chop it into small chunks. If you like a little variety in your head cheese, there's no shortage of extras you can add. Traditionalists will insist that the ears go in, though you may want to trim away the tougher bits around the edge. The tongue is also essential, though you should cut away the coarse outer skin first before slicing it.

When the stock is reduced, taste it and adjust the seasoning, adding salt, freshly ground pepper, and lemon juice or vinegar. When you're done chopping the meat, season with ground allspice, nutmeg, a little cinnamon, crushed juniper berries and ground cloves if you can stand them. Fill your loaf tins with meat to about the three-quarter mark, add the reduced stock, and let cool. Then cover with wax paper, add a weight such as a brick, and refrigerate for a couple of days. Serve cold, with Oxford sauce.

Oxford Brawn Sauce

I spent some time eating in Oxford and, such is progress, never encountered this delicious nineteenth-century accompaniment to brawn, as head cheese is known in England. Allowing for the obvious differences (the olive oil, for a start), this piquant sauce, from

Elizabeth David's *Spices, Salt and Aromatics in the English Kitchen*, is very similar to the sweet mustards served with the sauerkraut-covered hot dogs that are a breakfast treat in Southern Ontario's German markets.

Blend together 2 tablespoons of brown sugar with 2 teaspoons of Dijon mustard. Add a little salt and pepper, then stir in 6 tablespoons of olive oil and two tablespoons of wine vinegar.

I like to think this sauce is Oxford's way of combining brawn and brains.

John Allemang's "On the Table" column ran for several years in *The Globe and Mail*; he is now the newspaper's television critic. A food enthusiast since he first made the child's improved version of scrambled eggs (add ketchup *while* cooking), he has been writing about the pleasures of eating since 1977. He lives with his family in Toronto and is the occasionally grumpy father of two teenage vegetarians.